CW00350641

Gay, Inc.

Gay, Inc.

The Nonprofitization of Queer Politics

Myrl Beam

University of Minnesota Press
Minneapolis
London

Portions of chapter 4 were published as "At the Limits of 'By and For': Space, Struggle, and the Non-Profitization of Queer Youth," *Scholar and Feminist Online* 13, no. 2 (Spring 2016).

Copyright 2018 by Myrl Beam

All rights reserved. No part of this publication may be reproduced, stored in a retrieval system, or transmitted, in any form or by any means, electronic, mechanical, photocopying, recording, or otherwise, without the prior written permission of the publisher.

Published by the University of Minnesota Press
111 Third Avenue South, Suite 290
Minneapolis, MN 55401-2520
http://www.upress.umn.edu

The University of Minnesota is an equal-opportunity educator and employer.

Library of Congress Cataloging-in-Publication Data
Names: Beam, Myrl, author.
Title: Gay, Inc. : the nonprofitization of queer politics / Myrl Beam.
Description: Minneapolis : Univ Of Minnesota Press, 2018. | Includes bibliographical references and
    index. |
Identifiers: LCCN 2018001926 (print) | LCCN 2018020173 (ebook) | ISBN 9781452957760 (e-book) |
    ISBN 9781517901783 (hardback) | ISBN 9781517901790 (pb)
Subjects: LCSH: Nonprofit organizations—Middle West. | Gay liberation movement—Middle
    West. | Neoliberalism—Middle West. | BISAC: SOCIAL SCIENCE / Anthropology / Cultural. |
    BUSINESS & ECONOMICS / Nonprofit Organizations & Charities.
Classification: LCC HD2798.M58 (ebook) | LCC HD2798.M58 B43 2018 (print) |
    DDC 362.89/6457630977—dc23
LC record available at https://lccn.loc.gov/2018001926

Contents

Introduction

We, the Left, have been described as being weak, fractured, disorganized. I attribute that to three things: COINTELPRO. 501(c)(3). Capitalism.

Susanne Pharr, Plenary Session, "The Revolution Will Not Be Funded: Beyond the Non-Profit Industrial Complex" Conference

More insidious than the raw structural constraint exerted by the foundation/state/non-profit nexus is the way in which this new industry grounds an epistemology—literally, a way of knowing social change and resistance praxis—that is difficult to escape or rupture.

Dylan Rodriguez, "The Political Logic of the Non-Profit Industrial Complex" in The Revolution Will Not Be Funded

In June of 2013, timed to hit right before Gay Pride events, the Ali Forney Center in New York City—the largest social service agency for LGBT homeless youth in the country—released a video to promote a fundraising collaboration with the gay-owned design house Nasty Pig. Nasty Pig donated T-shirts designed by gay celebrities like Alan Cumming, Michael Stipe, and Adam Lambert to be auctioned off to benefit the center. In the video promoting this fundraiser, Carl Siciliano, the executive director of the center, articulates a familiar explanatory narrative for queer youth homelessness—family rejection. According to this narrative, the primary cause for queer youth homelessness is homophobia within, and rejection from, the family. "Homophobia," he says, "has a way of making children—teenagers—destitute. They come out and then they are put out."[1] According to Siciliano, the root cause of this *queer* kind of homelessness is homophobia—it literally is making children destitute.

Homophobia, on its own, is *not* making children destitute. Being destitute is making children destitute. Racialized poverty, not homophobia, is the root cause of homelessness, including queer youth homelessness.[2] This is certainly not to say that many queer youth who are homeless do not have fraught relationships with their families of origin, experience homophobia, and get sent away from the home they knew. That can be the case for some young people, but it is only ever a piece of the story, and importantly, it doesn't explain *homelessness*, especially persistent homelessness. When a young person with access to resources gets put out, that doesn't necessarily translate into homelessness, and, when it does, the homelessness is not often long lasting. Instead, for most queer youth experiencing homelessness, that homelessness is due to entire families and communities living in poverty, without access to affordable housing, trying to survive in the rubble of the failed social safety net. Public housing, public hospitals, and public benefits have been decimated over the last forty years while the prison system has expanded and a shift toward temporary and tenuous labor in the service sector has occurred. Why, if this broader context of racialized poverty is really at the heart of queer youth homelessness, is homophobia so frequently identified as the culprit, especially by organizations that should know better, working, as they do, with queer young people experiencing homelessness? The family rejection narrative is important insofar as it is a compelling story for Ali Forney's prime donor base: middle and upper income white gay and lesbian couples. In order to have that cash value, the narrative obscures the systemic political economic realities of racialized poverty in the United States, and it constructs *queer* youth homelessness as exceptional, separate from the figure of the *undeserving* poor so readily at hand. In other words, like so many organizations across the LGBT movement, Ali Forney's approach to an issue it wants to address is driven by what wealthy donors need to hear in order to motivate them to give money.

For two years I was employed in a queer youth nonprofit in Chicago as a case manager, working with young people experiencing homelessness and housing instability, most of whom were queer, many of whom were gender-nonconforming, and the large majority of whom were young people of color. For those young people who had experienced family rejection, that was only ever one factor among many that attributed to their homelessness, and for many it wasn't a factor at all. The actual factors— Chicago's crumbling public health and education systems, the destruction of fifty thousand units of public housing, intense residential segregation and racialized policing, exclusion from labor markets, gentrification, and a punitive and policing public benefits system—are much less appealing to wealthy white gay donors, without whom organizations like the Ali Forney Center and The Broadway Youth Center, where I worked, would not exist. This contradiction—between the complex systemic violences that structure reality for young people and the direct service staff who worked with them, and the simplistic and individualized narrative used to sell those services to wealthy donors—is merely one frustrating contradiction among many that make working in queer nonprofits so maddening. I remember very clearly during my tenure at the Broadway Youth Center a staff meeting full of shared irritation about the neighborhood gay chamber of commerce organization's attempts to pressure the Chicago Police Department to install a "blue light" surveillance camera at the intersection where our drop-in space was located. This proposed camera would enable increased policing of the young people who accessed the drop-in, young people who were trying to get a meal, see the medical provider, perhaps meet with their case manager, or just connect with friends. Many had outstanding warrants, typically for the kinds of economic crimes engaged in by young people doing what they need to do in order to survive: loitering, shoplifting, turnstile jumping, writing bad checks, sex work, or petty drug sales. In the face of this potential for increased surveillance there was amazing solidarity among the staff, a shared recognition that increased policing would make homeless queer youth less safe and leave their ability to negotiate hostile systems even more tenuous, and that it would have a differential impact on youth of color.

I also remember, though, the shame I felt hours later as I, while staffing the drop-in, interrupted a young person rolling her way past the food table, filling her paper plate, chatting with her friends, giving them shit, and told her to put one of the pieces of pizza she grabbed back on the table so that everyone who came that afternoon would have something to eat. Me, a white college educated trans-masculine person reprimanding an African American trans woman, maybe sixteen, for "taking more than her share"—as if I was not actually the person in that situation who had received more than my fair share. I remember trying to make a joke, to be as kind as one can be while policing the eating choices of someone else, to make it less humiliating and dehumanizing for that young person, but the power dynamic was stark, and there was no room for humor. Me, with my belly full, telling this person to leave drop-in hungry, knowing that those two pieces of pizza were all she would eat that day, perhaps all she'd eaten in days. And she looked at me incredulously, like "are you really doing this?"—but that was my job. Of course, I don't know what she was thinking or feeling—this may have been an injustice that felt commonplace to her by that point in her life. But *I* felt it, whether or not she did. It certainly made clear to me that though my job was many things, uncomplicatedly "good" it was not.

To go from solidarity around a shared resistance to the policing of young people to actually policing an individual young person was a devastating moment. After years of working in nonprofits, though, a familiar feeling rose up in my chest: awareness crept in that the work I *wanted* to be doing—making the world a more just place—felt very far from the work I *was* doing—helping sort through wreckage, helping order chaos, witnessing, watching, trying to resist, or even just see, the systems *that I was a part of* that are intended to make poor people feel less than, like objects of pity, of punishment, of control. And, of course, on bad days, I knew I was actually the agent of those systems, making people into objects, disciplining their behavior, trying to diminish their individuality and complexity into the kind of deserving victim that a shelter would house or mental health program would serve. I was struggling to grapple with the fallout of the collapse of social possibility in the lives of poor queer youth of color, and the only resources made available to me by the organization I worked for were the bare minimum necessary to sustain life—some food, a shower, a pair of underwear, a blanket, referrals to shelters—and "life skills" programs that promised individual solutions to systemic problems.

This book emerged as an attempt to reckon with the desperate sadness that I, and those around me, experience in LGBT nonprofits—and also the profound attachment we nonetheless have for them; to grapple with how these spaces and organizations eat people up—staff, youth, clients, volunteers—but also the investment we retain, the belief and hope and love for the people, the relationships, the solidarity, the *idea* of community, and the vision of justice articulated there. These two examples—the reality of working with queer homeless youth and the stories told about them to raise money—illustrate the disjuncture between mainstream articulations of LGBT community centered on privatization and consumption, a narrative LGBT nonprofits must address in order to raise money, and the profound social crisis experienced by the queer people who often constitute those organizations, whether clients, participants, or frontline staff.

The pages that follow are intended to contribute to an emerging critique of the danger that the nonprofit form poses to our social movements, the kind of organizing we do, the systems through which we distribute care, even our ability to imagine justice. Initially I imagined this book would offer concrete solutions to a clear-cut problem. But as you will see in the pages that follow, the uneven landscape of our organizations—and our desires—are much more complex than simple solutions: though the structure of the nonprofit does tend to have a conservatizing effect on organizations—primarily through the pressure of fundraising—these are also spaces of lifesaving connection and profound political analysis. I hope to do justice both to the insidious constraints built into this organizational structure as well as the inspiring and energizing work often undertaken within them.

The Rise of Gay, Inc.

This book specifically addresses the impact of nonprofitization on LGBT social movements, investigating how the institutional location of movement organizations—the nonprofit system—impacts their politics.

In the wake of the 2015 *Obergefell v. Hodges* decision that legalized same-sex marriage, the LGBT movement is faced with a set of existential questions about its purpose, its direction, and its very existence. This book is intended to contribute to that introspection. For the past twenty years, marriage increasingly became the central animating goal of the LGBT movement, to the great consternation of many on the queer left, this author included, who believed marriage represented a retreat from queer politics rather than the advancement of it. Now, as life for many becomes more precarious following the election of Donald Trump, queer movements are at a crossroads: will this movement be able to shift its focus—and its money—away from the narrow goal of marriage and address the myriad ways that this new and dangerous precarity is deployed through the regulation and policing of gender and sexuality? In order to answer this question, it is worth investigating why marriage, of all things, became the primary focus of the movement. It wasn't, as many have noted, because the majority of queer people were desperately clamoring for that right.[3] On the contrary, marriage mattered only to a very select few.[4] But those select few wield incredible power to determine the agenda of the movement with their money, through donations to the nonprofit organizations through which the LGBT movement largely operates. Though much ink has been spilled in critique of the politics of marriage, much less has been said about the institutional arrangement that allowed the voices of these few wealthy individuals to have such an outsized role in determining the future of the movement. This book is concerned with that institutional arrangement.

Scholars over the last twenty years, from Cathy Cohen to Lisa Duggan, have decried the dominance of what they term "single issue politics" in queer social movements: the exclusive focus on the part of LGBT movement organizations on issues that are solely "gay"—legal equality, hate crimes, military service, for example—at the expense of issues that affect the majority of LGBT people, who also occupy other marginalized identities, issues like immigration reform, universal healthcare, progressive taxation, or education policy.[5] They argue that the only people for whom specifically and solely "gay issues" like marriage are the foremost concern are those already most privileged within the LGBT community, often wealthy white gay men, and to a lesser extent wealthy white lesbians. That the issues deemed most important by those most privileged within the LGBT community have come to be so exclusively dominant is, I argue, a function of the structure of the movement itself, the nonprofit system. These privileged members of the community are the "major donors" that LGBT nonprofits court, appeal to as "leaders," and to whom they are therefore beholden. The single-issue politics of the contemporary LGBT movement is a function of economic dependence, and that relationship of dependence is, as I will show throughout the book, a core feature of the nonprofit system.

In addressing the profound impact the nonprofit form has on queer movement politics, I do not mean to suggest that there is no queer movement outside of nonprofits; on the contrary, many people who would consider themselves part of the movement, activists who push and critique the politics articulated by national mainstream organizations like the Human Rights Campaign and the National Gay and Lesbian Task Force, have no formal nonprofit affiliation. But many of those individuals donate money to nonprofits, volunteer their time, and, perhaps most importantly, would think of various kinds of queer and social justice organizations as constituting "the movement." This is the case for two major reasons: first, the nonprofit form *is* used on a massive scale by social movements as a way to organize resources, to turn money from people into staff time advocating for a cause. It is also because these organizations monetize the *idea* of "the movement" in order to capture the hearts and pocketbooks of potential donors. Nonprofits imagine *themselves* as constituting the movement, which is, I argue, just as important as the degree to which they actually do.

The LGBT movement is not unique in the degree to which its politics are overdetermined by its structure. In fact, since the mid-1960s, there has been a massive expansion of the nonprofit system: from only three thousand 501(c)(3) organizations in 1965 to more than 1.5 million today. Contemporary social change organizing is structured through the nonprofit form on a massive scale. However, though nonprofitization is an issue with which many social movements are grappling, LGBT nonprofits are uniquely illustrative locations from which to theorize both the expansion of the nonprofit system as well as transformations in queer politics. It is during the period of rapid proliferation of nonprofits, beginning in the late 1960s, that the modern LGBT movement has taken its present shape: a vast network of community centers, rights organizations, social service agencies, and other nonprofits explicitly working in and for LGBT communities.

This expansion of the nonprofit system—and its pernicious effect on queer politics—is an important, and undertheorized, engine of the so-called homonormative turn in queer politics.[6] Now more than ever, dominant voices in the LGBT movement are focused on a narrow "equality" agenda, organizing for inclusion into existing systems of power through marriage, hate crimes penalty enhancements, and access to an inclusive military service. This, Lisa Duggan argues, is a "politics that does not contest dominant heteronormative assumptions and institutions, but upholds and sustains them, while promising the possibility of a demobilized gay constituency and a privatized, depoliticized gay culture anchored in domesticity and consumption."[7] For Duggan, this shift in politics is due in large part to neoliberalism, with the stripped down politics of homonormativity reflective of larger trends toward hollow multiculturalism and a broader cultural politics discursively buttressing corporate profits and the upward redistribution of wealth. Homonormativity is, Duggan argues, a "new window-dressing for a broad, multi-issue neoliberal politics."[8] This book builds on the work of Duggan and other scholars concerned with the politics of homonormativity, by demonstrating the degree to which the structure of LGBT movement organizations has facilitated this political shift.

The Work of Feeling

There is an animating paradox at the center of this project: the nonprofit structure actually entrenches the very inequalities that it purports to ameliorate. Illustrating that this is indeed the case is not actually the project of this book.[9] Instead, *Gay, Inc.* probes the *why* of this paradox. Why do we remain so deeply, personally invested in a system that fails over and over to achieve the results we hope for? At the center of this paradox is *feeling*. Throughout the book, I explore the feelings built into the nonprofit structure—shame, fear, hope, desire, frustration, isolation, connection— and analyze how these feelings inform queer politics, how they inform the LGBT movement's approach to poverty, to the state, and, importantly, to its understanding of itself. A key intervention of this project, therefore, is centralizing affect—the political economy of feelings—in understanding the nonprofitization of queer social movements. In fact, nonprofits are actually *legally mandated* to operate according to explicitly affective logics: to qualify for 501(c)(3) nonprofit status, an organization must operate for "charitable purposes" to promote "the common good" and "in the public interest."[10] In what seems like surprisingly imprecise language for the tax code, these organizations and their relationship to individuals and to the state are reliant on, and produce, a set of "common sense" assumptions about compassion, deservingness, community, and citizenship. Their very right to exist as nonprofits depends on their ability to produce and promote an affective landscape that is legible to the state. These discourses are made materially real in and through nonprofits, imbricated as they are in relationships of power and circuits of capital.

In this work I am utilizing the insights and tools offered by scholars contributing to what Patricia Clough has termed the "affective turn" in social theory, much of it building on the groundbreaking work of Raymond Williams, who argued that scholars must be attentive to "structures of feeling," analyzing "meanings and values as they are actually lived and felt."[11] Though much exciting work is being done exploring affect as a precognitive capacity in the Deluzean tradition, this project relies instead on those who take up political feeling, the feeling of politics. Scholars like Lauran Berlant, Ann Cvetkovich, Sara Ahmed, and others offer tools to understand how social movements are felt, how capitalism is experienced, refracted, enjoyed, and despaired of. In analyzing the circulation of affect with queer nonprofit spaces, Ana Agathangelou, Morgan Bassichis, and Tamara Spira's concept of "affective economies" is particularly helpful. Affective economies, they argue, index "the various ways we become invested emotionally, libidinally, and erotically in global capitalism's mirages of safety and inclusion."[12] Rather than simply analyzing the historical and political changes that have enabled the nonprofitization of queer movements, this book investigates how those changes are felt, contested, re-fracted, lived with, and grappled over.

In particular, this book builds on the work of Deborah Gould, who, in her important text *Moving Politics: Emotion and Act Up's Fight Against AIDS*, theorized the "emotional habitus" of the gay and lesbian community in the context of AIDS.[13] Gould investigates what she calls "the emotional work of movements," suggesting that affect has a central, and often over-looked, role in "generating, and foreclosing, political horizons."[14] I extend that project into investigating the ways that feelings are animated within institutions, the way that LGBT nonprofits operationalize and monetize feeling, targeting and intensifying some affective orientations and limiting others.

The case studies at the heart of *Gay, Inc.* are organized around the ex-ploration of the economies of feelings that queer nonprofits generate, rely on, capitalize upon, and evoke in a range of actors, from funders to partici-pants to staff and volunteers. This stems from both a theoretical and meth-odological commitment to excavating the role of affect in maintaining the primacy of an institutional form that, perversely, often undermines its own "mission." Methodologically, I analyze nonprofits as what Ann Cvetkovich calls "repositories of feelings and emotions."[15] These nonprofit sites "be-come sticky, or saturated with affect, as sites of personal and social ten-sion."[16] Affect is a key conduit through which the power of the nonprofit system flows, reliant as it is on feelings of generosity on the part of donors, their sense of connection, their understanding of themselves as citizens, as community members, as "leaders" with something to offer. It is also through affect, though, that we can glimpse the system breaking down, the ruptures and inconsistencies, failures and contradictions: "clients" who are expected to feel grateful but don't, the frustration and sadness of staff de-spite the cultural narrative that holds that they are "doing such *good work.*"

The chapters that follow trace four distinct but overlapping affective orientations: *compassion, community, capital,* and *crisis.* Each of these frameworks is material and discursive, and is built on a series of implicit and explicit *affective transactions*: the exchange of a wealthy donor's guilt for money, for instance, or the expectation of a client's gratefulness in ex-change for services. Fundamentally, each is *felt.* Further, each has a par-ticular salience in queer social movements.

Compassion, which lies at the heart of the U.S. charity model—a sys-tem of control over populations made surplus by capitalism—grafts older disciplinary models of poverty governance onto new approaches to issues like queer youth homelessness, HIV/AIDS, sex work—even ideas of queer community itself. Compassion has always been a defining logic of poverty governance in the United States, and throughout U.S. history the figure of the "deserving" poor is used to rationalize the abandonment and policing of those deemed "undeserving." In this sense, compassion has always served as a disciplinary form of power, directed at particular bodies—poor people, immigrants, unwed mothers, the homeless, and the sexually deviant, among others—intended to reform, control, manage, and police behaviors and moral postures. Of course, as scholars and activists have shown again and again, compassion is a stance specifically intended *not* to disrupt current configurations of power, but rather to ameliorate the harm it causes while simultaneously entrenching the wealth of the ruling class. Compassion, I argue, has seen a resurgence through the nonprofitization of poverty management since 1970, and, as such, has had a profound—but largely unremarked upon—impact on queer politics.

The impact of disciplinary logics of compassion has been buttressed and augmented by the logic of *community*, a paradigmatic discourse of late capitalism—and of contemporary LGBT movements—which conceptualizes nonprofits as sites of togetherness and shared identity, in which difference falls away. Community has been a particularly salient framework of neoliberal multiculturalism, where political power is often exercised through consumption, and queer people have been reconfigured as target niche markets. Community is not just what Nikolas Rose and Soo Ah Kwon refer to as an "affirmative" form of governmentality, however, since producing "the community" also produces threatening others who fall outside it.[17] For LGBT nonprofits, the techniques of hailing and mobilizing queer community rely on the policing of racialized others, especially poor queer and gender-nonconforming people of color. Thus for contemporary queer movements, community is both affirmative— fostering a sense of unity through consumption, desire, and the articulation of uniquely LGBT identities and issues—and negative: the reliance on urban policing, gentrification, exclusion, and segregation. In this sense, community is what Foucault describes as a "biopolitical" form of governance: the power—directed at the population, rather than at individual bodies—to increase the life chances of some while "exposing [others] to death, increasing the risk of death for some people."[18] The dual nature of community—both affirmative and policing—is what Jasbir Puar calls a "bio-necro collaboration," directing some bodies toward life and other, queerly racialized bodies, toward death. It is within "the interstices of life and death" that I locate LGBT nonprofits: an apparatus that produces, disciplines, and regulates particular queer subjects.[19] Nonprofits, then, operate as a form of hybrid statecraft, a critical relay in circuits of governance that knit the disciplinary technologies of the welfare state to the biopolitical scope of the neoliberal security state.

Connected to the logics of compassion and community is a contested discursive and material orientation toward *capital* within contemporary LGBT nonprofits, in which the nonprofit system is structured to consolidate and upwardly redistribute wealth, even as actors within some queer nonprofits actively work against it. Although often difficult to approach as an affective project, capitalism is profoundly *felt*, in myriad ways: the feeling of efficiency, of lavish corporate-style fundraisers, and, just as acutely, the felt experience of never having enough. These feelings are at the heart of the nonprofitized queer movement. Despite the work of activists within queer nonprofits to grapple with and contest the profound inequalities caused by racialized capitalism, nonprofits themselves increasingly adopt businesslike structures, use corporate-style management techniques and language, and operate according to increasingly market-driven principles. Although numerous scholars have critiqued the consumption-oriented turn in queer politics, less attention has been paid to the degree to which LGBT nonprofits increasingly articulate queer identity and issues through the corporate language of logic models, return on investment, efficiency, and branding.[20] LGBT nonprofits offer a unique window onto late capitalism: within queer nonprofits, capitalism is both more and less complete than is often imagined. Nonprofits are certainly not outside capitalism, as some naively imagine, but neither are they wholly corporate: they reveal the fractures, inconsistencies, and contradictions of advanced capitalism, even as they document its ascendency. Central to this project is recognizing the degree to which market logics are resisted and refracted on a daily basis, in small and large ways, in the actual practice of capitalism in nonprofits. Further, nonprofits also offer a somewhat contradictory case study of state power under advanced capitalism. Rather than reflecting a withdrawal of the state, as many scholars of neoliberalism have theorized, nonprofits instead illustrate the expansion of state power through governance that is increasingly nodal, operating through a fragmented web of nonprofit locations, which are, nonetheless, sites of policing and discipline.[21]

Finally, this book explores multiple levels and discourses of *crisis* operating within nonprofits, as organizations struggle to deal with the social and economic catastrophe produced by advanced capitalism: crumbling public infrastructure, militarized urban policing, segregation, and entrenched and expanding inequality among the people seeking their services. Meanwhile, the structure of the nonprofit itself is perpetually in crisis, dependent on an untenable funding structure based on a gift economy. The financial structure of the nonprofit sector at large is based on donations, monetary gifts predicated on the largesse of wealthy donors, donors often unwilling to fund the long-term systemic changes that are necessary to truly address the social crisis with which nonprofits contend— changes that might disrupt the system of power that creates such wealth for those donors. These structural factors imbue nonprofits with a constant sense of impending devastation, as managers hustle for the next grant or major donor, as frontline staff try to find time to deal with their grief and trauma amidst pressing need, as clients piece together a web of inadequate services, and as clients, staff, volunteers, and community members alike invest the hope they have for another, more just, world.

I am not interested in celebrating the "good works" of nonprofits, nor am I interested in rehearsing a declension narrative about the uncontested domination of neoliberalism. This project instead exposes the murky world of practice, of complicity, and of complex personhood—it lives in the world of committed people doing the best they can, and the structures in which they participate, rail against, ignore, and make do.

An Embedded Nonprofiteer: A Note on Method and Theory

Exploring the blurry lines between the radical imaginary of queer social movements and its institutional iterations is central to this project, exposing the conflicting logics that structure nonprofits, the limits of community, and how "we" imagine—and organize toward—a better world. In order to do so, I employ an interdisciplinary approach involving ethnography, interviews, archival research, and personal reflection. The book centers on case studies at four Midwestern LGBT nonprofits, two in Chicago and two in Minneapolis. Using interviews—with staff, volunteers, participants, donors, and board members—and analyzing archival records—including local gay newspaper coverage, internal communications, strategic plans, grant applications, and fundraising appeals—I examine the ways that individuals and organizations grapple with the constraints of private and state funding, the pressures of austerity, the dynamics of the charity framework, and the way that community is articulated and enacted through the 501(c)(3) apparatus. The organizations at the center of this book are not the spaces that typically come to mind when one imagines "the LGBT movement." They did not directly engage in marriage advocacy, and as that issue became increasingly paramount in the last fifteen years, so too did the organizations that advocated for it come to stand for "the movement." But the organizations discussed in this book, and hundreds like them, do indeed constitute the imagined community of "the movement": they produce and police ideas about queer community, they articulate the horizons of queer politics, and they operate within the same affective—and structural—world as advocacy organizations.[22] Though the formal legal equality agenda has become dominant, and legislative and legal advocacy the movement's most prominent tools, this is a fairly recent phenomenon. In the earlier days of the movement, in the 1970s and 1980s, queer politics was envisioned and enacted in a wide range of spaces, and as the movement sought legitimacy through nonprofitization, it did so through a similarly wide variety of organizations: community centers, clinics, youth spaces, social services, legal services, and theaters, alongside more traditional legislative advocacy. Even now, though legal advocacy has come to dominate our imagination of the movement, some of the most important political work is happening in community organizing spaces that critique legislative advocacy as a tactic. The politics and tactics of organizations like the Human Rights Campaign and the National Gay and Lesbian Task Force, two national organizations that are often invoked as constituting "the movement," have been widely critiqued. Organizations like those discussed in this book have not. Nonetheless, all of them—from radical grassroots organizations, to corporate-style community centers, to national legislative advocacy organizations—operate within the same constraints inherent in the nonprofit form. At the organizations I analyze, therefore, the strong interplay of neoliberal discourses of community, disciplinary logics of compassion, contested orientations toward capital, and the pervasive sense of crisis are just as glaring as those at mainstream national movements, but they are nonetheless largely unmarked.

The organizations I examine are also all spaces to which I am connected, to greater or lesser degrees. At one space, I was an employee for two years;

at another, I was a board member.[23] The other two I engaged with as a community member and, at one, in my capacity as a staff member at a partner organization. This proximity simultaneously offered me unique access and posed interesting methodological challenges. I approach these spaces as what Sara Ahmed calls "contact zones" between institutional and everyday forms of contact. According to Ahmed, contact writing does "not simply interweave the personal and the public, the individual and the social, but show[s] the ways in which they take shape through each other, or even how they shape each other."[24] The people with whom I spoke are critical actors—they know what they are doing as much, if not more, than I know what I am doing—they struggle, they make choices, they are constrained, and their ideas about the world are produced, as are mine, through powerful and pervasive cultural narratives about difference, inequality, merit, citizenship, and "the good life." I share with them an investment in queer nonprofits, an investment of emotional and physical energy, and I share with them the frustration that the work we want to be doing through those nonprofits is often constrained, co-opted, or just out of the reach of our imaginations. At various points I also deeply disagree with them and their assumptions about the organizations they work for or believe in.

This proximity did not resolve the fundamental impossibility of representing the other, a challenge at the heart of all ethnographic work, and one with which I have struggled mightily throughout this project. One area in which this struggle has been particularly acute has been in the question of whether and how to chronicle the experiences of clients and participants of the nonprofits I study, participants who occupy a particularly vulnerable position in relationship to those organizations and to me as a researcher. When my location was one of case manager rather than researcher, I often received calls and emails from scholars investigating queer youth homelessness, or transgender teens, or HIV/AIDS. Those researchers sometimes wanted to host a focus group, have clients complete surveys, or conduct one-on-one interviews, often in exchange for a ten or fifteen dollar Target gift card, or something comparable. I often went to great lengths to reroute or dissuade those researchers, out of a concern that the cost for participants—unearthing traumas—outweighed the benefit—a few dollars to spend at Target. In conversations with my colleagues—many of whom are now, years later, my informants—we discussed what we felt was the ethical failure of asking these people who work every day to survive to let down their guards and expose traumas often held at bay, out of necessity, through sheer force of will, sometimes with the help of substances, simply so that someone could write a book.

Now, of course, I am the researcher, a position that frequently demands documenting, however partially, the experiences of those who are often absent from popular and scholarly discourse, and whose absence is necessary for power structures to remain as they are. This paradox—the importance of documenting the experiences of marginalized subjects out of a concern with justice coupled with the exploitation inherent in doing so—has been a central methodological, theoretical, and ethical quandary for this project. What this has meant for my particular project is that I rely much more heavily on the experiences and perspectives of staff of nonprofits—as well as volunteers, donors, board members, and the like— rather than clients and participants. I chose not to conduct focus groups or offer monetary compensation for interviews. When I do interview clients or participants they are people with whom I have a relationship—for example, fellow board members—or they are in a position where the cost of sharing their experiences is mitigated somewhat by their circumstances— their basic needs are met, and they have the emotional and physical space to wander through their memories without significant trauma. This is what Johannes Fabian calls a practice of "not-writing," an ethical approach to gathering and interpreting ethnographic "data" that recognizes that what is *not* written is sometimes just as, if not more, important than what is.[25] While there is certainly another book to be written that centers the experiences of clients of nonprofits, this methodological choice has also opened a particular affective window, one onto the emotional lives of staff, board members, volunteers, people who believe in nonprofits, who invest in them, who are let down by them, who try to make them better.

Finally, in writing about these spaces, I use the actual organization names, but obscure the names of my informants and refer to them throughout using pseudonyms. The organizations are each unique in the Midwest—the only trans-specific youth organization, for example, or the only LGBT health center—so obscuring their names would not actually obscure their identities. Instead, I have changed the names of my informants, and often their personal characteristics, job titles, or the dates of their involvement, and at times, even split one informant's narrative into two pseudonym identities.[26] Because I ask informants to speak candidly about leadership failures, questionable decisions, unhealthy workplace dynamics, frustrations, and fears, and because, in the case of clients and staff, they are reliant on these organizations for either services or a paycheck, it is critical that their contributions to this project not jeopardize their relationships with the organizations. Despite obscuring these details of their identities, I have carefully crafted pseudonym identities that represent similar, if not identical, positionalities.

Chapter 1 offers critical context for analyzing the case studies that follow. In particular, chapter 1 investigates the role of the voluntary sector in the political economic history of U.S. approaches to poverty in order to outline the stakes of the contemporary nonprofitization of social movements. The chapter begins by considering the expansion of the nonprofit system as a key feature of neoliberalism, the political economic framework that has risen to ascendency in the United States and globally since the mid-1960s. Since the waning years of the 1960s, decades of erosion of public services and the social safety net have outsourced the provision of basic services to a patchwork network of nonprofit organizations, which have, in turn, expanded on a massive scale in order to meet those needs. The role of charity in facilitating capitalism is not new, however, and chapter 1 further contextualizes the contemporary nonprofit within the history of the voluntary sector in the United States, arguing that the nonprofit has always been central to the ascendency and power of capitalism in the United States. Ultimately, chapter 1 provides the framework for the case studies that follow, illustrating the ways that the nonprofit structure that is now so widely used by social movement organizations was not inevitable, does important social work, and has had a profound impact on the political horizons of social movements.

Chapter 2 addresses the murky space between social movements and social services at the Howard Brown Health Center (HBHC) in Chicago, my former employer. I focus on the development of their HIV/AIDS programs in the 1980s as well as the contemporary story of their youth homelessness program, the Broadway Youth Center (BYC). Both of these moments illustrate the limits of the institutional logic of *compassion*. This site reveals the legacy of an older charity framework, animated by discourses of worthiness and uplift, inherited by the modern nonprofit. I first trace how the particular narrative of AIDS mobilized by HBHC, necessitated by the quest to corporatize their institutional structure, imagined HIV positive people of color as outside "the community," at risk because of injection drug use and not same-sex sexual behavior. Instead, as Howard Brown turned toward major donors and corporate sponsorships, they mobilized a compassion narrative of the deserving victim made poor by illness, an alternative to the racialized antiwelfare discourse of the period that was palatable to white, suburban, affluent donors and corporate sponsors. Ultimately this strategy relied on and endorsed the same narrative of compassion and charity that was, during that very period, being mobilized by Reagan to dismantle the social welfare system. In contrast, the issue of queer youth homelessness presents a fundamental challenge to the single-issue identity politics of Howard Brown, and the alignment between the BYC and its parent organization has always been uneasy. At Howard Brown, after three decades of corporatization of management systems, the consolidation of a traditional development and administrative machine, and the incorporation of neoliberal values at every level, the BYC hardly fits into Howard Brown's strategic positioning as a "boutique" clinic that wealthy, insured, LGBT people would choose to utilize.

Chapter 3 addresses the production and management of *community* at the Center on Halsted, the Chicago LGBT community center: its appeal, the mechanics of its production, the affective economies on which it relies, the moments it exceeds the terms under which it was mobilized, and the possibilities it enables and forecloses. This chapter analyzes a series of conflicts over who constitutes "the community" of the community center, why, and to what ends. First I trace a viral campaign to "Take Back Boystown" from the increasing numbers of queer and gender-nonconforming homeless youth of color accessing the community center, and the idea held by some in the neighborhood that the Center on Halsted was a "magnet" drawing those "undesirable" youth to the fashionable and gentrifying gay neighborhood of Boystown. A second conflict focussed on the Center on Halsted Anti-Violence Program's acceptance of an anti-sex trafficking grant from the Cook County State's Attorney's office despite the seeming knowledge that it would do very little to increase the safety of the young people it targeted—and perhaps even further endanger them—once again illustrating the institutional structures which butt up against and enforce the limits of "community." I argue that community, in the institutional arrangement considered in this chapter, functions according to a biopolitical rather than strictly disciplinary logic. In the context of neoliberalism's ever-expanding ability to incorporate particular queer bodies into the national imaginary and technologies of control, community is increasingly the logic through which some queer bodies are protected and folded into (national) life, and others are located outside the life of the nation, a threat to it, and exposed to early death. At the Center on Halsted, some queer lives are optimized through therapy, social programs, educational offerings, job resources, and networking, while other lives are located outside "the community," and regulated through explicit relationships with the police, the on-site security guards, and conflicts over the space itself.

Chapter 4 turns to an LGBT youth space in Minneapolis, District 202, documenting its (contested) transformation from a social justice organization into a "social entrepreneurship" organization pursuing "mainstreaming" through collaborations with corporate partners, culminating in its eventual closure and the loss of its nonprofit status. The transformation of this organization offers a useful window into the role of *capital* in contemporary LGBT social movements in the United States. District 202 was envisioned as an organization "by and for" LGBT youth, a direct critique of the compassion logic of the charity model, in which only the elites "know what's best" for the targets of their services. But what does "by and for" youth mean for the structure of the organization? Is a nonprofit infrastructure compatible with true leadership of marginalized people? This chapter considers one of the core questions of this project, whether the nonprofit form can be used to advance social justice, a question that hinges on the nonprofit's structural orientation toward capital. The transformation of District 202 illustrates that the danger is in assuming the nonprofit form is benign, simply "good," or vacant of power, ready to be occupied by the progressive politics of the organization.

Chapter 5 analyzes a Minneapolis organization with which I worked for many years, the Trans Youth Support Network (TYSN). TYSN was founded by a group of primarily white youth workers after a series of instances of violence against trans women of color in Minneapolis in 2006. Those young, white, queer lefties wanted to challenge social services to become more accessible to trans people, believing that if trans youth had more of their basic needs met they would be subject to less violence. This chapter considers under what terms trans youth of color, who occupy a particularly precarious social position, engage with the nonprofit structure. TYSN points to the necessity of what Avery Gordon calls a "stance of undefeated despair," the simultaneous grief and rage over the ubiquitous violence directed at brown trans bodies, that "is the basis for the carrying-on-regardless that the struggle for emancipation and happiness requires."[27]

Exploring the various ways that activists take seriously the nonprofit structure and attempt to work their way around it, thwart it, take it, and use it for liberatory ends, the conclusion takes up the stance of undefeated despair and considers the value of melancholia, disidentification, mourning, and other practices of resistance. In the months following TYSN's decision to become youth-led, the organization did indeed lose funding. Youth staff worked for months without pay before deciding to close the doors. The conclusion takes up this closure and considers the value of failure as an analytical frame, as well as concrete practices that queer organizers can use to resist the co-optation of their work and politics that the nonprofit structure invites.

1

Neoliberalism, Nonprofitization, and Social Change

Despite the present ubiquity of nonprofits in the United States, in 1960 there were only approximately 3,000 501(c)(3) nonprofits in the United States. By 2015, that number had risen to 1,571,689.[1] In 2013, the largest sector, public charities, held just over $3 trillion in assets.[2] The total assets held by nonprofits increased by 106 percent in just ten years, from 1998 to 2008, reflecting a level of growth that far outpaces both the state and business sector. Nonprofits accounted for 9.2 percent of all wages and salaries paid in the United States in 2010, and in 2012 contributed $887 billion to the U.S. economy. Charitable giving totaled $390.05 billion in 2016, and further, approximately a quarter of adults in the United States volunteer.[3]

Despite this ubiquity, the nonprofit form is fascinatingly elusive. Called NGOs, or nongovernmental organizations elsewhere in the world, in the United States the nonprofit occupies a legal status within the tax code, 501(c)(3), that indicates tax-exempt status, although even this is only a partial definition: many small community organizations that we would imagine to be nonprofits do not have that designation, while many large corporations, like hospitals, do.[4] Despite this ambiguity, the nonprofit occupies a constitutive place in the American imaginary, believed to exist outside the market as well as outside the state, and therefore exempt from both profit motives and venal political power. Nonprofits are imagined to constitute a mythical "third sector," the "civil society," the incorruptible outside, the proverbial public square. This is a constitutive fiction. Instead, I argue, the nonprofit form is deeply imbricated in both the state and the market, both materially and discursively.

Materially, these organizations are typically funded by individual donations; by philanthropies, largely with wealth accumulated via profits and held by families or corporations; by corporations themselves, as a tool of profit-seeking via targeted image-management; or by the state, often providing services subcontracted by the state—housing, after-school programming, education, and medical care, to name a few such services.

Further, they apply to the state for nonprofit designation, the 501(c)(3) tax-exempt designation, according to regulations created and managed by the state. But these organizations are also constitutive of our very ideas of the market and the state themselves. In imagining what constitutes an *outside* of capitalism or state power, we produce and reiterate ideas about the role of the market, its limits, the purpose and proper objects of state power, and the fundamental characteristics of each. The case studies that follow demonstrate both these material relations as well as their corresponding discursive function, both equally powerful.

This chapter is intended to provide the historical context and conceptual frameworks necessary to analyze the case studies that follow. In particular, this chapter argues that in order to comprehend the conservativizing effect of the nonprofit form on queer politics, we must recognize the nonprofit form as critical to the development, ascendency, and primacy of capitalism in the United States. Therefore, this chapter begins by outlining the political economic engine for the massive expansion of the nonprofit system in the United States: neoliberalism. It then traces the development of the voluntary sector in the United States, the emergence of which was critical to the development of a uniquely American form of capitalism. Placed in this context we can then analyze the impact of this structural form on U.S. social movements—and in particular, LGBT movements—of the last half-century.

Neoliberalism and the Rise of the Nonprofit Industrial Complex

The massive expansion of the nonprofit system that began in the mid-1960s has been facilitated by a wholesale transformation over the same period in the way the needs of people living in poverty are, and are not, met. This transformation is one feature of neoliberalism, a set of economic and social policies championing fiscal austerity, deregulation, privatization, and "free trade" that was articulated in the early Cold War by followers of Austrian political philosopher Friedrich von Hayek—among them American economist Milton Friedman—and rose to global ascendency in the 1980s with the Reagan administration in the United States and the Thatcher administration in the United Kingdom. Neoliberalism continues to be the dominant political and social framework of both the left and the right in the global north, and through multilateral organizations like the World Bank, World Trade Organization, and International Monetary

Fund, neoliberal reforms have been coercively instituted in many global south economies through structural adjustment schemes.

Neoliberalism is, however, not just a set of policy frameworks; perhaps more insidiously, it is a way of seeing the world, an orientation, and a set of "common-sense" assumptions about capital, consumption, the state, and inequality. According to Foucault, American neoliberalism is not simply a policy choice, but a "whole way of being and thinking"[5] in which the market is generalized to become a "principle of intelligibility"[6] through which subjects are produced and made meaningful. For Wendy Brown, this rationality "exceeds particular positions on particular issues" about which those on the right and those on the left might disagree, and instead forms the very horizon of possibility for the enunciation of "issues" and "positions."[7] Therefore, while Reagan and Clinton, for example, certainly differed on particular policy approaches to poverty, they shared the fundamental framework of neoliberalism.

It is in this context that we must place the massive expansion of the nonprofit system in the United States, as well as its sanctified place in the national imaginary that has largely shielded the system from critical scrutiny. Although initially spurred by Great Society funding in the 1960s, the exponential expansion of the nonprofit system in the 1980s and 1990s reflects in the inverse the demise of the social safety net in the United States, and the discursive tools used to facilitate the demise. At the same time that right-wing politicians were mobilizing narratives demonizing poor women of color as welfare queens gaming the system, a parallel discursive project championed volunteerism, charity, and community togetherness as alternatives to the supposedly bloated welfare state. Beginning in the mid-1960s with Barry Goldwater's failed presidential run, and solidifying during the Nixon administration, politicians mobilized powerful antiwelfare rhetoric demonizing people of color living in poverty and rhetorically linking urban civil unrest with racialized crime, in order to simultaneously undermine civil rights movements and underwrite massive spending cuts to social welfare programs.[8] However, to bolster support for vast reductions in the social safety net—a safety net on which the majority of those who rely are white—fear-based hysteria about lazy welfare cheats and bloated government bureaucracy was not enough. Buttressing this narrative was an affirmative nationalism centered on volunteerism and community. Instead of government programs, they advocated volunteerism, private charity, and faith- and community-based "solutions" to the dislocations and inequality caused by advancing capitalism. On the occasion of the centennial of the United Way, Reagan articulated this narrative:

> Since earliest times, we Americans have joined together to help each other and to strengthen our communities. Our deep-rooted spirit of caring, of neighbor helping neighbor, has become an American trademark—and an American way of life. Over the years, generous and inventive people have created an ingenious network of voluntary organizations to give help where help is needed.[9]

And to a great extent, this discursive project has been wildly successful, with the nonprofit system largely escaping critical scrutiny.

In her book *Sweet Charity: Emergency Food and the End of Entitlement*, Janet Poppendieck argues that the offloading of core social safety net provisions onto the nonprofit sector "is at once a *symptom* and a *cause* of our society's failure to face up to and deal with the erosion of equality."[10] The expansion of the nonprofit system, she argues,

> works pervasively on a cultural level by serving as a sort of "moral safety valve"; it reduces the discomfort evoked by visible destitution in our midst by creating the illusion of effective action and offering us myriad ways of participating in it. It creates a culture of charity that normalizes destitution and legitimates personal generosity as a response to major social and economic dislocation.[11]

Further, she argues, this new array of small, disconnected, underfunded nonprofit organizations is wholly inadequate to the task of providing the kinds of services that the centralized state-run welfare programs once offered, and their maintenance "absorbs the attention and energy of many of the people most concerned about the poor, distracting them from the larger issues of distributional politics."[12] It is not surprising, then, that "poverty grows deeper as our charitable responses to it multiply."[13]

The proliferation of nonprofits further dovetails with waning public approval for direct benefits for people living in poverty, meaning that nonprofit organizations can only provide "stuff"—food, case management, services—but not cash benefits, just at the moment when public cash benefits are slashed. Nonprofits are regarded as bastions of good works and volunteerism, while welfare is demonized as bloated and habit-forming. National conversations about income redistribution, conversations that had come briefly to the fore in the 1960s, have faded into the distance, while people living in poverty have even fewer resources to maintain their tenuous grasp on life. Though these faith-based appeals to charity are often understood as examples of the Christian moralism of neoconservatives—George W. Bush's "compassionate conservatism" for example—to the extent that appeals to charity serve as a pretext for the erosion of public services, they reflect what Wendy Brown calls "neo-liberal political rationality."[14]

Jennifer Wolch describes this new constellation of organizations—what she terms the shadow state—that rose in the wake of welfare state reorganization: "a para-state apparatus comprised of multiple voluntary sector organizations, administered outside of traditional democratic politics and charged with major collective responsibilities previously shouldered by the public sector."[15] One defining characteristic of this new array of organizations is the degree to which it is influenced by corporate wealth, both in its reliance on private philanthropy and through direct funding by corporations and corporate foundations. This distinctly neoliberal feature allows corporations to cleanse their image through support for "good causes" and to appeal to particular identity groups, as evidenced by corporate support for Pride festivals as a bid to appear "gay friendly" to consumers despite policies that make life even more precarious for their poorly paid workers, both gay and straight.[16]

Dylan Rodriguez terms this the nonprofit industrial complex (NPIC): "a set of symbiotic relationships that link together political and financial technologies of state and owning-class proctorship and surveillance over public intercourse, including and especially emergent progressive and leftist movements, since about the mid-1970s."[17] The expansion of the NPIC does not, however, represent a retreat of the state. On the contrary, as the subsequent chapters illustrate, the NPIC is a vehicle for the expansion, rather than retraction, of state power, exercised through the governance function of nonprofits dispersed throughout the social body. The NPIC legitimizes structural social inequality both morally and materially, and it works alongside more overtly policing institutions like prisons, urban schools, and the low wage labor markets to manage, direct, and discipline bodies.

Transnational NGOs

Neoliberalism is a fundamentally transnational phenomenon that produces rationalities and economic realities that are at once deeply local as well as profoundly imbricated in global networks, flows, and the differently enabled movement of wealth and bodies. U.S. nonprofits, therefore, are both specific to their local contexts and deeply tied to these transnational systems. The larger process that I take up in this book—namely, the co-optation, management, and recuperation of social movements in and through neoliberal capitalism—is similarly a global phenomenon. Sangeeta Kamat, in her foreword to the edited volume *NGO-ization*, quotes Arundhati Roy in quipping that "the greater the devastation caused by neoliberalism, the greater the outbreak of NGOs."[18]

The signifier nongovernmental organization, or NGO, was created by Article 71 of the 1945 United Nations charter, a capacious term which includes any kind of organization that is, at least in theory, independent of the state and not a profit generating enterprise. A recent social media campaign entitled #NGOfacts, organized by Nonprofit Action, has popularized the idea that there are ten million NGOs worldwide.[19] Michael Edwards and Alan Fowler estimated that by the year 2000 NGOs were dispersing between twelve and fifteen billion dollars per year.[20] In fact, the Johns Hopkins Center for Civil Society Studies estimates that if NGOs were a state they would have the fifth largest economy in the world. Further, many critics have noted that the NGO sector is often more powerful than the state itself. Though the critique of the nonprofit system is nascent in the United States, burgeoning especially since the 2006 publication of the groundbreaking anthology by Incite! Women of Color Against Violence, *The Revolution Will Not Be Funded,* the critique of NGOs in the global south has a decades-long history. Global south activists, as well as transnational feminists and scholars of development, have produced detailed and nuanced critiques of the deceptively central role of NGOs in globalization, in controlling and co-opting people's movements, and in advancing neoliberal rationalities through "empowerment" programs.[21] NGOs have been widely criticized as advancing a fundamentally neocolonial relationship of power.[22] Some scholars argue that NGOs maintain Western hegemony, even after former colonies gain independence, by undermining the power and sovereignty of the state by funding a civil society that advances Western norms and power.[23]

It is not just Western funding itself, but rather the mode of NGO intervention that causes James Ferguson, among other scholars, to argue that development NGOs are also fundamentally depoliticizing for social movements and popular uprisings.[24] Tania Li calls this mode "rendering technical," in which asymmetries of power are transformed into "problems" that require "technical" solutions. Li describes how the practice of "rendering technical" "confirms expertise and constitutes the boundary between those who are positioned as trustees, with the capacity to diagnose deficiencies in others, and those who are subject to expert direction."[25] In this way, people's protest movements are undermined by a turn toward a culture of experts providing models, "capacity building," and "best practices," and then tying those approaches to funding. These experts are, of course, funded largely in the West and operate within a development framework, and they are therefore unwilling to identify the violences of structural adjustment regimes or the fundamentally disempowering nature of their "empowerment" programs.

Though my own analysis would not be possible without this important work, it is worth noting that U.S. nonprofits have largely escaped the attention of critical NGO scholarship. This gap is telling. It primarily has to do with the different affective regime within which U.S. nonprofits operate. For instance, the editors of the volume *Theorizing NGOs: States, Feminisms, Neoliberalism* note that the long-standing assumption of the basic good-ness of NGOs is no longer a given. While this may be true of the organizations reported on by authors in that volume, primarily in the global south and the former Soviet Union, it is not, by and large, the case in the United States, where the nonprofit form is still venerated as essentially good, and moreover, a site of American Exceptionalism, of all that is supposedly distinctly good about America: cooperation, community, faith, charity, volunteerism, kindness, and self-reliance. This exceptionalist notion insulates U.S. nonprofits from the kind of critique leveled against the NGOs elsewhere in the world.

Because this kind of exceptionalism is so effective at shielding the U.S. nonprofit sector from scrutiny, in order to understand how and why the U.S. nonprofit structure has so powerfully shaped movement politics with so little critical attention, it is essential to trace the prehistory of the contemporary nonprofit system, investigating the relationship between settler colonialism, early capitalism, state power, and the establishment of a distinct, and distinctly American, voluntary sector.

"Repressive Benevolence": Compassion and the Disciplining of Difference

Though U.S. nonprofits have come to exert an especially powerful role in the management of poverty in the context of neoliberal governance, the nongovernmental organization has always been important in the development of uniquely American forms of both capitalism and statecraft. In fact, as David Wagner writes, "the origins of our charitable institutions are integrally connected with a vision of repression over those deemed different, dangerous, or 'deviant.'"[26] At the center of the development of U.S. capitalism, state power, and national identity are two massive projects for accumulation of land and wealth: the genocide of Native American populations and chattel slavery. And at the center of slavery and genocide, we find missions, voluntary organizations, and other charities. In his book *What's Love Got to Do with It?* David Wagner traces charity as a "moral technology" that functioned alongside military violence for disciplining various social others.[27] Missions to "civilize" Native Americans, for instance, were key activities of a wide range of religious, and later secular, voluntary organizations, ones that later turned these same technologies on other "deviant" populations such as immigrants and single mothers. Under the cover of "doing good" those organizations were able to undertake a kind of violence that might have otherwise aroused resistance from voters or lawmakers. "While most colonizers wanted the Indian's *land*," Wagner notes, "the repressive philanthropists also demanded their *souls* and their *culture*."[28] The overtly moralizing tone and the discourses of racial difference deployed in benevolent societies' undertakings toward Native Americans were incorporated into charitable institutions targeting poor whites, and ultimately made their way into federal poverty policy.

Wagner and historian Peter Dobkin Hall note that early American approaches to poverty policy differed significantly from English Poor Laws, which provided direct aid. Informed by the civilizing missions targeting Native Americans, Wagner argues that colonial approaches to poverty focused on spiritual uplift rather than tangible benefits. Unlike the vague acknowledgement of entrenched class inequality reflected in English Poor Laws, in the colonial United States poverty was associated with personal moral failure; instead of cash benefits, coaching and instruction on the ways of right living were offered, thus creating an "American" form of poverty management: wholly more judgmental, moralistic, and individualized. Cotton Mather, for instance, informed by missions proselytizing to

Native Americans, entreated his congregants to "always bear in mind that charity to the *souls* of men is the highest form of benevolence."[29] Mather went further, in fact, and demanded that those with charitable inclinations use caution, because "giving wisely is therefore an even greater obligation than giving generously; and withholding alms to the undeserving as needful and essentially benevolent as bestowing them on the deserving."[30] The belief that poverty is essentially a moral and spiritual failing came to influence greatly both the development of early capitalism and the state's approaches to its management, underwriting a patchwork system of alms and charity mixed with moral uplift as the commonsense and correct way of organizing care in the United States.

The individualizing and moralizing approaches of charity in the United States became further entrenched through the development of private philanthropy during the Progressive Era, beginning in the 1890s with the publication of Andrew Carnegie's *Gospel of Wealth,* in which he called for proactive philanthropy. He wrote: "The best means of benefitting the community is to place within its reach the ladders upon which the aspiring can rise."[31] Carnegie believed that outright charity, however, encouraged "the slothful, the drunken, the unworthy," and that the responsibility for addressing poverty must lie with men of industry. During this same period, John D. Rockefeller, who shared Carnegie's zeal for philanthropy, was soon overwhelmed with requests for aid to his foundation, a $100 million endowment for the "betterment of mankind." He hired staff to implement the principle of "scientific giving," and as the legal structure for the foundation became clearer, the modern foundation—with its open-ended endowment, gifts to organizations rather than direct involvement, and staff rather than direct donor control—was born. The first foundation of this type was the Russell Sage Foundation, chartered in 1907 for the "permanent improvement of social conditions."[32] These industrialists intended to create what Hall calls a "private sector alternative to socialism," one that would buttress the social system that produced their wealth, but ameliorate the most devastating impacts of its accumulation.[33] These foundations had and retain important additional functions: they are fundamentally tax shelters, in which vast private fortunes are spared taxation and, thus, public direction over their distribution. Contemporary foundations are required to disperse only 5 percent of their holdings in the form of charitable contributions—far less than the rate of taxation to which those fortunes would otherwise be subject. Thus, exempt from taxation, these private fortunes accumulate in value and are used to great effect in targeted social manipulation.

As Hall notes, however, one of the seeming contradictions of the Progressive Era was that the entrenched power of industrialist elites co-existed alongside populist anti-big business rhetoric and increasing political might of the working class. Theodore Roosevelt is famous for saying, in reference to Rockefeller, that "no amount of charity in spending such fortunes can compensate in any way for the misconduct in acquiring them."[34] A combination of militant trade-unionism, populism, socialism, and later the Great Depression forced political leaders to adopt some aspects of a social welfare state, much to the distaste of philanthropists and charity leaders. These public gains, however, were short-lived, as in the buildup to World War II, business leaders were welcomed back into the fold, leading big business to have an important voice in crafting post-war social and economic policy. As a public welfare state rose and waned, the private alternative only increased in power.

Even during Johnson's War on Poverty in the mid-1960s, thought of as the high water mark for the welfare state in the United States, the programs of the Great Society reflected the preferences of big charity more so than they established an enduring welfare state. One of the lasting legacies of the Great Society is government funding for community-based organizations in the form of block grants. Instead of centralized public social services, government provided partial funding to private organizations, outsourcing the services demanded by social movements. These block grants did not entirely fund community programs, necessitating the reliance on volunteer labor, additional fundraising, and low wages for paid staff. Not a welfare state at all, then, but what Loïc Wacquant calls a "charitable state": "limited, fragmentary, . . . informed by a moralistic and moralizing conception of poverty," and "subcontracted to private and non-profit agencies, which distribute and administer [resources] in the name of the national collectivity."[35] This intricate and unwieldy public–private mesh is, Jacob Hacker argues, "dedicated to preserving the private tilt of U.S. social policy."[36]

Throughout the history of philanthropy and organized charity, actors at various points along the political spectrum have critiqued the power held by these private entities. Only a few years after the Russell Sage Foundation was founded in 1907, the Wash Commission, in 1916, issued a report calling foundations a "grave menace" that concentrated political and social power in promoting an ideology and public policy favorable to big business. In 1959, the Senate Finance Committee decided to liberalize the tax code and allow unlimited deductions for charitable contributions. The dissenting minority wrote in their report:

> The tax base is being dangerously eroded by . . . tax exempt trusts and foundations. [Further], even more harmful social and political consequences may result from concentrating, and holding in a few hands and in perpetuity, control over large fortunes and business enterprises. The attendant inequities resulting from the tax treatment of contributions, particularly in the form of capital, to foundations are being magnified daily.[37]

In fact, one of the only major differences between the contemporary NPIC and this earlier incarnation of the "charitable state" is that throughout their history the twins of organized charity and big philanthropy have been mistrusted by the working class, targeted by social movements, despised and contested by socialists and unions. Now, of course, those same social movements have institutionalized themselves in and through the very charitable structure that they once railed against. The case studies in the following chapters demonstrate the profound impacts that the "moral technologies" of charity that are *built into* the nonprofit system are having on queer social movements, now that so many social movement organizations are literally incorporated into the nonprofit form.

"In the Shadow of the Shadow State": The Nonprofitization of U.S. Social Movements

The massive expansion of the nonprofit system in the United States since 1960 has had a substantial impact on social movements, as activist organizations incorporate into the nonprofit structure and are pulled into the technologies of power carried within what Hall calls the "private alternative to socialism."[38] In *Black Awakening in Capitalist America*, Robert Allen documents the powerful effect of the Ford Foundation in shifting black nationalist organizations away from revolutionary organizing and toward civic engagement and community economic development. According to Allen, in 1967 the Ford Foundation awarded a Harlem-based think tank $500,000 to conduct "civil rights fellowships," and ultimately focused on funding a Congress on Racial Equity (CORE) chapter in Cleveland in order to "calm" racial tension in that city. Ford funded a voter registration and education drive as well as a youth leadership program intended, according to a CORE report, "to identify and train urban ghetto youth in those . . . skills which can serve as an alternative to frustration and violence."[39] Allen notes that, according to the director of the youth leadership program, its intent was to "show that 'the legitimate hostilities and aggression of black youth' could be 'programmed' into socially acceptable channels."[40] And with the election of Carl Stokes as the first African American mayor of a major American city, due in large part to Ford-funded voter registration drives, "racial tensions" in Cleveland were indeed eased, though not through substantive change in the underlying systemic causes of that tension, but by greater integration of black revolutionary social movements into existing systems of power.

Critics of the NPIC argue that its expansion during the later movement era, post-1968, was in fact a backlash against those revolutionary movements, an attempt by big business and the state—through mechanisms like the Ford Foundation—to co-opt and redirect radical social protest. Dylan Rodriguez argues that expansion of the nonprofit system has functioned alongside more visible repressive policing technologies to restore and safeguard white supremacy in the face of black and brown power movements. According to Rodriguez, "the spectacle of Hooverite repression obscures the broader—and far more important—convergence of state and philanthropic forces in the absorption of progressive social change struggles that defined this era and its current legacies."[41] Funders have material power over what kinds of organizing and programs can be funded and what cannot, but they also wield considerable discursive power to set the limits of "common sense" ideas about social change.

The stifling effect of the nonprofit system is not merely limited to the sector's historic and resurgent charity function, although the transfer of social services from the state onto former movement organizations has had a significant impact. According to sociologist Stanley Aronowitz,

> One of the key mechanisms for transforming social movements from independent adversaries of the state to collaborators is the service contract. . . . Once militant groups . . . find themselves caught in the contradiction of the welfare state, . . . [becoming] adjunct[s] of state and local governments seeking to enhance their own legitimacy . . . like antipoverty groups and other community

organizations since the 1960s, [they are] effectively demobilized by these relationships.[42]

Nowhere is this seen more clearly than in the nonprofitization of the domestic violence movement in the United States throughout the 1980s and 1990s. Activists like Incite! Women of Color Against Violence document increasing professionalization, medicalization, and bureaucratization as movement organizations accept government and foundation funding to provide shelter and advocacy, displacing a political analysis of gendered and racialized violence for an individualized approach to "healing." Now heavily reliant on government funding, these organizations collaborated with the state in the 1980s just as Reagan's law and order politics mobilized the specter of racialized threat to bolster support for prison and policing expansion. In turning to the state for financial support and legitimacy the political aims of the movement were co-opted and used as a rationale to expand the prison industrial complex and increase surveillance and policing of urban communities of color—forms of violence that the earlier domestic violence movement placed at the center of their critique.[43] Now activists describe a domestic violence sheltering system that is punitive, individualized, led by white professional social workers rather than survivors of violence, and focused on "healing" rather than justice or systems change. It is, in fact, frustration with this system that generated and popularized a critique of the NPIC; Incite! Women of Color Against Violence, a group founded by antiviolence activists of color to protest the racism of the contemporary mainstream domestic violence movement, expanded its critique to address what they see as one major underlying cause for this co-optation: the nonprofit industrial complex.

It is not just nonprofits that provide direct social services like shelter, however, that are demobilized by these relationships. Ruth Wilson Gilmore argues that those "grassroots groups that have formally joined the third sector" exist in the "shadow" of what Jennifer Wolch calls "the shadow state."[44] Gilmore writes:

What's wrong is not simply the economic dependencies fostered by this peculiar set of relationships and interests. More important, if forms do indeed shape norms, then what's wrong is that the work that people set out to accomplish is vulnerable to becoming mission impossible under the sternly specific funding rubrics and structural prohibitions that situate grassroots groups both in the third sector's entanglements and in the shadow of the shadow state.[45]

All nonprofit organizations, even small, politically radical grassroots organizations, are implicated in this web of state power, corporate wealth, and the disciplining function of charity. This dynamic is one with which the LGBT movement has had to contend

The Nonprofitization of the LGBT Movement

It was at this pivotal moment in the history of U.S. social change activism—the dawn of neoliberalism and the retraction of the social safety net—that the modern LGBT movement intensified. Much critical work on the contemporary queer movement, including, at times, my own, has flattened the history of the LGBT movement for the sake of critique. That flattened history is simple: what was once a radically contrarian, intersectional, antiauthoritarian movement against sexual and gender norms has become a narrow, conservative attempt to secure inclusion within dominant social institutions for a select—white, middle class, monogamously coupled—few. However, this history is misleading in at least two ways: it diminishes the critical left edge of the contemporary queer movement, and it obscures the power wielded by the more moderate, tactical, and rights-focused organizations and organizers within the nascent movement of the 1960s and 1970s. There is a rich body of scholarship documenting the complexities of both the early and more recent LGBT movement, providing critical context for the following chapters. As I outline the broad contours of that history, I am particularly interested in reading the oft-fraught relationship between queer organizing and the nonprofit form.

Across the last fifty years, four fairly distinct strains of LGBT organizing emerge: 1) antiracist, intersectional, antipoverty, anti-imperialist, revolutionary organizing; 2) service-based organizing, including healthcare, poverty, homelessness, HIV/AIDS, youth; 3) electoral, legal, and rights-focused organizing; and finally, 4) community centers. There is certainly overlap between these frameworks, both at the individual level—for instance, activists who perhaps volunteer for the antiviolence hotline and participate in antiwar organizing—and at the organizational level, as perhaps an antiracist, queer people of color led organization might plan their next direct action at the community center. But in a practical sense these approaches are nonetheless distinct: they rely on different funding streams, donor bases, staff or volunteer labor, and have differing political goals, values, and structures.

Contrary to the simplified version of queer movement history, these four approaches were all active in the early movement era, and they still are. In the 1970s all of these kinds of organizing were almost exclusively volunteer led and funded via ad hoc, pass-the-hat style donations. Some of them still are, particularly those that are people of color led, grassroots based, and social justice focused. That some types of organizations and political approaches still operate on shoestring budgets, passing the hat among an already depleted cadre of volunteers and small-time donors, while others rake in corporate sponsorships and multimillion dollar grants from major private philanthropies—this is the story of nonprofitization and its effects on queer politics. The shift in politics I describe in this book, the so-called "homonormative turn" in queer movement politics, isn't so much a turn, as if the politics of particular organizations changed, but rather that some approaches and politics, those that most dovetailed with prevailing neoliberal diversity rhetoric, were amplified through funding, staffing, communications, media, and other types of organizational infrastructure—while others were not. Of interest here is the degree to which this was an infrastructural shift rather than solely a political one, facilitated by the nonprofit structure, the state, and private philanthropy.

Although there were always influential white-dominated assimilationist strains within the early gay and lesbian movement, in the years immediately following the Stonewall Riots there were also powerful voices and organizations spurring the nascent LGBT movement toward a radical, intersectional critique of state power and normativity. Emily Hobson, in her important book *Lavender and Red: Liberation and Solidarity in the Gay and Lesbian Left*, challenges the notion that gay and lesbian politics existed only in one of two expressions: separatist radicalism and liberal electoral politics. Instead, she documents a ferocious and wide ranging anti-imperialist politics that animated gay and lesbian organizing in San Francisco across three decades. Activists were involved in other New Left organizing or black and brown revolutionary people's organizations, organized for an end to the Vietnam War and against police violence, and mobilized a critique of not just sexual normativities but capitalist heteropatriarchy.

Out of the work of those New Left-aligned activists was born the short-lived Gay Liberation Front (GLF), which is an instructive example of the ways that organizational structure informs, and is informed by, political framework. Terrence Kissack, in his history of GLF describes a profoundly anti-institutional organizational structure:

> Rejecting parliamentary procedure and representative government as hopelessly hierarchical and inequitable, the Front embraced participatory democracy and the ideal of consensus. . . . Facilitators were chosen by lot, served for four meetings, and were then replaced by someone of the opposite sex. There were no membership fees, no officers, and anyone who came through the door was made a member in good standing. Because of this system, the participants at the weekly general meeting varied greatly over time. Since there was a constant influx of people and no clear agenda, debates could and did repeat themselves endlessly.[46]

While this free-flowing style encouraged lively debate and certainly facilitated a broad intersectional analysis of systems of power, it also felt frustrating to members: simultaneously fabulously wide-ranging yet stagnant, powerful but with no concrete strategy or goals.

By December of 1969, Kissack documents, moderates and those formerly involved in homophile organizations broke off and formed the Gay Activists Alliance (GAA). Along with more moderate political goals, GAA had bylaws, elected officers, clear rules for membership, and operated via Roberts Rules of Order, a decidedly hierarchical system for discussion and decision-making. Further, by 1971, as attendance at meetings waned, GLF adopted membership guidelines and began to take minutes, presumably to limit the frustration caused by such wide-ranging and structure-free meetings.[47] This, in turn, limited the kind of widely intersectional political project at the heart of GLF, and the organization itself closed by the end of 1971.

The same questions of strategy and institutional structure were being debated in nascent gay and lesbian health clinics in this period, as documented by Katie Batza in her book *Before AIDS: Gay Health Politics in the 1970s*. Batza recounts this debate in the early days of what became the Los Angeles Gay and Lesbian Community Center. Immediately following the decision on the part of the founders of the Gay Community Service Center to pursue conventional nonprofit status in order to gain tax-exempt status and increase potential funding, Batza notes that "the cracks in this relationship between services and politics began to surface."[48]

For the radical faction within the [C]enter, which blended the politics of gay liberation, feminism, the Black Panthers, the Brown Berets, labor, and other radical political groups of the time, accepting state funding posed a series of problems. First, they argued philosophically that, by accepting state funding, founders and management became extensions of the state. They viewed state funding, and the requisite prudence on the part of management, as in direct contradiction to the radical liberation politics that they saw at the core of the center's founding. From their perspective, the acceptance of state funds was tantamount to introducing and reinforcing within the center many forms of oppression radicals commonly associated with the government and mainstream society.[49]

Early gay and lesbian health clinics were in a difficult position, Batza argues. The gay and lesbian community relied on these community health clinics for necessary medical care, services that were not safe to receive from mainstream providers, or for which they were shamed, price gouged, or outed for receiving. In order to sustain and expand these medical services, gay and lesbian health clinics increasingly sought out and received state funding, often through the expanded funding for community health centers made available by Johnson's War on Poverty. However, as Batza so compellingly argues, this funding had an insidious effect on these organizations. "Under the second Nixon administration [the requirement] that clinics receiving federal funding meet building and licensure codes, use only trained and certified medical professionals, and comply with standard bookkeeping practices for billing and payroll called for massive changes in culture and protocol in some volunteer-run community clinics like the Fenway clinic."[50] Despite the pressure toward professionalization, formalization, bureaucracy, and specialized skills, we should not see the state as strictly repressive, Batza argues. Although in many ways the state actively discouraged queer community building, health, and life, she writes, "not only did the state facilitate the emergence of gay health services through funding and licensing, but it helped to ensure that gay health services would survive the conservative political swing of the 1980s by forcing clinics' professionalization, regulation, and political pragmatism."[51]

So, paradoxically, it was *because* the state forced emergent gay and lesbian health organizations to comply with funding stipulations demanding professionalization and formalization that many gay and lesbian organizations were able to weather the Reagan years, a period of massively diminished public funding, by utilizing this organizational infrastructure in order to pursue private funding. And this was not true just of gay and lesbian health clinics. As Tamar Carroll describes, intersectional feminist antipoverty organizations like the National Congress of Neighborhood Women (NCNW) and the Mobilization for Youth (MFY) relied heavily on state funding to provide services to low-income individuals, services that enabled those individuals' participation in political organizing. When Reagan cut funding available through the Comprehensive Employment and Training Act (CETA) and eliminated much funding for Community Development Block Grants (CDBG) and other funding for community programs, those services and programs became more tenuous. Carroll describes the impact of those cuts: "As federal funding became scarce and highly restrictive, activists increasingly relied on foundations and the nonprofit sector. However, foundations were also influenced by the ascendency of conservative critiques of social programs and implemented their own requirements for evaluation."[52]

It was also in large part because of this fundraising infrastructure, which cultivated individual donors and private philanthropy, that electoral and advocacy organizing—now the dominant strain of LGBT organizing—was able to flourish. As Amy Stone demonstrates in her book *LGBT Rights at the Ballot Box*, though there were antigay ballot initiatives around which LGBT communities organized as early as 1974, it wasn't until the 1990s that there was a nonprofit infrastructure capable of advancing a cohesive gay rights policy agenda.[53] During the period of the 1990s, due, in part, to the professionalization and formalization demanded by prior eras of state funding—and with the support of key LGBT major donors and foundations—the LGBT movement developed a cadre of professionals experienced in electoral campaigns— skilled in polling, get out the vote efforts, communications and messaging, addressing legal challenges, volunteer management for phone banking and door knocking, lobbying, and the like.

Again, it is important to note, the fact that this type of organizing rose to the fore was not because it was simply so compelling to ordinary queer people—or even ordinary queer activists—as an issue or approach. In fact, for nearly the entire history of electoral and policy organizing, legal advocacy and organizing goals have in many ways been driven by the right rather than the LGBT movement. Anti-LGBT ballot initiatives have been widely used by the right in order to drive conservative voters to the polls—

and the development of an organizational infrastructure to support professional lobbying and electoral organizing as a response to these attacks
was not simply a self-driven, strategic choice on the part of movement
leaders. Rather, it represents the result of a dialectical relationship between
politics and infrastructure. This type of electoral and policy-focused infrastructure was appealing to the cadre of wealthy funders cultivated during
the 1980s and 1990s, and then, once active, that infrastructure had its own
momentum, one with which we are still grappling.

Longtime movement leader and public intellectual Urvashi Vaid helps
us assess this complex organizational landscape:

> The organized infrastructure has done the unsexy work, day in and
> day out, of building support in state capitols to get LGBT people to
> the point where, as of this date, nineteen states have some form of
> anti-discrimination law. This infrastructure, which includes LGBT
> community centers, HIV/AIDS organizations, youth groups or the
> Gay/Straight Alliances, campus LGBT programs offices, statewide
> LGBT advocacy organizations, is a vital resource for future activ-
> ism and to sustaining the pressure in fallow times. On the other
> hand, the institutionalization of social movements always carries a
> downside—a bureaucratization, the professionalization of activ-
> ism, a more conservative politics than street action affords, even a
> shrinking of leadership as ordinary folks just let others do the work
> and become checkbook activists.[54]

Vaid argues that we should think of the contemporary LGBT movement
not actually as a "movement" per se, but as two parallel sets of organizations: one national, policy-oriented, and doggedly single-issue, and the
other local, grassroots, progressive, and antiracist.[55] Among the former,
she lists the Human Rights Campaign (HRC), Lambda Legal, GLAAD,
National Center for Lesbian Rights (NCLR), and the Gay and Lesbian Vic-
tory Fund. Among the latter she lists FIERCE, the now defunct Queers
for Economic Justice (QEJ), Sylvia Rivera Law Project (SRLP), Southerners on New Ground (SONG), important queer progressive philanthropies
like Astraea, as well as, interestingly, the community center movement,
HIV/AIDS service organizations, and queer youth organizations—the
spaces taken up by this book. She writes: "These movements share a common history, they often share institutional origins, they overlap, they coexist,

they cooperate, and they compete." But importantly, she goes on, "they are not coterminous: their endpoint differs dramatically."[56]

To form a more progressive movement that expands beyond homonormative equality politics, Vaid calls for, among other things, changes to the organizational structure and operations of movement organizations. Vaid specifically critiques many features of the nonprofit, in particular the lack of representation by nonwealthy, nonwhite queer people who do not offer significant financial resources to those organizations. Further, she notes the lack of accountability built into nonprofit governance. She calls this hyper focus on those within the community with the greatest financial resources the "dirty little secret of LGBT movement organizations."[57] She believes that this focus has accelerated in the last fifteen years as the budgets of LGBT organizations have increased. She notes that the political consequence of this overrepresentation is that a very narrow set of concerns and life experiences are represented.[58] It is this overrepresentation, of course, that leads to marriage being the central goal of the movement.

The lessons we can draw from this history are twofold: first, the seemingly benign infrastructural choices of LGBT movement organizations have profound and often unanticipated effects. In particular, the kind of infrastructure necessary to cultivate donors and raise funds—an infrastructure that involves careful fiscal tracking, bookkeeping and auditing practices, donor database tracking and management, savvy communications and marketing, and high-value events—tends to overvalue particular specialized skill sets and demobilize ordinary activists. Further, this type of infrastructure tends to produce its own momentum and values its own reproduction over any political goal. The second lesson is that the nonprofit structure was not—and is not—a foregone conclusion. Since the early days of the movement people have been engaging in explicit conversations about how structure informs the political project of queer movement organizations. Those organizations that chose a more formal structure, and accessed funding and developed infrastructure, were, in turn, pushed by their own structure toward more conservative politics. But this relationship is dialectic rather than causal. And further, even those who resist that formal incorporation nonetheless find themselves grappling with the same pressures, the necessity of funding, and the demands of funders. The four case studies that follow illustrate the daily work of navigating these structures, structures that are all at once overdetermined, laden with inescapable meanings and histories, and at the same time fragile spaces of unmaking and renewal.

2

The Work of Compassion

Institutionalizing Affective Economies of AIDS and Homelessness

I cannot for the life of me figure out how the organization that I helped form has become such a bastion of conservatism and such a bureaucratic mess. The bigger you get, the more cowardly you become; the more money you receive, the more self-satisfied. You no longer fight for the living. You have become a funeral home. You and your huge assortment of caretakers perform miraculous tasks of helping the dying die. . . . I think it must now come as a big surprise to your Board of Directors that the GMHC [Gay Men's Health Crisis] was not founded to heal those who are ill. It was founded to protect the living, to help the living go on living, to help those still healthy stay healthy, to help gay men stay alive.

Larry Kramer, Open Letter to Richard Dunne, New York Native

Compassion may itself be a substitute for justice . . . compassion always already signifies inequality. The compassionate intend no justice, for justice might disrupt current power relationships.

Hannah Arendt, On Revolution

The above epigraph was one of a handful of photocopies of national LGBT press coverage of HIV/AIDS and HIV/AIDS organizations found in the Howard Brown Health Center archive at Gerber/Hart Library in Chicago. In this article, the controversial founding executive director of GMHC, Larry Kramer, laments what he perceived as the bureaucratization, corporatization, and loss of political mission of one of the earliest and most important community responses to HIV/AIDS. He goes on to argue that the mission of gay community responses to HIV/AIDS must exceed offering direct services only, or else they will simply be providing cover for the city or state not to provide those services. He writes: "but in taking our money, you are, in essence, asking us to pay twice for what you are doing—once in our contributions to you, and once in our taxes to the city."[1] Instead, he argues that gay community responses must have a specifically queer politics, "something our city will never provide."[2] Sadly, he writes, "you have become only another city social service agency, and at the rate one hears about your inner squabblings . . . it will not be long before you are indistinguishable from any of the city departments—health, police, parking violations—that serve our city so tepidly."[3] Although certainly describing a very different local political dynamic and set of organizational politics, this critique offers an important perspective on early LGBT community health responses to HIV/AIDS—important enough to have been photocopied and saved by someone at what was then called Howard Brown Memorial Clinic, an LGBT community health center in Chicago. As I argue in this chapter, amidst the intense pressure of the AIDS crisis, the social service model that many of the first wave of LGBT organizations adopted had a profound impact on the kind of response HBMC could have. Ultimately, that social service model relied on a narrative of compassion and charity that endorsed the violences of the state that turned AIDS into a targeted weapon: privatization, abandonment, funding cuts, policing, and wholesale attacks on the social safety net.

In this chapter, I turn my attention to that organization, a Chicago LGBT clinic and social service organization founded in 1975. Named after the first out gay health commissioner for New York City, Dr. Howard Brown, Howard Brown Memorial Clinic (HBMC), now Howard Brown Health Center (HBHC), was the brainchild of a small group of out gay medical students.[4] With the institutional backing of the then also fledgling local organization Gay Horizons, they began to offer STD testing in a tiny storefront on Chicago's north side. Due in large part to federal funding to research hepatitis B and then test the subsequent vaccine, HBMC already had an infrastructure in place when the first AIDS cases hit Chicago. Throughout the decade of the 1980s, the organization built its services significantly: expanding its research wing to include, among others, the MACS study (Multi-Center AIDS Cohort Study), adding a volunteer-staffed buddy system called the AIDS Action Project, offering case management, an AIDS hotline, and, in 1985, testing services. Alongside these programs, its administrative infrastructure also grew, such that in its 1990 annual report, the organization reported that "during the late 80s, HBMC completed the successful transition from grass-roots community clinic to a professional research, health and human services center."[5] Currently the organization has a budget of more than $22 million, serving more than eighteen thousand people a year in their primary care clinic, case management, behavioral health, research, HIV/STD prevention, elder services, off-site homeless youth drop-in, and three resale shops.

I begin by exploring the logic of compassion, how it functions as a mode of governance, and the affective economies on which it relies. Using this theoretical frame, the rest of the chapter analyzes the institutionalization of this organization in and through two significant—but very different—moments of crisis, one in the 1980s and the second in the more recent past. In the 1980s, organizational dysfunction maps onto a landscape of trauma, as fully half the organization's clients died of AIDS, failed by a social safety net ravaged by Reagan's antistatist policies. I begin by exploring how the group's very conventional white gay professional founding organizers relied on "common-sense" ideas and technologies of nonprofit structure, tracing their attempts over the decade of the 1980s to build their institutional infrastructure according to those logics. I then analyze how this process of institutionalization was impacted by the trauma of AIDS, looking in particular at how the organization mobilized an affective narrative about AIDS in order to raise necessary funds—a narrative, while effective, that was fundamentally a white, middle-class story of crisis. As Howard Brown turned toward major donors and corporate sponsorships, they mobilized a narrative of the deserving victim made poor by illness, an alternative to the racialized antiwelfare discourse of the period that was palatable to white, suburban, affluent donors and corporate sponsors. I then examine how that "fundable" AIDS narrative mobilized by Howard Brown imagined HIV positive people of color as outside "the community," at risk because of injection drug use and not same-sex sexual behavior. Ultimately this strategy relied on and endorsed the identical narrative of compassion and charity that was, during that very period, being mobilized by Reagan to dismantle the social welfare system.

Nearly thirty years later, Howard Brown's queer youth homelessness intervention, the Broadway Youth Center (BYC), must grapple with the limits of the compassion narrative mobilized in the 1980s. In my years as a case manager at the Broadway Youth Center, I observed how that logic of compassion produced crisis within its youth homelessness programs and, more broadly, entrenched the social crisis that produces that homelessness to begin with. Queer youth homelessness has increasingly been "discovered" as a social—and fundable—issue by national and regional LGBT organizations, albeit primarily through a narrow, identity-based lens that fails to account for the racialized and gendered impact of poverty, lack of affordable housing, welfare "reform," law and order criminalization, and gentrification. The issue of queer youth homelessness presents a fundamental challenge to the single-issue identity politics of HBHC, and the alignment between the BYC and its parent organization has always been uneasy. At HBHC, after two decades of corporatization of management systems, the consolidation of a traditional development and administrative machine, and the incorporation of neoliberal values at every level, the BYC hardly fits into Howard Brown's strategic positioning as a "boutique" clinic that wealthy, *insured* LGBT people would choose to utilize.

Although much about these two historical moments is very different, organizational dysfunction marks this contemporary period as well. In 2008 the organization was found to have misused federal funds associated with the MACS study, by using restricted funds—those designated for certain programmatic activities—for general operating costs, specifically to cover the unreimbursed cost of providing medical care to uninsured patients. A very public scandal ensued, and the organization was forced to return $500,000, leaving HBHC with a major shortfall in its operating budget. In order to raise the funds necessary to keep the doors open, the organization—using a public relations firm—launched a "lifeline appeal," utilizing YouTube testimonials from staff, clients, and supporters to raise $500,000 in fifty days. I analyze the conflicting affective logics at work in this appeal in order to think about the limits of compassion. The appeal raised the money successfully, due in large part to the affective narrative about crisis that simultaneously hailed and mobilized "the community."

Unlike the AIDS crisis, which emerged as a point of connection and solidarity, the poverty and homelessness experienced by so many BYC clients has, instead, the feeling of what Lauren Berlant calls "crisis ordinariness": a systemic crisis that is not exceptional, but instead "embedded in the ordinary."[6] Despite the degree to which the BYC is used as a "golden jewel" for fundraising purposes, the program is devalued and under-resourced, and ultimately the politics of the organization do not fully claim the work of the BYC. In many ways the precarity of the program mirrors the precarity of the young people who access it to meet their basic needs—and for similar systemic reasons.

My purpose here is to think about the relationship between crisis and compassion: materially, affectively, and discursively. The very strong role of the state in this particular organization makes it an ideal site from which to analyze the logic of compassion and the disciplinary technologies of the welfare state at work in queer nonprofits: the legacy and institutional apparatus of the charity framework grafted on to a putatively political project. AIDS and homelessness—and the moral economies, institutional structures, funding narratives, and service frameworks that have developed to manage them—offer two particular, contextual, and specific alignments of these structures of power.

Governance through Compassion

Candace Vogler writes: "Of the many species of tenderness directed towards others' troubles, compassion falls squarely in the range of affective orientations with a built-in hands-clean clause."[7] She differentiates compassion from other affective postures like regret and mercy by stressing how the compassionate person "sympathizes with misfortunes that she did not cause and that would not otherwise touch her life." "Accordingly," she writes, "any intervention that she undertakes from compassion . . . will involve generosity or kindness. . . . While it's good to help strangers now and then, you do not owe aid and comfort to particular strangers." This has, of course, been the defining logic of the social safety net in the United States since colonial times, the framework behind what Loïc Wacquant calls "the charitable state." He is referring both to the material function of nongovernmental organizations in the provision of care—the state provides services through charities themselves—but even more so to the affective tilt of the safety net:

> The guiding principle of public action in this domain is not solidarity but *compassion*; its goal is not to reinforce social bonds, and less still to reduce inequalities, but at best to relieve the most glaring destitution and to demonstrate society's moral sympathy for its deprived but deserving members.[8]

Wacquant demonstrates that this logic has been critical in the transformation into what he calls the "carceral society," in which "the criminalization of marginality and the punitive containment of dispossessed categories serve as social policy.[9] Compassion, then, is both an engine and an effect of neoliberal social and economic changes, including both the retraction of the social safety net and the deployment of new punitive and moralizing systems like workfare and Temporary Assistance for Needy Families (TANF), as well as the vast expansion of the prison system as a poverty management technology. Lauren Berlant writes that compassion is "at the heart of the shrinkage [of the welfare state], because the attendant policies relocate the template of justice from the collective condition of specific populations to that of the individual, whose economic sovereignty the state vows to protect."[10] Much has been made of George W. Bush's "compassionate conservatism," and Bill Clinton famously "feels your pain." Though compassion has been an important mode of governance throughout U.S. history, it has become useful in a renewed way under neoliberalism as the moral logic of transformation of the social safety net, which knits the disciplinary function of earlier incarnations of the welfare state to the new affirmative modes of governance found in community-based nonprofits. At the same time that right-wing politicians were mobilizing narratives demonizing poor women of color as welfare queens gaming the system, a parallel discursive project championed volunteerism, charity, and community togetherness as alternatives to the bloated welfare state. This was George Bush Sr.'s famous "thousand points of light" alternative to welfare: compassion, administered by community and church, as an alternative to a state-based social safety net.

Though neoliberal governance is increasingly affirmative, as I explore in the next chapter, and encourages individuals to internalize market logics and become self-governing entrepreneurial subjects, the heavy hand of surveillance, policing, and bodily discipline has not dissipated. The punitive moralism of compassion is built into workfare, TANF, public housing—all public benefits that remain after welfare "reform"—through systems like time limitations, work requirements, drug testing, child limits, marriage incentives, and other, less tangible, mechanisms of surveillance. But the punitive moralism of compassion is also vitally embedded into the charity model of social services, and as those services increasingly provide services once offered by the state, the disciplinary power of nonprofits intensifies.

Berlant argues that compassion is a "social and aesthetic technology of belonging;" it is this approach to compassion that animates this chapter. As the example of Howard Brown demonstrates, nonprofit organizations must appeal to a narrative of compassion, to incite compassion in others, literally in order to exist; donors give because it *feels* good, and nonprofits, in order to get that donation, must make donors feel good, feel heroic, feel pleasure in that gift. Marjorie Garber notes, however, that compassion is "felt not between equals but from a distance—in effect, from high to low."[11] Moreover, Berlant describes the posture of compassion as one that "denotes privilege: the sufferer is *over there.*"[12] The compassionate one must never be made to feel at fault, implicated in the social condition that produces the suffering they see and in response to which they feel compassion. So in order to incite compassion in donors, nonprofit organizations must exhibit particular affects and not others, must produce the correct conditions among staff, clients, participants, volunteers, and donors. This becomes most readily apparent through the relation of "deservingness": the organization must articulate its clients—and through its clients, its services and programs—as uniquely deserving.

Deservingness is always, of course, articulated against its other, the figure of the "undeserving" poor. But there are additional postures that invite compassion: thankfulness, neediness, desperation—although clients can't be *too* desperate, lest their pain produce discomfort in the giver, or suggest that the clients *deserve* something and perhaps even that the giver *does not.* Compassion is a tricky affect; one, to reiterate, wholly counter to the project of actually creating justice. Its impact on the kind of queer politics that can be articulated from within LGBT nonprofits is profound. This conservativizing effect on queer politics is largely because compassion cleaves onto homonormativity, as in order to be "deserving," one must be made the same, must mirror back the identities and values of the dominant class.

Despite the fact that it is, I maintain, deeply damaging to queer social movements, compassion is, nonetheless, sincerely felt, and powerful. One of its powers, I argue, is that it demands, *and creates*, crisis. In order to be deserving of compassion, one must constantly be in crisis; if the objects of compassion begin to thrive, they are no longer deserving of compassion. For example, one constant source of frustration during my years working at Howard Brown was that it was very difficult for uninsured transgender clients to access trans-specific healthcare, *unless* they were HIV positive. If they were positive, medical care was funded through Howard Brown's many contracts with the state Department of Public Health and the Centers for Disease Control and Prevention (CDC). In a cruel irony, uninsured trans clients were often unable to access the affirming care that would make it less likely they would be exposed to HIV, but once they became HIV positive, they could access hormone care and other services that would have reduced their risk in the first place.

As an animating feature of neoliberal governance, compassion also produces crisis on a broader social scale, and these two scales of crisis reflect and amplify one another. Communities must be in crisis, or "at risk" of crisis, in order to appear deserving of resources. In both historical moments that I explore in this chapter, these two scales of crisis are apparent, as the institutional dysfunction, burnout, financial strain, and frustration of staff mirrors the precarity in the lives of the people with whom they work.

Dynamics of Institutionalization: Neoliberalism and Ideas of "Nonprofitness"

The inception of HBMC was enabled by a particular alignment of forces: the need was there, but also the queer political and cultural climate in Chicago offered a self-identified community of patients, volunteers, and eventually, donors. Prior to the opening of the clinic there was nowhere that gay men could go to get safe and accessible care for sexually transmitted infections. In her book, *Before AIDS: Gay Health Politics in the 1970s*, historian Katie Batza traces these early days of Howard Brown, noting that the history of the HBMC differs significantly from that of other gay and lesbian community health organizations that began in the same time period, like Fenway Community Health Center in Boston.[13] HBMC, Batza argues, was much more conventional in its political stance and organizational structure, in large part because it was started by a group of gay doctors and medical students fully immersed in the professionalization of their field, rather than Fenway's group of community activists. Batza goes on to describe how HBMC combined the more formal concern with medical research and scholarship of the Chicago-based American Medical Association with the political proponents of socialized healthcare that was a major focus of the healthcare movement at that time. HBMC has had a very strong relationship with the state, particularly through federally funded medical research, throughout its history. Beginning in the period in which money was still flowing strongly through the Great Society-era funding for community-based organizations, HBMC managed to persevere in the 1980s when other organizations were hard hit by the Reagan administration's funding cuts, due in large part to this already strong medical research funding infrastructure. Although this medical research money continues to be a major part of their funding model, HBMC did follow the increasingly neoliberal nonprofit model adopted by most organizations during the 1980s and 1990s. With gala fundraisers, mass mailings, corporate sponsorships, foundation funding, donor tracking databases, and logic models, Howard Brown is a perfect example of the neoliberalization of major LGBT nonprofits, replete with the constant crisis atmosphere of high staff turnover, widespread dysfunction, and a constant state of fiscal instability.

HBMC's early history helps contextualize the path of corporatization that the organization took throughout the 1980s and 1990s. The shape of the organization in its early years—all professional white gay men—is perhaps informative as to their assumptions about the nonprofit form. The archival record of HBMC's early years depicts an organization that, despite its sex positivity, creative programming, and strong community and volunteer support, also adopted an overly formal and conventional organizational structure. For instance, the decision-making model relied on Roberts Rules of Order, with decisions recorded in detail—"all in favor so signify." The use of Roberts Rules of Order suggests that the organizational culture was built to mirror the professionalism of these young white doctors. The founding organizers simply relied on their "commonsense" ideas about what constitutes a "real" organization. A casual note from a 1980 board of directors meeting to hire a "girl Friday" to take on part-time administrative labor at the clinic further evinces these blind spots.[14]

The archival record reveals ongoing tension around organizational sustainability, as the organization tried to institutionalize through traditional nonprofit mechanisms, which, as I argue throughout, are themselves fundamentally untenable by design. Despite receiving federal medical research funds very early, for instance, they didn't begin having regular board meetings until 1980 and didn't receive their first foundation grant until 1984. Over the decade there was considerable turnover in leadership staff, particularly of executive directors, who left with alarming regularity, reflecting and contributing to enormous organizational instability. Some cited the pressure of dealing with the ravages of AIDS on the community, but many named organizational dysfunction as the primary reason for their exit. One departing executive director helpfully outlined many of these dynamics in a fiery resignation letter. He wrote:

> It is clear to me that no executive director can succeed at HBMC unless there is fundamental change in management, expectations, and philosophy. The reorganization that occurred last February is

deficient and indicative of the failure to identity problems. . . . The reorganization, subsequent position descriptions and role defini- tions do not reflect a mature understanding of an organization, nor the functions required to maintain the organization. . . . What is striking about the position descriptions is the strong emphasis on control and finance, and the lack of emphasis on program and the functions and skills necessary to manage. . . . What has occurred is a classic textbook situation. An inexperienced Board, with a strong President finds itself with operational (internal) problems. The Board (and for HBMC the problem is historical), unsure of its role, mistrustful of the ED, becomes distracted from Board functions and involved in operations.[15]

The departing executive director, Jerry Tomlinson, describes what he calls "textbook" organizational dysfunction. I would argue that the "textbook" to which he refers is a set of shared frameworks and technologies of non- profitization, which, despite being fundamentally unsustainable in and of themselves, are understood to be simply a set of managerial tools that can be applied, tweaked, perfected, and managed to peak efficiency. This fundamental ruse of nonprofitization is wildly successful—people at every organization I study absolutely believe that there is a way to make their organizations stable and sustainable over the long term, a belief that is nec- essary, I know, for people to get up and go into work every day, especially in the context of profound and urgent need.

What is significant in this example is the degree to which clearly wide- spread organizational dysfunction is individualized. Although Tomlinson begins the letter by naming fundamental organizational dynamics, much of the letter singles out a set of individuals. He writes: "compounding this classic situation is the history of Abramson, Johnson, and Keppling with the clinic. There are people who had major *responsibilities* for directing and the guiding of the clinic *prior* to the reorganization. They cannot ex- empt themselves from HBMC's problem[s]."[16] Interestingly, when Tom- linson was hired—to replace an ED who resigned with little notice—he was immediately given personal responsibility for an intimidating array of broad organizational failures. In a memo to the newly hired Tomlinson from the executive committee of the board, they outline some of the tasks to be undertaken immediately and reported on after only one week. They wrote:

The members of the Executive Committee and the entire board are extremely happy to have you aboard. We realize that the scope of the challenges ahead of you may seem a bit overwhelming at first.

Consequently, we thought it would be helpful to you to set forth for you the areas that require your immediate attention.

1. Implement a system for monitoring cash flow.
2. Determine whether a feasibility study should be conducted on primary care.
3. Develop a funding proposal for the US DHHS [Department of Health and Human Services] grant which can be submitted by HBMC in case the AFC [AIDS Foundation of Chicago] proposal is inadequate.
4. Develop a plan, which can be implemented immediately, to increase Benefit and Foundation Income to the levels set forth in HBMC's 1987 budget.
5. Monitor HBMC's billings on Federal, State, and City grants to ascertain that billing is timely and reimbursement is maximized.[17]

What progress the board imagined that the new ED could make in his first week on increasing event and foundation funding, clearly below budgeted levels, is unclear. However, the level of responsibility placed on this one individual to "fix" broader organizational problems reflects the corporate-style desire for a dynamic, entrepreneurial leader who will "take control."

It is critical to analyze this kind of organizational dysfunction in the context of the AIDS crisis: an organization grappling with stunning and terrifying need, having to navigate for the first time a public benefits system wholly inadequate to the task, and the grief and numbness of the daily deaths of friends, clients, lovers, and coworkers. One funding proposal noted that while the government standard was that each case manager have thirty to forty clients, Howard Brown case managers had a caseload of eighty to ninety Persons with AIDS (PWAs).[18] In the archival record, amidst memos about resignations, firings, management training, executive consultants, and strategic planning, were monthly surveillance reports on AIDS-related deaths. As of 1987, 58 percent of those who had AIDS were dead. In January through July of 1987, 22 percent of Howard Brown's clients died.[19] The precarity of Howard Brown's institutional infrastructure in many ways reflected the precarity of Howard Brown's clients, and the demise of the social safety net that exacerbated both.

In the wake of Tomlinson's departure, the board hired an outside management consultant to help them engage in another round of organizational restructuring (having, according to Tomlinson, just undergone a fairly unsuccessful restructuring). A handwritten record in a folder entitled "Management Consultant" lists "raw issues," including: "no mgmt. leadership," "too much Board meddling," "no goals," "no staff input in decisions (the 'little people' syndrome)," "poor community PR," "no set policies and procedures," and "unrealistic expectation of staff member effort." Beneath this list is another, entitled "real issues." It reads:

1. Lack of clearly designed mission statement from BoD, backed up by clear strategic plan and specific management and budgetary objectives.

2. Need to develop employee position charters (not *job descriptions*) outlining how each position feeds into Clinic annual plan.

3. Compensation tied directly to performance against approved plan, with quarterly review and deficiency analysis.

4. Policies and procedures designed to minimize bureaucracy and maximize service to client.

5. Revised volunteer policies and procedures to match assignments to highest possible use of individual talents.

6. Volunteer stroking.

7. Service to clients—MAKE THEM NUMBER ONE!!
   a. Let no person or procedure supersede this policy!

8. Intensive training in *management skills* for SMS concurrent with development of management plan.

9. *Managing change* takes precedence over technical work.

10. PLANNING—ORGANIZATION LEADING CONTROLLING[20]

This list is interesting for a number of reasons. First, there was clearly an acknowledgement of how difficult it was to work at Howard Brown during this period, of how overburdened the staff was and how low their morale. And further it is clear from this list that members of the leadership team genuinely wanted to improve the experience of clients of HBMC, recognizing that the impact organizational dysfunction had on clients was the most critical failure. The key evidence it provides, however, is of a strongly neoliberal set of answers to the problems listed under "raw issues." This document imagines that the problems faced by this organization— problems mostly related to the scarcity that is endemic to the nonprofit structure—can be solved by better management training, by tying pay to performance, by streamlining bureaucracy to make operations more efficient, and by setting specific management and budgetary objectives. This list reflects broader discursive trends that are, by now, quite familiar: a mistrust and disdain for everything bureaucratic, fetishization of management techniques, streamlining, efficiency, and "achievable objectives."

The adoption of this set of rhetorics is uneven over the course of the decade, but it is most clearly evident in HBMC's efforts to develop their fundraising and development systems. In 1984 HBMC submitted a proposal to the Chicago Resource Center requesting funding to assist their transformation into a "professional corporate foundation, [with] major donor fundraising capability."[21] They also requested funding in the same proposal to "enable HBMC to develop a comprehensive strategic plan which will allow quality service to be delivered in a structured, cost effective manner."[22] Their objective was:

> To initiate a professional corporate, foundation, and major donor fundraising capability, including the development of a multi- faceted fundraising strategy, in order to provide a broader base of funding for the operation and expansion of services to the gay and lesbian community.
>
> During its years of service, HBMC has depended heavily on the gay and lesbian community for financial support of its charitable services. It is money from this source that has financed rent subsidy and patient emergency fund programs. . . .
>
> The projected service needs mandate HBMC change its funding base through the hiring of a full time development manager who

can be given the tools to implement a program. Major donor solicitation as well as foundation/corporate exploitation require particular expertise and talent.

... HBMC believes that a professional, objective-oriented approach will be necessary to meet the needs of persons with ARC [AIDS-Related Complex] and AIDS and the gay and lesbian community. In these times of new and formidable challenges to the well-being of these people, it is mandatory that thoughtful, well-conceived strategies be developed.[23]

The proposal ends with the statement: "The problems are great, ever-changing and growing; models for response are non-existent." This is, of course, untrue. The objectives put forth by HBMC followed a well-established social service framework, albeit one undergoing a significant period of neoliberal transformation in that period. The context of AIDS was new, but the model on which HBMC chose to pattern its response was not.

This proposal, however, does reflect the limits of HBMC's original financial model. Medical research funding could not support the kinds of services the organization wanted to provide to PWAs—emergency rent subsidies, social and psychological support, and case management assistance navigating the many public benefits systems. Instead, over this period, HBMC turned its focus to developing major donors, soliciting corporate sponsorships, holding major gala fundraisers, and significantly expanding its foundation funding base. In the context of Reagan's antistatist policies, HBMC was forced to turn its attention toward private sources of funding, sources that might fund some of the services the state would not, but only if they were able to craft a narrative that appealed to those private donors—donors that, paradoxically, had benefitted from Reagan's punitive moralism and trickle-down economics.

Crafting the Fundable AIDS Narrative

By 1990 the board had hired a new executive director with a background in for-profit healthcare administration and began to implement fully the more neoliberal fundraising machine that it had spent the 1980s building. The year 1991 saw the organization's largest fundraiser yet, a gala at suburban Arlington Race Track, dubbed "An Unbridled Affair." For this event, the organization contracted with an outside event manager, who prepared for them a press packet following the event containing this article in the *Daily Herald* entitled "Arlington Party to Raise AIDS Research Funds." It read:

> The fight against AIDS may soon receive an extra boost by northwest suburban residents who attend a black tie gala at Arlington International Racecourse in Arlington Heights. The track will hold a party Saturday, sponsored by Neiman Marcus Oakbrook store in Oak Brook, to benefit the HBMC clinic on Chicago's near North Side. The center is renowned for its efforts in research and support services for those afflicted with Acquired Immune Deficiency Syndrome. . . .
>
> The event is expected to draw 500 people, all with the opportunity to bid for jewels, a trip, a shopping spree and other items at a silent auction that evening. In addition, various prizes—including a 1991 Jeep Wrangler—will be raffled off.[24]

One article noted that former president Gerald Ford sent three pairs of cufflinks for the raffle. The department store Neiman Marcus hired models for the evening to roam the party adorned in jewels that party attendees could bid on. The article quotes "Barbara McClure, vice president general manager of Neiman Marcus Oakbrook," who says "that the store is pleased to sponsor Howard Brown and recognizes the acclaim that the center has earned." It goes on:

> Neiman Marcus has been committed to supporting non-profit organizations that work to improve the social health and economic conditions in every community in which it has a store. McClure adds "It's a tremendous opportunity for the people in the suburbs to help us fight a disease that is affecting people throughout the northwest suburbs and the nation." Majsek [event coordinator for HBMC] says of the fundraiser: "our success in being able to provide the essential services to people living with AIDS depends on the suburban population joining the fight."[25]

A fascinating instance of early corporate branding around HIV/AIDS, this is an illustrative example of an organization mobilizing a particular narrative of AIDS in order to appeal to an affluent, white, suburban wealth base in order to fund services for an urban, gay constituency reliant on a public benefits system often demonized by suburban voters.

The script of the slide show presented to attendees that evening reflects this particular narrative of AIDS. Against a backdrop of photos of clients and staff, the ED said:

> With the onset of AIDS and HIV infection, the Clinic has grown in response to ever-expanding needs. . . . Howard Brown has four divisions . . . but the division that I want to focus on with you today is our social services division. . . . At the heart of our social services division is our case management department. During 1990, direct services were provided to 716 individuals having a full diagnosis of AIDS. Our clients are primarily gay men; 71% are white, 23% are Latino or Hispanic.
>
> In many ways Howard Brown is their lifeline to obtaining help. . . . These individuals face considerable prejudice and [stigma] in their daily lives. Many are turned away by their families; some lose jobs; all must confront a life-threatening disease that is fatal to over 80% within a two year period from the time of diagnosis.[26]

For this suburban audience, the executive director mobilizes a traditional narrative of charity and compassion, even going so far as to say that the "lifeline" of case management is the "heart" of the division. The ED depicts PWAs as truly pitiable: turned away from family and dying, with Howard Brown their beacon of light in the darkness. The speaker closes the presentation with this entreaty: "To face today's needs—and prepare for tomorrow's challenges—we need to depend on support from individuals and businesses throughout the Midwest to come to our aid. With your support we can keep our promise to lead the fight against this disease until a cure is found." In the background the slide show closes with an image of a clear donation box with coins and dollar bills in it, with the words "Your Money Helps In the Fight Against AIDS" printed on it in black letters.[27] This narrative of AIDS allows wealthy suburbanites—people who may have supported and certainly benefit from the kinds of political economic policies that deepened inequality, reduced public benefits, closed public hospitals—to feel as though they are "supporting a worthy cause" as race-track owner Ed Duffy, president of Arlington International Racecourse, Ltd., said in the *Herald* article. It is an odd trade-off: their support for such a "worthy cause" absolved those individuals and corporations from their support for policies that were literally killing PWAs living in poverty, while

Howard Brown ekes out enough money to continue to offer programming that could provide some comfort and support, some emergency rent assistance, all the while allowing the underlying systems to remain unchanged. In this way they had indeed, as Larry Kramer wrote of GMHC, become "a funeral home. . . . helping the dying to die."

Unlike explicitly activist organizations like ACT UP, which as Deborah Gould demonstrates, relied heavily on anger to fuel its organizing, in this period Howard Brown increasingly relied on and mobilized the traditional narratives of compassion and charity, even as those narratives were being retrofitted to serve as discursive logic for neoliberal reforms. So as Reagan and Bush touted the fundamental American-ness of charity as a rationale for decimating the public health, housing, and benefits systems, Howard Brown was adopting a version of the same logic in order to fund the increased demand caused by that state abandonment.

Whiteness, Wealth, and Imagining the Community of AIDS

Before discussing the racialized implications of this narrative, I would like to dwell for a moment on why and how compassion works, or *the work that compassion does*, and on the real affective connection Howard Brown mobilized and literally capitalized upon. In what was easily the most moving of archival finds, an easy-to-miss manila envelope dated from 1992 contained approximately eighty letters, accompanying checks ranging from ten to three hundred dollars, given in honor of loved ones who had died of AIDS. Each letter tenderly described the connection that many who died of AIDS felt to and at Howard Brown. One letter read:

> Enclosed find a check in the amount of $300.00 as a memorial donation in the name of my brother. Bruce's birthday is this coming Thursday . . . and I wish to remember him on this day and the love he showed and shared with his family and friends. I know Bruce spoke highly of HBMC and the services and support of the staff for not only him but all people who had or are now living with HIV and AIDS.
>
> I would appreciate it if you would acknowledge this memorial donation to my parents (and Bruce's) as this will help them through their loss and on May 12th as they think of Bruce. Thank you.[28]

These letters offer us a critical insight into the affective world of giving and fundraising. It is not simply perfunctory—people *feel* and imagine into being a real sense of connection. Of course this connection is, also, strategic: a remittance form that went out in every Howard Brown newsletter often accompanied these letters, demonstrating that Howard Brown encouraged and solicited these memorial donations. But this is not simply exploiting the grief of families and loved ones. Memorial contributions allow family members, sometimes estranged from the life of a child or nephew or family friend, to feel a sense of connection and shared purpose. One letter-writer, whose cousin died of AIDS, acknowledged and even welcomed the mechanical aspects of giving. He wrote: "I am sure you will send us reminders to donate in the future, and we plan to do so. Thanks for the good work." These gifts remind us of the affective framework that all of these exchanges discursively call upon, the actual monetization of feeling on which nonprofits rely.

The acknowledgment letter further demonstrates this affective dimension. Unlike the form letters intended for tax purposes that often acknowledge receipt of a tax-deductible donation, the letters sent to acknowledge these gifts were very personal. One reads:

> On behalf of all of us here at HBMC—staff, volunteers, and the people living with AIDS and HIV-disease that we serve, I am writing to acknowledge receipt of a memorial donation made in the name of Craig Augustine.
>
> We receive much of our client services funding from individual donors . . . we find little joy in memorial contributions. We realize all too frequently the loss of another beloved friend or family member. Our comfort must be found in the memories of all that we have shared with them, and in the knowledge that they will always be part of our hearts, our minds, and our souls.
>
> Mere words at a time like this are inadequate to express our feelings. Know that we really do understand all that you have gone through, and that we empathize with you in your loss.
>
> The men and women of HBMC hope that you find solace in your memories and that your spirit will be gladdened by the good works that will be carried out in your brother's name.
>
> Sincerely,
> Howard Brown Development Director[29]

These very personal donation and acknowledgment letters reflect the context of grief and loss, but also the context of broader social abandonment felt by those who loved people with AIDS. They also reflect the class and race dynamics of charitable giving, with the development director calling on the same narrative of compassion—"we hope your spirit will be gladdened by the good works that will be carried out in your brother's name"— that the script at the suburban gala relied upon. Such narratives work because people do have feelings about them; their spirits *are* gladdened. It isn't just that individual nonprofits rely on the monetization of feeling, the entire system, both the harsh realities of capitalism that produce profound desperation, the retraction of the state social safety net which intensifies that desperation, and the nonprofit sector which absorbs it. And our feelings about this massive collapse are channeled into charitable giving, it is one way we mediate and make sense of this social reality.

This mode of fundraising calls forth the narrative of charity and volunteerism that Presidents Reagan and Bush, Sr. mobilized to support the privatization of public institutions. These privatization schemes were having immediate negative effects on PWAs and organizations serving them, Howard Brown included. A decade of closures of public hospitals, public housing, and major cuts to the Community Development Block Grant program meant that there was no longer any safety net to prevent people from dying homeless and in poverty. Organizations like Howard Brown, whose client base was primarily white and middle class, and consequently never had to navigate the public benefits system with its clients prior to the AIDS crisis, was therefore left scrambling to piece together various remaining benefits and programs with its own emergency relief. Howard Brown supported the creation of Chicago House, the first housing program for homeless HIV positive people and PWAs.[30] It also publicly opposed the state's regressive AIDS-related legislation, which included mandatory testing for prison inmates and those seeking marriage licenses, and it refused to give the names of those it tested despite the state authorizing public health officials to collect identifying information of anyone tested HIV positive.[31] But its response to these policing gestures was contradictory. On the one hand, staff clearly believed that HBMC had a responsibility to fight actively on behalf of PWAs. In his July 1987 monthly report to the board, the executive director shared his conviction that Howard Brown should refuse to share the names of HIV positive patients.

He wrote: "I have also said that we would *not* report names. I recognize that this is a Board policy decision; but, events required that I address the subject."[32] Clearly aware that he had overstepped his power in making that decision, or at least the board might feel that he had, he provided justification for that refusal: "The community expects HBMC to take a proactive stance on issues affecting the gay community—it puts us in a leadership position."[33] But the following document in the archive, dated the same month, seems to indicate that the board's response to the executive director's small rebellion was to shore up the "nonpolitical" nature of the organization. The bylaws committee met that very month, likely in response to this action, to review and modify the bylaws to ensure that they obeyed the statutes restricting the political involvement of tax-exempt organizations. In the minutes for that meeting the committee reported:

> For legal reasons, the statement shall remain in the Bylaws that provides "that the corporation shall not participate in, or intervene in (including the publishing or distribution of statements) any political campaign on behalf of any candidate for public office." The Committee discussed whether this statement should be extended to cover all political matters and determined that, for the time being, this statement was sufficient. . . . The Bylaws Committee also recommended that the Clinic re-emphasize the decision-making process on matters with political implications, noting the Board (or its Exec Committee) must approve all policy statements before they are made public.[34]

The final sentence, reemphasizing the exclusive power of the board of directors to make decisions on "matters with political implications" is clearly a rebuke of the executive director for exceeding his authority by taking a political stance without the approval of the board.

This hesitance to advocate vocally for policy change is understandable, given the scrutiny organizations like Howard Brown were under. How could it have done so, while simultaneously begging for funds from the very people those policies benefitted? But not only did they not advocate for particular policy changes, they did not, at any point, begin to address the systemic causes of the crisis—not the disease itself, but the state abandonment, privatization, and antipoverty policies that turned the disease into a targeted weapon. Even as Reagan and Bush touted the fundamental American-ness of charity as a rationale for decimating the public health, housing, and benefits systems, Howard Brown was adopting a version of the same logic in order to fund the increased demand *caused* by that state abandonment.

The Imagined Community of AIDS: Race and Deservedness

The power of the narratives of AIDS mobilized in the previous two funding appeals lies in their ability to imagine into being a community of PWAs, a community of fellow travelers, friends, lovers, family, volunteers, and donors. A community that was critical to how Howard Brown imagined itself, to the story it told about itself, and on whose behalf donors imagined themselves to be contributing. It did *not*, however, reflect the actual community of people with AIDS in Chicago. Howard Brown, located as it is on Chicago's nearly all white north side, served a client population that was disproportionately white and affluent, compared to the overall population of PWAs. In numerous grant proposals, however, HBMC described its racial composition as mirroring the demographics of PWAs, but this math only worked according to a particular narrative of AIDS: one that imagined African Americans as primarily exposed to HIV through injection drug use rather than same-sex sexual behavior.

The narrative that HBMC told about its client population was this: they had been upstanding, employed, tax paying, out gay men, who then, once struck down with HIV and reduced to poverty as they were no longer able to work, were forced to rely on a public benefits system inadequate to their needs. This is hauntingly familiar to anyone conversant with the markedly different discourses around Social Security and TANF, both of which are public benefits, but one—Social Security—made sacrosanct by the racialized moral economy of deservedness that surrounds it, while the other—TANF—constantly under threat and maligned as fostering a "culture of dependence." This discourse similarly relies on the notion of the deserving poor, those who have paid into the system and deserved to draw on it when they were disabled through no fault of their own. This was, of course, in contrast to the ever popular "welfare queen" and other racialized symbols of the *undeserving* poor: lazy, dependent, and unemployed. A memo from the director of the HBMC social services department to the ED and the board advocating for continued funding for emergency financial assistance for PWAs depicts this narrative. In it, he writes:

The provision of even $200 every 90 days meets a critical need for
a large percentage of our clients. . . .

In assessing the value of this component of the Social Services
program, it is important to be cognizant of the financial predica-
ment many PWAs find themselves in.

In sum, the $200 grant allows the client to supplement his
severely reduced income just enough to meet fundamental human
needs. It may allow him to catch up on rent, buy adequate food,
pay his health insurance premiums, take care of non-reimbursed
medical bills, or buy a monthly CTA pass.

The cessation of the program will have unfortunate consequences to our overall AIDS service package. Although we have an
outstanding group of emotional support services, most people in
crisis must first meet basic needs before being able to appropriately
utilize less tangible services.[35]

This narrative describes someone who was employed until they were no
longer able to work, and who needs financial assistance to pay for necessary life expenses. The client is imagined to be savvy with money, rea-
sonable, not greedy, and unfairly excluded from the workforce, in marked
contrast to the way other welfare recipients are discursively constructed as
gaming the system. It is worth noting that this kind of emergency financial
assistance would never be offered by Howard Brown to homeless youth
clients of the Broadway Youth Center. In fact, the impetus for this memo
was the impending closure of this program, an outcome which the social
services director warns would harm Howard Brown's image in "the community." He writes: "Our financial assistance program does help solve the
most pressing day-to-day problems and thus serves as a primary, concrete
reminder of the value of HBMC's overall PWA services. The positive PR
value we generate through this service will not only be lost if it ceases,
but may indeed reflect very negatively on us."[36] He goes on to entreat the
board to "let the community know of our plight (detailing need, expenses,
etc., via press release or similar medium) *and* solicit donations vigorously
for the sole purpose of continuing this program."[37] It is not only important
that the organization would provide such no-strings-attached financial assistance, but that they believed the community would support it, which
clearly they did. Were the client population of Howard Brown less white,
as it is in their Broadway Youth Center programs, it is very doubtful that

the community would support such financial assistance, no matter how critical in the lives of clients. "The community" supported a program like this because of how "the community" was imagined—primarily, but not exclusively, white, middle-class, north-side, and gay-identified.

In his work on the conflation between race and risk, historian Timothy Stewart Winter describes the impact of race, segregation, and the discourse of risk on HIV positive people of color in Chicago. He describes the great "conflation" between race and risk group, allowing men who have sex with men to be understood as code for white, and injection drug user to be code for African American.[38] Howard Brown believed their client demographics were appropriate to the population of PWAs because they understood people of color to be at risk primarily because of injection drug use, although this was not, in fact, the case.[39]

This reliance on the racist crack hysteria of that period is clearly evident in an internal memo entitled "Minority Outreach Program," which had the goal of "[educating] Gay/Bisexual and heterosexual individuals about AIDS and safe sex practices, targeted to and in minority communities."[40] The first aspect of this program, apparently, was to identify "cultural factors" for each "minority" community. For "Blacks," the four so-called cultural issues were: "1. Drug abuse," "2. Teen pregnancy," "3. Strong influence of the Baptist Church," and "4. Strong influence of the family." Similarly for "Hispanics," the "cultural issues" were also drug abuse, strong influence of the family, the "language barrier," and the "strong influence of the Catholic church."[41] In an astonishingly blatant bit of racism, the action steps to be taken to address these barriers were to: "identify and approach black and Hispanic clinic employees (Mike and Tim, etc.) who would be able to make referrals to associates or friends interested in volunteering."[42] According to this program African American and Latino people were already imagined to be first IV drug users, confined, if they were also men who had sex with men, by their strong family ties and religious identities. In the case of African American's perceived issue with "teen pregnancy," they were presumed to be heterosexual, as well.

What was left out of this narrative, of course, is that absent social service organizations like Howard Brown, in the wake of the demise of the public health system wrought by Reagan, family and faith institutions were often the only sources of care and support available. Rather than being evidence of a not fully "gay" identity, representing cultural "issues," the importance of family and faith institutions to HIV positive people of color is actually evidence of the racism of organizations like Howard Brown and the disproportionate impact that the closure of public facilities have on people excluded from private healthcare organizations whether through poverty or geography. Winter reports that one-third of all people with AIDS were treated at Cook County Hospital and that of those, 70 percent were people of color. Winter describes how the decade of hospital closures under the Reagan administration had "disconnected south and west side communities from health care and drug and alcohol treatment," further exacerbating the risk of HIV for individuals in these areas.[43] Howard Brown's particular narrative of AIDS, a white, middle-class narrative, identified the "community" as consisting of out, gay-identified, community-minded men, and the organization consigned HIV positive people of color to a crumbling public infrastructure, imagined outside of "the community," not a part of the story. This failure of imagination continues to resonate as we look ahead to the issue of queer youth homelessness.

Is Homelessness an LGBT Health Issue? Crisis Ordinary, Race, and "The Community"

The kind of financial support available to PWAs experiencing poverty is simply unimaginable for the youth of the Broadway Youth Center (BYC)—unimaginable that the organization would offer it or that the community would fund it. The BYC is a drop-in program for homeless youth offering basic needs services like showers and food, as well as case management, medical care, HIV testing, and a GED program. From 2006 to 2008 I worked at the Broadway Youth Center as a case manager. Every day, young people who came into the drop-in space would get some food, sign up for showers, and meet with a case manager. While they waited they hung out with one another, played cards, had amazing impromptu dance competitions, and gathered supplies: underwear, hygiene necessities, makeup, blankets, and whatever other donations had been gathered that month. I met with young people in half hour increments, working with them to get a spot in one of the few youth shelters, or perhaps to run interference with a Department of Children and Families case worker, or some other figure from a system intended to help but which hurts, hurts, hurts. Frequently I tried to hook young folks up with mental health services or hormone access or basic healthcare. We worked together on applying for benefits, getting criminal records expunged, navigating the process of registering for school when one is homeless, and countless times, attempting to track down their identifying documents, which are a necessary first step to do almost any of the other tasks. I spent a lot of time sitting with young folks at a computer, looking for services that didn't exist or directions on how to navigate incredibly complex benefits systems that I am privileged enough to never have had to experience. Often the violence that youth faced on the street, while couch hopping, and in shelters was so immediate and traumatizing that these case management activities took a back seat to just getting through the day. Nearly everything in the lives of homeless young people is more complicated, precarious, and terrifying than I—or any case manager—could "fix." By far the most important aspect of my job was to be one person who actually *saw* homeless young people—as unique, as resilient, as messy in a human way—and I tried to reflect back to them that the many injustices they experienced on a daily basis were just that: *unjust*.

In many ways the Broadway Youth Center was incredibly unique—it was staffed by a group of younger people, nearly all under thirty, mostly queer identified, and many queer and trans people of color. Youth clients gave each other haircuts, did each other's makeup, and participated in a wide array of programming, much of which they themselves developed—writing poetry, discussing police violence, talking about trans identities. There were also terrible fights between youth, constant police scrutiny, profound mental illness, and it was hot, and packed, and loud. Stuff got stolen and lice ran riot. Staff was constantly trying to de-escalate conflicts to prevent the police from being called, and refusing the police access when they were called, to try and maintain the BYC as a space where youth with outstanding warrants—which are ubiquitous in the lives of homeless youth—could safely be. It was beautiful and devastating, and it reflected a reality of queer homelessness and poverty that Howard Brown has never quite known how to apprehend.

Developed in 2005, as a collaboration between Howard Brown and two homeless youth agencies (The Night Ministry and Teen Living Program), the Broadway Youth Center's development took advantage of the "hands-off approach from [the] senior management" at Howard Brown.[44] It has become a darling of Chicago's young queer and genderqueer community and is seen as one of the few northside LGBT programs that is multiracial and has intersectional politics. Despite its popularity, it has received paltry support from Howard Brown. Up until 2013 it was housed in a much too small space, riddled with black mold, lacking air-conditioning, with food and hygiene products provided by volunteers, where hundreds of youth would vie to get their needs met by a two person case management staff. Starting in the summer of that year, the situation became even more precarious: temporarily housed in the basement of a local church, without enough electricity to even support work stations for every staff member, let alone air-conditioning. In that new temporary space, staff had to pack up the entire drop-in every night so that other church groups could meet in that space in the evening, and the center was continually engaged in a battle with the church's neighboring homeowners for a permit to continue operations. It remained in that precarious position—in a stop-gap location only intended to last a few months—until a new space was finally acquired in 2016.

During this period, while the BYC struggled to continue meeting the basic needs of Chicago queer homeless youth, Howard Brown proceeded with plans to rebrand itself as a "boutique" healthcare provider to affluent, insured, LGBT people. While the BYC languished, literally in the basement, the organization poured millions into a new branded boutique imprint called Aris Health by Howard Brown. In what follows I examine Howard Brown's attempts and failures to wrestle queer youth homelessness into the compassion narrative on which it bases its fundraising, and the attachment people within the BYC have, nonetheless, toward their organization.

Lifeline Appeal: Feeling Crisis

The compassion narrative mobilized by Howard Brown in the mid-1980s as they turned toward individual and foundation donors got a recent workout in the form of a "lifeline appeal" launched by the organization in 2010 to cover a major budget shortfall. This appeal utilized YouTube videos by staff, clients, and volunteers in which they shared their personal stories of how Howard Brown has been a lifeline for them or for their community. This appeal was widely successful: it aimed to raise $500,000 in fifty days, a huge sum for any organization. After fifty days it exceeded its goal, raising $650,000. It did so through the skillful deployment of affect, of personal feelings for and about the organization: fear, crisis, love, solidarity, connection, and community. The BYC was made particularly visible in the lifeline appeal, with videos made by youth clients, BYC staff, and donors that made particular mention of the importance of the BYC itself, rather than solely Howard Brown. In what follows I explore this moment in detail, analyzing in particular what the visibility and invisibility of the BYC in the videos tells us about the limits of compassion and of community, and the relationship between AIDS and homelessness in the gay imagination.

On April 26, 2010, the *Chicago Tribune* reported that Howard Brown Health Center was under investigation by the National Institutes of Health (NIH) following allegations that they mishandled funds associated with the Multi-Center AIDS Cohort Study (MACS) grant, a long-running research project studying gay men who are HIV positive or living with AIDS.[45] HBHC, in partnership with Northwestern University Medical Center, was selected by the NIH in 1983 as one of five national sites, and MACS represented HBHC's longest-running research project and one of its most steady income streams. The funds associated with the project are "restricted funds," meaning that they can only be used to cover expenses explicitly budgeted and allowed for in the grant itself. In an interview, Tom, a senior member of the staff at the BYC, explains what happened:

> They used restricted funds to pay for admin overhead and medical expenses. And, well, for a lot of the medical services that we don't recoup any payment for, so a lot of the monies were basically being used for general operating support for medical services. I feel like the financial mismanagement was a combination of inadequate supervision of federal funding—and to the point where it became really apparent that it was going to really heavily impact cash flow, and that's really what precipitated the lifeline appeal campaign.[46]

Howard Brown revealed in a statement that upwards of $3 million was mishandled over a two-year period. In the immediate aftermath of this revelation there was a great deal of shuffling and purging of staff as the board and management tried to determine both who was responsible and who would seem responsible to donors. In the weeks following, two members of the senior administration were fired by the board: the executive director immediately, and then, a few weeks later, the development director, who had initially been moved into the interim-ED role following the ouster of the ED. The legal counsel for Howard Brown, Anton Jones, then moved into the executive director role, a move which dismayed many staff members with whom I spoke. The financial ramifications were immediately felt. As the *Tribune* reports, "after learning of the problems, Howard Brown made Northwestern University the lead agent for the AIDS study.

Jones said that the center had to give Northwestern $539,000 to make up for money that was pulled out and used to cover other expenses. 'We need to get that money back,' Jones said."[47] It was to recoup this money that Howard Brown launched its "lifeline appeal," which represented the organization's first major foray into social and new media.

Development staff made short videos featuring staff, clients, and volunteers describing why Howard Brown is their "lifeline." Accompanying each video was a message from the organization explaining the project: "These Lifeline Stories will be shared online over the coming weeks to tell the story of Howard Brown's life-preserving work and to inspire others to be a lifeline for Howard Brown! We're taking our mission and our message viral by sharing 50 Stories in 50 Days."[48] The affective appeal is immediately evident in the use of the word "lifeline" to describe the act of donating money. By donating money you become someone who would throw a lifeline to save another who is drowning; this implies, of course, that if you don't give, and Howard Brown is no longer able to do "life preserving work," then you are implicated in the resulting deaths. The campaign collapses the individual lives that might be preserved with the preservation of the organization itself. Johnna Redmond, a freelance journalist who reported on the scandal for the local queer media, described the power of the appeal:

> I really remember this urgent call going out, . . . "We will close our doors, and it's fucked up that this has happened, but we have to do something." All these queer people who have no money, myself included, throwing money into this. It was the first time I had seen in Chicago where the mainstream gay community found common purpose with radical queers, and that was to save this organization that all of us use. Howard Brown really brings us together, our lives really depend on it. This community that is already really strained in an economic sense really strained to pull it together.[49]

It is important to recognize that the sense of crisis mobilized in this campaign is not simply (just) a fundraising tool; the feelings expressed in the videos are clearly strongly felt, and those feelings did in fact truly resonate with the viewers who then opened their wallets. This is the importance of affect to this work, and to this project: it is not simple. Though affect is used to cue a particular set of actions—donating, in particular—this does not diminish its "real-ness." And although affect can be cued by particular narratives, it also can exceed those prescriptive narratives, as we will see. In this case in particular, as Howard Brown both authorized and released control over these stories, there is considerably more variation in the allowable narratives than would usually be available through a tightly controlled, message driven, branded fundraising campaign. In what follows I provide a close reading of a number of lifeline appeal videos to examine how affect is mobilized, and to what ends, by different actors within the Howard Brown constellation.

Nearly all of the fifty films are short, two-minute, confessional-style videos of individuals presenting how Howard Brown is a lifeline for them. One of the films, though, was long enough to be split into three parts. In it, the speaker, Lance, presents his own experience of Howard Brown, a story that is perhaps the closest to the story that Howard Brown would tell about itself. In the first of three videos we get a sense of the speaker: an older, perhaps sixty-ish, white gay man, recently retired from a professional career, who was out and active in the Chicago gay scene in the 1970s, before and during Howard Brown's early years. In the second video, he articulates the narrative of AIDS that is, by now, quite familiar. He says:

> My name is Lance, and for the last two years I've been a volunteer in the Outreach Department of Howard Brown. . . . I had a wonderful colleague and friend . . . that was my first real introduction to this terrible gay cancer. I won't go through, um, the terrible details of what Ken had to put up with. Most of you know what that was like in the early days. But Ken was the first person I lost to [AIDS]. *[begins to cry]* I lost a lot of friends to HIV and AIDS. But a remarkable thing happened; the gay community came together in a way I had never seen before. . . . They needed somewhere to coalesce around, and where was it, it was Howard Brown.
>
> Howard Brown was there leading the way in our fight against HIV/AIDS. I was not a joiner but I admired the work of Howard Brown and these courageous gays and lesbians who were out there demanding attention, demanding answers. . . . We know that it's moved from being a terminal illness to a horrible but chronic disease. I have every confidence that one day there will be a cure for HIV/AIDS. Howard Brown is in the forefront, is working, is sending out lifelines to literally thousands of people. They are alive because Howard Brown is alive to support them.[50]

Lance tells exactly the kind of story you would expect from a Howard Brown fundraising appeal: a story of the cruelty and devastation of AIDS, a story of redemptive community response, a response that has turned the tide, making a cure all but a foregone conclusion. A story about lives saved. And this is not at all to diminish the power of that story or to suggest that it is untruthful: it is indeed true, for Lance and for many others. It is also, for Howard Brown, a useful story, a story with "good cash value," to borrow a term from George Henderson. Lance was not an activist, "not a joiner," but he "admired" the work. In the third part of his video, Lance becomes visibly emotional discussing the importance of Howard Brown:

> When it came time for me to retire . . . I needed something to do;
> And I thought, "I want to do good works, but I don't want respon-
> sibilities," so I immediately thought of Howard Brown. I cannot
> tell you how my admiration has grown as I see the work that the
> people at this organization do. The lifelines are very real. Those of
> you who are of my generation remember what it was like before
> Howard Brown. Those of you who are younger than I am, I am tell-
> ing you, you don't want to know that reality. We cannot let Howard
> Brown Health Center disappear. We have to save this organization
> which has saved so many of us. *[Speaking emphatically]* . . . They
> inspire me, I'm moved by working with younger people who are
> really dedicated. And I'm asking you for *them*—they've sent out
> these lifelines for us, it's time for us to send lifelines back to How-
> ard Brown. I can't tell you how important this is to me *[choked up]*.
> Please help Howard Brown Health Center in its lifeline project.[51]

In this section his emotion is palpable: he emphatically entreats viewers to donate, both so that the community never knows what it is like to again go without an LGBT health center, but also, interestingly, to protect the staff who would lose their jobs if Howard Brown shut its doors. Again, his class position is clear: he retired early and was looking for something to fill his time. His use of the phrase "good works" harkens back to a Christian model of charity to the downtrodden and suggests how he understands his own involvement with Howard Brown.

But other videos present an alternative narrative, stories that point to the complexity of crisis and compassion within Howard Brown. In this analysis, I want to center the attachment that people feel to Howard Brown as an example of what Lauren Berlant calls "cruel optimism," in which the object of one's desire is actually a barrier to one's flourishing.[52] Howard Brown, which appears to be—and is—a site of connection and a source of life-saving services is also, I argue, complicit in the systemic violences that make those services necessary. To illustrate: another video features Peanut, a young person from the BYC, an African American gender-nonconforming queer person. He says:

> Hello everybody, it's Peanut again saying "Hi" to everyone out there in TV land. Let's get down to business. Howard Brown and the BYC have *helped us*. . . . When I was homeless they helped me get transportation, you know the train and the bus if I needed to sleep, food to eat, a shower, condoms, it really helped us! . . . They are like a lifeline to me and I just thank them all. I met Chanel [a case manager] at a church, she told me about the BYC, that I could go there show up and get food and meet people like me that was out on the streets, and I met people. And they say that you can have a family, your blood family, and it's just nothing, but you make your own family and they'll love you better than your real family. But Chanel is a good girl, and if you come to the BYC you'll meet her and she'll have your back. Chanel and the BYC is my lifeline.[53]

In this narrative, Howard Brown is eclipsed entirely and the space and staff of the BYC are the lifelines, *they* will "have your back." But according to an informant within the BYC, Howard Brown does not have the BYC's back. When asked how all of the transition following the MACS scandal and lifeline appeal had impacted the BYC, Tom reported:

> I guess we feel exploited; we're still the golden jewel of Howard Brown, but [we're] even more under-resourced. The building is falling apart; the power will go down for two and half days. Still there's no A/C in the drop-in, and so we have to create a protocol about what to do when it's making people sick because it's so hot and we have to close. There are no resources and no one cares.[54]

In my conversations with informants in 2013, with the BYC even more pre-cariously housed in a church basement, its physical resources even poorer, fighting a battle just to continue to occupy the church basement within the gentrifying neighborhood—a battle that could have been avoided had Howard Brown invested in a new space for the drop-in program—that sense of exploitation and frustration had only intensified.

Cruel Attachments: Love and Betrayal

A number of interviews with staff of the Broadway Youth Center revealed that they shared the strong sense that the BYC was exploited for fundraising purposes but that the money never made it back to the programs and services of the BYC. One informant described how they had to fend off a never-ending stream of fundraising ideas that would exploit the stories of BYC youth for financial gain. The informant described how, *in a job interview*, a candidate for a fundraising position—a person who was actually hired—described a fundraising idea that is straight out of the most paternalistic model imaginable: "In her interview the idea she had for building community with queer homeless youth was that they would get donated paper bags and youth will make cranes and sell them at the Brown Elephant [resale shop] for a dollar. Everything is a joke. The BYC reminds us what a joke everything is and how sad that is."[55] This marketing scheme, used to represent and commodify the suffering of everything from child cancer victims to starving children to, apparently, queer homeless youth has its roots in the most paternalistic and voyeuristic forms of charity. Through the production and sale of little paper cranes, wealthy donors can literally consume the pitiable tragedy of those they are "saving." Further, by taking up a strategy that has most often been used to commodify third world suffering, the same hands-off affective stance that has typified U.S. responses to hunger in the global south can be imported to distance wealthy donors from the effects of ravaging inequality just down the street from their condo. This desire to sell the suffering of BYC youth to raise money felt, to my informant, like a clear red flag, but the individual was hired nonetheless. How could that new hire represent the interests of the BYC, and fundraise on its behalf, when the BYC works with young people who don't fit the model of "deserving victim?" For that informant, who was sharing a sense of the mood at the BYC, everything is a cruel joke: it would be funny if it weren't so sad, if people's lives didn't depend on the services they struggle to provide.

It is with no small sense of irony that BYC staff described their precarious housing situation: a homeless service for homeless youth. One of the case managers, Montana, reflects on this cruel irony:

> The BYC should never have been unstably housed. Everyone knew the lease was ending at the end of 2012, and I can't blame one specific individual. It was about having an interim CEO and having a Board that didn't understand why the BYC's mission is critical, and the main operation person was fired; there's literally twenty different reasons why the BYC became homeless that are connected to forty different individuals. The crisis could have been averted. . . . But because there was so much crisis . . . the space was wholly ignored in terms of its physical needs. So it was unsafe and unhealthy a lot of the time, which perpetuated a lot of the crisis at the BYC, this is a regular way of operating.[56]

Despite this betrayal by the parent organization, the staff of the BYC continued to invest, even as they became burnt out, frustrated, and cynical. One long-time staff member, Shelby, finally decided it was time to quit. I asked her to take me through that process. When did she know it was time?

> When we moved from the permanent location, and we worked really really hard to ensure there was no stoppage in service, even if it meant rolling [equipment] out every day, [I thought], we could do that for six months. But then it became apparent [that] there was just no investment in finding a space. And I was just driving around the neighborhood looking for church basements, and I was in survival mode: if I don't find something, critical services will be cut, we'll have to return money, staff positions will be cut, and so I found this church basement. . . . The moment I had was when I walked into the drop-in space and it was maybe a hundred and five degrees and we couldn't even put window units in because the electricity couldn't handle it, and we just had fans that were super fucking loud. And there was a young person with as little clothes on as possible laying on the tile floor to cool themselves off, and that was the moment that I was so disgusted and angered, and I was like, "I can't condone what the larger organization is doing to young people." I just had this feeling that I can't keep anyone safe, I can't keep youth safe, . . . and

meanwhile cops were trying to get in the front door because they were trying to get to a young person, and just at every exit there was some metaphor for institutional violence.[57]

This relocation would not have had, in and of itself, such a great impact, she said, had it not come after years and years of existing in a crisis atmosphere. What were they doing instead, if they weren't looking for new spaces?

Based on interviews and coverage in the local gay press, it is clear that in the wake of the MACS financial scandal, the new executive director intensified the organization's investment in neoliberal tactics of efficiency, branding, messaging, and technological systems. New systems were created to fix problems—particularly the immediate fiscal distress and the widespread image problem—but the existing problems of underresourced programs, overburdened staff, and a need that far outpaced the capacity of the organization went unanswered. Instead, the ED focused on making the organization *seem* efficient and capable, primarily through the use of technology. Tom reported that "he's trying to clean house. 'It's a new day!' The messaging I'm getting is that it's important to build a corporate medical model, almost like a University Medical Center."[58] In the year after the scandal, Howard Brown posted a budget surplus, but according to Tom, it was made possible by "programmatic under-resourcing, so we can see how we're getting this surplus, but it comes at the cost of the programs themselves."[59] Despite this programmatic underresourcing, Howard Brown expanded its use of technology and even hired a PR firm. According to Tom, "you know there's an *interim logo*. We all cracked up about that . . . . Everything is a joke. . . . There's a new mission statement, but no one knows what it is. It's *interim*."[60]

For staff on the frontlines, the PR haggling over the messaging of the interim mission is far removed from the life and death struggles experienced by the clients with whom they work, and it is evidence that Howard Brown as an organization doesn't know or care about those struggles. In the context of that struggle Howard Brown's discordant "solutions" focused on management technologies become so cruelly ironic. Tom describes:

There's a new person, a friend of the ED's, who was hired for some unspecified senior position involving technology. His big projects have so far involved getting all of the senior staff tablets, so that everyone comes into meetings and all the senior staff have tablets and no one else does. . . . The other project is that he wanted to increase confidentiality in the waiting room so he got these Olive Garden-style vibrating discs, which of course don't work, they just sit in the basket on the counter vibrating all the time. So they numbered them, and now someone takes a vibrating disk with a number on it and they call out the number. So it's basically four hundred dollar numbers that could be laminated pieces of paper.[61]

For the staff and clients of the BYC, who are so immersed in a world of immediate crisis, homelessness, and poverty, working alongside youth struggling to find a meal, struggling to find a place to sleep that night, dealing with the immediate and long-term effects of terrible violence, and negotiating demeaning and diminishing social service programs—people for whom there are simply no good options anywhere—to see these hare-brained schemes must be absolutely crazy-making.

I asked Shelby, the longtime BYC case manager, about the toll of these wacky schemes amid the constant neglect of the program she worked so hard for. She described the long-term impact of years of grappling with crisis, both in the work with youth and within the organization itself. "I don't even know how to describe the physical and psychological toll, because it was severe," she said. "There were days where I would just spontaneously start crying, and I couldn't get it together, and I would have to leave [the drop-in space]. Do you remember LaTanya?" I did. A young African American woman, poised, quiet. She had a toddler that she often brought up to the space with her. She wasn't one of my case management clients, but I remember her around the space; she had been coming to the BYC since long before I was hired. I asked Shelby to jog my memory: "She worked with you, right?" "For years," Shelby said. She went on:

> She had a son who was killed, and then she committed suicide the next year. And it was a big turning point for me. For feeling broken. I can't do it. Spending all night at the BYC doing paperwork, it was just totally unsustainable. It was one hundred percent crisis all the time, but about people's real actual lives rather than about personnel issues, which are crises, but not.[62]

She paused for a moment. But, she said, "*I would do it all over again.* I don't know what that means."[63] Shelby spoke many times in our conversation about staying, in large part, because she felt that if she didn't stay and continue to pressure Howard Brown to support the BYC they would cut the program.

In an interview with a former manager of the BYC, Maleeka, who left her position some years ago now, she reflected on that phenomenon among staff. "You don't appreciate how unhealthy it could be until you're gone," she said. "I had a very special moment when I realized I don't need to carry Howard Brown on my shoulder, and lots of people on front lines or mid-level management are trying to carry it on their shoulders, or buffer young people, or be there because maybe no one else would be."[64] This is one aspect of the cruelty of our attachments to nonprofits. She explained: "You can sacrifice all you want to protect young people, but they [management] are having conversations about the BYC that you are not involved in, so it could be ripped away at any moment."[65] The Broadway Youth Center illustrates the degree to which, even amidst crisis, something important, something life sustaining, happens. Yet that space is so precarious, and those moments so fleeting. Montana reflects:

> What makes the work with young people hard is the, um, the continuous operating out of scarcity. There might be a flash of abundance, and it would be like "this could completely revolutionize the work if we had what we needed, or that there were housing options that were more effective or plentiful." You know? I think that what also makes it hard is that in the nonprofit system the priority is never the young people, but the preservation and protection of the nonprofit system itself.[66]

These flashes of abundance, when you could imagine what it would be like if there were actual resources that young folks could be connected to, keep people fighting for a little bit more here, a little bit more there, a grant to cover one more program. This is, of course, why compassion is useful for the neoliberal state: it occupies those people made surplus by the changing economic system—those who would be most likely to rise up and demand change—with the never-ending task of surviving, and occupies those who would fight alongside them in a never-ending quest to find *just one more grant* to try and ensure that such survival is possible.

Conclusion

Though most of the lifeline appeal videos narrate crisis in order to appeal to the compassion of donors, one lifeline appeal seemed to recognize and gesture toward the profound inequalities that underlie the appeal and the organization more broadly. Chanel, who was named as the staff member who would "have your back" in Peanut's video, read from a prepared statement for her video. She said:

> Dear friends and family and community. I love my work with young people and I love my work at the Broadway Youth Center. . . . It's a place for young activists and movement builders. I am privileged to bear witness to the magic, the hard moments, the really really really hard moments, and the small miracles that keep us struggling and loving and resisting and making it work against all odds. BYC youth are known for their resourcefulness, hilariousness, unrelenting toughness, and big loyal hearts. I learn from this every day. This is the first place that many young people come to ask us really personal and scary questions about their gender identity and sexual identity, about their bodies, about their lives. . . . It's the first place where people come after they've been incarcerated and need a place to get re-grounded. It's the first place where people reach out to us for support. We're here when people test positive and connect them to the resources they deserve. . . . We're here when young people have nowhere to go and we safety plan and safety plan and safety plan. *I do this work because I believe that young people are amazing lifelines to each other.* Howard Brown Health Center, our committed community partners, and BYC youth have built this space collectively, *so that now there's not just one lifeline, but hundreds and probably thousands.*[67]

This video explicitly rejects the idea that Howard Brown the *organization* is the lifeline, but instead describes the *people* who "have built this space collectively," as "lifelines to each other." She rejects the narrative that so many hold—even and especially Howard Brown donors—about home- less queer youth of color: as problems, delinquents, lazy, or the more be- neficent narratives of tragic paternalism. They do not fit the compassion narrative; they are not going to make paper cranes. Instead she describes the complex personhood, the barriers, resilience, constrained agency, and individual personalities that escape and exceed those narratives. This, according to both my own experience and to the many interviews conducted with staff of the BYC, is what made the BYC difficult, both for Howard Brown to claim unreservedly and difficult to build relationships with homeowners and business owners. It refused, at least when it could, to rely on the paternalistic and pathologizing narratives that dehumanized the youth who relied upon it, who built it, who peopled it. Its refusal of the compassion narrative made it impossible for Howard Brown to apprehend, or to contain, but the freedom thereby enabled to go "off script" is little comfort when it is one hundred degrees and there are a hundred young people with little access to hygiene supplies all trying to get their needs met.

I asked Shelby to reflect on why she stayed at the BYC for so many years, despite the crisis atmosphere and neglect on the part of its parent organization. She thought for a moment, and replied:

> I stayed because I really believe in my heart that there is and
> should be radical ways for people to have access to basic needs. . . .
> I also recognize that there were lots of flaws and under-resourcing;
> there was no one day that was perfect. And I loved the group of
> people who were so committed to the work. To creating a safer
> space for young people to show up and be messy and mad and
> angry and beautiful and kind, and there aren't a lot of spaces that
> are just open, especially for GLBT young people.[68]

In this chapter I have argued that for those who believe in queer nonprofits, our attachment, our longing, is an example of cruel optimism. But as Shelby reflects, many who grapple in and with those spaces are not so optimistic: there are no perfect days.

What is left, then, without the optimism? Only the cruel relation and the work of making do. Berlant argues that a "spreading precarity provides the dominant *structure* and *experience* of the present moment."[69] Neoliberal economic transformations have produced a class of precarious, "flexible" workers, contract-based, without benefits, without union representation, with wages undercut by outsourcing; alongside this, we see the privatization of the social safety net, diminishing public institutions, and competition and scarcity among nonprofit agencies. Precarity and crisis are the mode of the present.

In response to the crisis of the present, a precarity that frays fantasies of the good life, Berlant asks "what happens to optimism when futurity splinters as a prop for getting through life?" She argues that we find ourselves at an *impasse*: "managing the presence of a problem/event that dissolves the old sureties and forces improvisation and reflection on life-without-guarantees."[70] For Berlant, rather than simply denoting stuckness, an impasse is a way of making do. She writes:

> The impasse is a stretch of time in which one moves around with a sense that the world is at once intensely present and enigmatic, such that the activity of living demands both a wondering absorptive awareness and a hypervigilance that collects material that might help to clarify things, maintain one's sea legs. . . . The holding pattern implied in "impasse" suggests temporary housing.[71]

The seeming affective contradiction that Shelby articulates, a clear-eyed indictment of the nonprofit system coupled with deep hope and longing, seems to be shared by many of my informants—and is, in fact, a contradiction I often feel acutely. This contradiction embodies this impasse, one strategy for making do, for reimagining life after the demise of the fantasy of the good life.

3

Community and Its Others

Safety, Space, and Nonprofitization

In this post-disciplinary context, discipline does not fall away. Though welfare state institutions begin to lose distinct form under internal and external pressures, this does not mark the disappearance of techniques of social control associated with schools, hospitals, prisons and the lot. Rather, accounts suggest that these techniques have become unmoored from their institutional arrangements, allowing for a more general distribution of abstract disciplinary practices across what had been known as the social. Further, in the context of the coming-to-dominance of biopolitics, the remains of disciplinary enclosures may begin to serve new functions. The opening up of enclosures, the multiplication and diffusion, suggest that the organization of the individual and its confinement in space is no longer the primary goal of disciplinary mechanisms. Rather, disciplinary mechanisms in this context may serve as flashpoints between an individual and biopolitics.

> Craig Willse, "'Universal Data Elements,' or the Biopolitical Life of Homeless Populations"

But what began to take shape here was a new way of demarcating a sector for government, a sector whose vectors and forces could be mobilized, enrolled, deployed in novel programmes and techniques which operated through the instrumentalization of personal allegiances and active responsibilities: government through community.

> Nikolas Rose, "The Death of the Social? Re-figuring the Territory of Government"

One of the rare formal collaborations between the Broadway Youth Center and the Center on Halsted (COH) is occasioned by Transgender Day of

Remembrance, a yearly event held throughout the country to mark those trans people who did not survive the violence directed at them. The two organizations come together to host the "Night of the Fallen Stars" celebration in the Center on Halsted's well-appointed facilities. In 2012, however, a telling conflict marred the proceedings. Just days before the event, the COH's transgender program coordinator resigned her position in protest of the center's decision to accept a donation from the Human Rights Campaign (HRC) in order to "offset costs of the event."[1] In a letter posted to her Facebook page, Violet Stanlet, who had held the position as a volunteer for more than five years, wrote: "when the Director said to me: 'We couldn't turn down the money,' it felt like a slap in the face, not only for me, but for my community as well."[2] Stanlet is referring to the Human Rights Campaign's longstanding dismissal of trans issues, most recently their decision to pursue federal employment nondiscrimination legislation that did not include gender identity as a protected category. After it had been the target of nationwide protests by trans people, Violet found it particularly galling that the HRC would offer a donation in support of Transgender Day of Remembrance—and even more so that the Center on Halsted would accept it.[3] She wrote: "I can not be a part of putting money above principle. I can not be a part of enabling HRC's attempt to buy their way back into the Trans communities' good graces. I can not be associated with an organization which would show such disrespect for the Transgender community."[4] Implicit in Stanlet's critique is an assumption about "community": of whom it is comprised, where it is located, and that "it" can reasonably make demands on and be represented by the Center on Halsted.

In this chapter, I turn to what Terry Stone, executive director of Centerlink, a network of LGBT community centers, calls the "spirit of the community": the LGBT community center.[5] The first LGBT community centers opened in Albany, New York, and Los Angeles in 1971, and since then, they have sprung up in most urban areas in the United States, reflecting the emergence of the contemporary queer "community"—and the institutional formations that purportedly house it—during the time period I consider in this book.[6] This emergence and expansion has been facilitated by a very different set of alignments than the more charity- and discipline-oriented Howard Brown Health Center of the previous chapter. The community center, in contrast, sits at the nexus of state power, yes, but even more so corporate wealth, foundation giving, and LGBT philanthropy.[7]

Whereas the previous chapter explored the affective, institutional, and disciplinary logic of *compassion,* this chapter addresses the production and management of *community:* its appeal, the mechanics of its production, the affective economies on which it relies, the moments it exceeds the terms under which it was mobilized, and the possibilities it enables and forecloses. Community, in its institutional arrangements considered in this chapter, functions according to a biopolitical rather than strictly disciplinary logic, offering a window into a scene of contestation over which bodies are of the community, who must be regulated, how they must be regulated, and for what reasons. Community, in the context of neoliberalism's ever-expanding ability to incorporate particular queer bodies into the national imaginary and technologies of control, is increasingly the logic through which some queer bodies are protected and folded into (national) life, while others are located outside the life of the nation, a threat to it, and exposed to early death. Within this framework, we can then explore the nonprofit's struggle to produce something called "the LGBT community" as the bureaucratized, regulatory nonprofit apparatus acting as the connective tissue between affect and the biopolitical management of life and death. The community center illustrates both sides of what Jasbir Puar calls a "bio-necro collaboration," in which life is fostered for some, while others are rendered irredeemably undeserving. At the Center on Halsted, some queer lives are optimized through therapy, social programs, educational offerings, job resources, and networking, while other lives are located outside "the community," and regulated through explicit relationships with the police, the on-site security guards, and conflicts over the space itself.

The Center on Halsted is, ironically enough, just down the street from the Howard Brown Health Center and its Broadway Youth Center—both are located in the gentrified Lakeview neighborhood in Chicago, or "Boystown" as it is known. But the differences between these two organizations are important. In 2007 the COH opened a brand-new "green" space, the first floor of which is rented out to a Whole Foods grocery store. The space is furnished with contemporary furniture and art and equipped with a computer center, a theater, conference rooms that are rented out for earned income, therapist offices, and a youth space—even a cubical farm in the center of the building that houses its expansive middle management. The airy and contemporary feel is somewhat at odds with the picture of homeless youth sleeping on a $3,000 couch in the middle of the day, and consequently fierce and unanticipated battles have erupted over public space, gentrification, race and racism, and homelessness, over what kinds of bodies and affects comprise "the community."

After first exploring some of the theoretical underpinnings of my investigation of community, I investigate how the disciplining power of the charity model became fused with a new neoliberal logic of community, specifically looking at a period in the 1980s when the role of the membership of the organization shifted and came to constitute a new community of donors. I then examine three instructive instances in the larger institutional efforts to produce and police "the community." The first is a series of procedural changes undertaken by the youth program soon after the center moved into its new space in order to more explicitly police who counted as the community of queer youth, and to limit the access of those deemed not a member of that community. These changes were enacted as a direct result of the increasing numbers of homeless youth of color accessing the youth programs; the sexuality of these youths was under question by the organization, and their efforts to police who did and did not belong illustrates the limits of community and the contestation over its boundaries. The second section traces these conflicts forward a few years, when, following a series of incidences of violence in the Boystown neighborhood and a video gone viral purporting to "capture" that violence, a campaign to "Take Back Boystown" was launched with COH occupying center stage.

The third site of conflict within this organization that I analyze is the uneasy relationship between the community center and one of its programs, the Chicago LGBT Anti-Violence Project (AVP). In 2011 the center's AVP accepted an anti-sex trafficking grant from the Cook County State's Attorney's office despite the seeming knowledge that it would do very little to increase the safety of the young people it targets—and perhaps even further endanger them—once again illustrating the institutional structures which butt up against and enforce the limits of community. The first two sites of conflict clearly illustrate the exclusionary function of community, while this third example traces the complex routes by which some bodies can become "deserving," can be reclaimed by community, and under what affective and discursive terms.

Looking at the struggle of the Center on Halsted to produce and police the boundaries of community, I ask: What kinds of subjectivity, what kinds of political horizons, are imagined by these efforts to achieve community? What possibilities are foreclosed? How do such entreaties to community mobilize affect—desire, fear, hope—and to what ends? How has community, in the context of the NPIC, come to function as the bridge between affect and biopower? How does community function to produce—both discursively and materially—not only those that are "in the community," and those that are not, but also those outside any imagining of community, the other "Others" Anna Agathangelou writes of "whose life and death do not even merit mention or attention?"[8]

Community and Neoliberal Governance

As I have argued, nonprofits escape scrutiny in large part through a widespread affective narrative that understands them as fundamentally "good," as constituting what David Wagner calls "the sanctified sector."[9] This affective narrative is about more than the supposed "good works" undertaken in nonprofits, though; this chapter analyzes how the idea of *community* is produced and lived through nonprofits, and how community functions as a tool of neoliberal governance, governance through feeling. A key part of the affective narrative that "sanctifies" the nonprofit sector has to do with the kinds of citizenship imagined to exist and be fostered within such organizations. Nonprofits are commonly understood to constitute "civil society," an instructively imprecise term intended to demarcate a sector outside of the state and the market, the so-called "public square" of citizenship, debate, care, and shared American identity. This assumed location outside the market and the state is a critical component of the benevolent narrative of nonprofits, obscuring, as it does, the key function of nonprofits in maintaining neoliberal governance—particularly their role in both entrenching economic inequality and managing the resulting poverty. Instead, nonprofits are understood, according to Miranda Joseph, to be "a metonym" for community, with a responsibility to "shape, define, and direct that community."[10]

In her important book *Against the Romance of Community*, Joseph challenges this narrative, arguing that community is, in fact, critical for and constitutive of both the nation-state and capitalism. For Joseph, capitalism and, "more generally, modernity, *depend on and generate* the discourse of community to legitimate social hierarchies."[11] Using Marx, Joseph demonstrates "the supplementarity of community with capital," arguing that "social relations are implied in material relations of production," and further that it is through community that the use value of commodities is established.[12] The idea of community that is nurtured and mobilized within nonprofits is one key mechanism, then, through which the contemporary nation-state and neoliberal economics function.

For Nikolas Rose, community is especially salient as a form of neoliberal governance. As neoliberal multiculturalism invites a stripped-down form of inclusion in the place of substantive systemic change, individuals in marginalized groups are invited to feel their connection to the newly welcoming state through their community identification. This is the kind of self-governance that Foucault describes, in which the logics of neoliberalism become enunciated and lived at the level of subjectivity. Rose reminds us that while the idea of community certainly predates neoliberalism, it "becomes governmental, however, when it is made technical."[13] He continues: "what began as a language of resistance and critique was transformed . . . into an expert discourse and a professional vocation. . . . Communities became zones to be investigated, mapped, classified, documented, interpreted, their vectors explained . . . and taken into account in numberless encounters between professionals and their clients, whose individual conduct is now to be made intelligible in terms of the beliefs and values of 'their community.' "[14] Contemporary nonprofits, I argue, are one key apparatus through which community is rendered technical. It is through nonprofits that community can be investigated, mapped, documented, interpreted, and, as I demonstrate, made profitable.

Queer community is an interesting example to consider, constituted, as it is, primarily through what it is not: heteronormative. This has meant that queer community has been historically positioned oppositionally to the state, resisting state regulation of sexuality. However, under the cultural politics of neoliberal capitalism, some queer subjects are offered access to normativity, contingent on their participation in other neoliberal projects like policing, private property, consumption, and nationalism. Scholars like Lisa Duggan and Alexandra Chasin have illustrated this profound turn toward the market, and Chasin in particular documents the degree to which queer community has been articulated through market participation. From boycotts to "gay money," corporate Pride sponsorships, and niche advertising, LGBT community is constituted in large part through its relationship to the market. As I demonstrate in this chapter, one important mechanism through which this invitation to neoliberal belonging is issued is through the rhetorical and material remapping of oppositional groups into communities of donors. This invitation into neoliberal self-governance is an example of what Soo Ah Kwon calls "affirmative governmentality," in which subjects are enlisted—through their understanding of themselves as community members—as willing participants in the cultural and economic project of neoliberalism.[15] Drawing on Foucault's concept of governmentality as productive of subjectivity, throughout this chapter, I analyze how particular kinds of queer subjects are produced, managed, mobilized, and policed. As access to the community of the nonprofit is increasingly managed by economic proximity—donor or client—subjects across that spectrum are invited to understand themselves and orient themselves toward entrepreneurial self-governance in an economic and cultural order in which queerness is not oppositional, but rather responsible, upwardly mobile, and *included*.

Understanding community as produced through the affirmative governance apparatus of the nonprofit is not at all to say that such communities are not "real"; on the contrary, they are powerfully real, both materially and affectively. Rose writes,

> Government through community, even when it works upon pre-existing bonds of allegiance, transforms [communities], invests them with new values, affiliates them to expertise and reconfigures relations of exclusion. This does not make "communities" in some sense false. But it should alert us to the work entailed in the construction of community, and the implications of the logics of inclusion and exclusion, of responsibilization and autonomization, that they inescapably entail.[16]

What Rose points to here is not just the invitation of unity and belonging issued by the promise of community, but also the exclusions that must then be managed as well. If the nonprofit system is one often-overlooked apparatus through which community is rendered technical, part of that technical capacity must be articulating and policing exclusions—those who are constitutively outside of community. In her scholarship on nonprofits that work with so-called "at-risk" youth, Soo Ah Kwon describes the state as "both caring and ruthless": the "powers that promote youth empowerment," she writes, "are not separate from those of youth criminalization."[17] This continuity between the affirmative technologies of community belonging and the policing technologies of exclusion are an example of what Jasbir Puar describes as the "bio-necro collaboration" of homonormativity.[18] Puar draws on Foucault's concept of biopolitics, a mode of power directed at populations, fostering life for some via tactics like public health campaigns—or in this context, community center programming—while exposing other populations to early death. In this way, community functions biopolitically, and as the example of the Center on Halsted demonstrates, some queer bodies are targeted for living, for entrepreneurial neoliberal subjectivity, while others are understood as criminal, irredeemably deviant, and oriented toward incarceration.

The critique that I level in this chapter is not simply that queer community is exclusionary. Instead, I am interested in the mechanisms and logics of exclusion *as well as* those of inclusion. The technologies of inclusion, of affirmative governmentality, are just as deserving of scrutiny and critique. The goal is, of course, not simply to widen those technologies of inclusion to target more subjects—as they are already doing. Miranda Joseph suggests that this common feminist and queer critique of the false universality of community usually, after demarcating the exclusions, calls for greater access to community. Joseph writes: "U.S.-based critics of identity politics have often instead pursued even more finely grained measures of authenticity, producing not a critique of community but a proliferation of communities."[19] My intention in this chapter is to trace the mechanisms through which community is produced and managed in order to think through what kinds of possibilities for social movements are enabled through community and what possibilities are foreclosed.

From Charity to Community

The Center on Halsted was founded in 1974 as Gay Horizons, a social service organization intended to meet the social, emotional, and mental health needs of Chicago's gay population. In 1996 they changed their name to Horizons Community Service, in part to side-step the ongoing conflict about whether to add "lesbian" to their name, as well as to reflect both their continuing social service orientation and their desire to become a community center. Their major early program was the gay hotline, which received hundreds of calls a month, meticulously documented, from individuals looking for everything from mental health support, to sex partners, to gay friendly electricians. By the late 1970s it began providing one-on-one and group mental health services, for which it charged a sliding scale fee, and which provided the major income stream that carried the organization through its early years. The organization began applying for its 501(c)(3) nonprofit status in 1977 and received it in 1978. The speed with which the organization sought and received their tax-exempt status suggests fairly significant cultural capital wielded by the founding members; the legal and financial skills necessary to navigate that bureaucratic process are quite daunting, let alone to achieve the status so quickly. It also reveals an uncritical embrace of the nonprofit form very early on. The question of *why* pursue 501(c)(3) status cannot be answered definitively by the extant archive, since the decision was in many ways a forgone conclusion—it was never debated and no other paths were considered.

This particular outlook is further illustrated by many other aspects of the organization's early history. The board of directors held regular meetings, which unfailingly followed Roberts Rules of Order.[20] The organization adopted a fairly corporate lexicon, with "annual corporation meetings" and very formal written documentation. By 1979 they were pursuing a relationship with the Chicago chapter of the United Way, first to receive training on "proper" fundraising and nonprofit management, and eventually for funding. A 1979 board meeting documents this early turn toward traditional charity funding models:

> Steven Larson and Cathy Schmidt had a meeting with a Senior
> Planner for The United Way to discuss planning techniques, etc.
> The woman from the United Way was very helpful and concerned
> about helping Gay Horizons, Inc. in anyway [sic] she could. She
> was somewhat optimistic about the chances of Gay Horizons get-
> ting financial assistance from the United Way. Some of the topics
> discussed were the necessary documentation required for funding,
> the purposes and programs of the organization, and budgets.[21]

Directly following is a description of their first cocktail party fundraiser in which "the purpose would be to give a talk about Gay Horizons, Inc. and its programs then to solicit donations."[22] This is a fascinating picture of the strong sense of inevitability and rightness of the turn toward traditional nonprofit models. It also presents a clear picture of the impact of that funding model on documentation, programming, and financial management. In many ways the history and vision of this organization, like all of the others in this book, was written for funding purposes, and so is fundamentally shaped by an idea of what is "fund-able."

In 1979 the first Gay Horizons youth program began, following the

solicitation of "professionals" to serve as group leaders. Also in 1979 the first
mentions of a community center appear in the notes, although that is a vision not to be realized for another twenty-five years. I am interested in *why*
the community center was envisioned, especially for a social service organization that was very clearly rooted in the charity model. While there is
clearly a sense of affinity based on identity, especially, and really only, among
white gay men, the idea of community did something else for Gay Horizons:
it produced and mobilized a group of donors who understood themselves
to be "the community." The example of Gay Horizons and its eventual transition into the Center on Halsted illustrates very clearly Miranda Joseph's
claim that community is a process of production and consumption.

Throughout the late 1970s and into the early 1980s board meetings
reflect a desire for greater funding in order to expand programmatic offerings and hire more than one part-time staff person. In a 1985 grant application to the Chicago Community Trust, the organization reports on
the reorganization of the board of directors undertaken in 1983 and 1984.
They write:

> In the spring of 1983 the Board of Directors was reorganized from
> representatives of our programs and external gay and lesbian
> organizations to permit us to recruit individuals committed to
> and capable of Board work, that is, financial development, agency
> and financial management, planning and evaluation and public
> communications. The reconstituted Board has designed a financial
> development plan, kicked off in December with a hearteningly
> successful membership drive, which will enable Horizons to be
> self-supporting after three years.[23]

There are two important shifts happening here: the first is a transformation on the board and the second is a transformation in the organization's
understanding of its membership, both of which reflect a marketization of
community. The grant narrative describes the prioritization of recruiting
individuals "committed to and capable of Board work." In order to achieve
the results they desire, they believe this means greater access to wealth,
which would enable greater fundraising—what they are calling "financial
development"—and the skills afforded by cultural capital to manage that
wealth. Prior to this 1983 reorganization, the board of directors had been
composed primarily of gay social workers and other mental health pro-

fessionals. These individuals had, in the early years of the organization, worked the hotline and provided the individual and group counseling that were the core programs of the organization. The 1983 reorganization is an explicit turn, not necessarily *away* from this social service framework, but *toward* a new community of wealth.

This new orientation on the board of directors is further illustrated in 1985. During the March board meeting one member, in referring to the year-end financial report, remarked that "financial development must be the top priority of the Board in the coming year. All Board members, in addition to their other committee and project activities, will be expected to support all Horizon's fundraising activities."[24] By 1992, qualifications for membership on the board of directors included "regular, personally significant financial gifts to Horizons, according to one's means." A second qualification for all board members was to "implement agency fund-raising strategies through personal influence with community contacts, including individuals, foundations, government agencies, corporations, etc."[25] This prioritization of personal wealth and networks of wealth as a qualification for board membership was, of course, not unique to Gay Horizons; the Howard Brown Memorial Clinic was undergoing a similar reorganization of its board of directors during this same time period. What is unique, however, is how this reorganization played out on the level of membership, changing the understanding of the wider community of the organization.

In the 1985 grant application to the Chicago Community Trust, the reorganization of the Board to prioritize financial acumen and access was illustrated by the board's new financial development plan, "kicked off in December with a hearteningly successful membership drive."[26] This is not the first slippage between member and donor, but it is a significant one. In its early years, Gay Horizons was constituted by a membership of volunteers who staffed the hotline, offered counseling services, did filing and administrative tasks, and kept up the office space. Managing the great number of volunteers was clearly a main administrative challenge for the board, and, once they were hired, for staff. The bylaws contained in their 1977 application for 501(c)(3) status made a distinction between "program members" and "general members": people who are active participants— volunteers or participants in programs—and those who simply pay "yearly dues of not less than $1.00."[27] Volunteers were considered members, and for a period in the early 1980s, minutes from every board meeting were even sent to every member in a gesture toward transparency.[28] Following the reorganization of 1983–1984, however, the membership was reimagined as a community of donors. Much work among the board of directors went into choosing from among six possible logos in advance of the 1984 membership drive—clearly an effort to make that drive more lucrative by appealing to a donor base that valued a polished, professional image.

By the mid-1990s, what was once a member drive had become an individual donor drive, making the shift from member to donor complete. Reflective of this shift, in 1995 tickets to the organization's annual gala fundraiser were $175 for an individual ticket and a stunning $400 for a pre-event cocktail reception and preferred seating at the dinner![29] Clearly the imagined community of the organization had shifted considerably, a shift that was invited in many ways by the organization's response to ongoing fiscal distress.

Throughout the 1970s and early 1980s Gay Horizons operated on a shoestring budget. In 1984, revenues totaled just under $24,000, and of that, only $7,019 was spent on staff—for one part-time executive director position.[30] Ten years later the budget had increased to nearly $1.2 million, with an executive director salary of $42,000, as well as numerous other staff positions that managed specific programs. Alongside this exponential budget increase, however, remained constant financial stress.[31] In 1992, for instance, there was a $92,000 budget shortfall from the previous year, primarily due to "significant shortfalls in development."[32] At that time they had a loan from the Non-Profit Assistance Foundation for $25,000, and the treasurer "reported that he believes the agency will have sufficient cash to operate through March."[33] They received a letter from the United Way "which indicated that based on the Agency's audited fiscal year 1991 financial position and results of operations, the Agency failed to achieve three of four financial ratio tests used by United Way to monitor the relative financial health of not for profit organizations."[34] By 1996 the financial distress became acute enough that staff were laid off. In the minutes of the January 1997 board meeting, the treasurer reported:

> On January 26 Sandra and Holly met with staff about the financial status of the agency; the staff was informed that Joel Trenton would be laid off, salaries are frozen with no mid-year salary adjustments given, and Holly authorized two "floating" holidays per employee. Holly asked that more meetings with donors be set up soon and that board members participate in cultivating donors.[35]

At the March board meeting of that year, Holly, the executive director, asked that board members adopt a line item of office supplies and either donate the money to cover it or provide the supplies themselves.[36] Given these fiscal demands, and absent a countervailing political pressure from inside the organization, it is no wonder that the organization turned toward cultivating increasingly wealthy donors and soliciting corporate sponsors.

It is alongside this organizational shift that Gay Horizons's longstanding desire to become a community center was imagined, planned for, and realized. The capital campaign began in 1997, and at that time they expected to break ground for a new center in 1999. In the appeal letter that was sent out that year, the executive director, Holly, wrote:

> This facility will be a concrete symbol of the contributions we—The Gay and Lesbian Community—are making to Chicago. Our community will work together to define the structure and services for this Gay and Lesbian Community Center. Through education, outreach, counseling, and advocacy, we promote community cultural awareness, wellness, and empower community members to better understand themselves and the places in which they live and work.[37]

Of course the community that would imagine this new community center was the one that had been fostered over the past ten years, a community intentionally cultivated to ensure access to wealth. The community center that Gay Horizons eventually became, the Center on Halsted, which broke ground in 2005 and opened in 2007, reflects this orientation toward the market. It is this center, and its efforts to grapple with the community that it spent twenty years cultivating, with which the rest of the chapter is concerned.

"Gangbangers," Troublemakers, and Other "Others"

A *Chicago Free Press* article from March 2008 details, in an interview with the executive director of the COH, the center's struggle to define its constituents—the LGBT community. The article details a series of procedural changes that the center enacted in order to "respond to trouble makers who've threatened the safe space that the [community center] had tried to create for GLBT youth."[38] These procedural changes are affective too, as they rely on a shared sense of threat to build the "us" of community.

The executive director goes on to explain that the center is "trying to create membership programs that help us identify the youths we're trying to help [because] we're getting a lot of complaints of kids on the street. . . . In our community we're already dealing with problems related to racism, and now we've got gangbangers on the corner." Lest the "real" LGBT youth feel alienated by such efforts, he clarifies that it is important that "the GLBT youths who are part of the Center's programs know they're still welcome at the center."[39] The article reads:

> It's also important, Valle said, that they feel safe there and respect others who are using the building and live in the neighborhood. "You can be here if you are respectful to one another," Valle said. "Those kids are welcome here. But there are those kids who are just trying to ruin it for everyone else, and right now they're just exploiting our kids." Aldermen Helen Shiller (46th) and Tom Tunney (44th) are involved in helping to address the issue, he said. . . . Ultimately, he said, the Center's goal is to provide a better environment, not a more restrictive one, for GLBT youths.[40]

The executive director of the community center positioned these changes as necessary in order to respond to "troublemakers" and "gangbangers." He further explained that "gangbangers and others seeking to exploit the GLBT youths who come to the [community center] have led officials to be more stringent in identifying youths who . . . we're trying to help."[41]

To contextualize this article, and understand the materiality of the project of defining and policing the LGBT community it describes, it is important to note that the center moved into its brand new building in the gentrified Boystown neighborhood less than a year before this article was written, a move not just from a smaller building with a focus on social services to a more expansive "community center" model, but also to the mobilization of a particular notion of "community"—a community that I argue is actively produced through techniques of normalization and surveillance.

It is important to note here that Chicago is both one of the most highly segregated cities in the United States, as well as one in which poverty is most clearly racialized. Due in part to the collapse of the welfare system

in the 1990s and the lack of compensatory social services, and exacerbated by the demolition of 18,000 units of public housing, which displaced
more than 42,000 public housing residents, the Chicago Coalition for
the Homeless estimates that approximately 33,000 young people experienced homelessness in Chicago in the year that the center moved to its
new space.[42] The National Gay and Lesbian Task Force estimates that approximately 40 percent of homeless young people are LGBT.[43] The Boystown neighborhood—although it is predominantly white—is, as a "gay"
neighborhood, one area in which homeless LGBT youth of color, especially those who are gender-nonconforming, make community and support themselves. Due to neoliberal law and order policies and the war on
drugs/poverty/crime, the economic crimes homeless youth must commit
in order to survive—squatting, loitering, shoplifting, sex work, turnstile
jumping, and so forth—are heavily policed as so-called "quality of life"
crimes. Coupled with the unwritten police mandate to police gender itself,
trans and gender-nonconforming homeless youth of color in Boystown are
heavily targeted by police profiling, subject to widespread police violence,
and incarcerated at disproportionate rates. Therefore, when the Center on
Halsted moved into this neighborhood, it entered into contested territory,
finding itself already embroiled in powerful conflicts that highlight profound fissures and dislocations in the idea of LGBT "community."

In analyzing this instance I make three related claims: the first is that
the continued fetishization of "community," which privileges narrow,
(homo)normative formulations of identity, underwrites larger discourses
of neoliberalism, ultimately serving to authorize and participate in the
regulation and policing of those queered by capitalism and other systems of
power: gangbangers, troublemakers, and other Others. The second, related
claim is that this production and policing of queer community increasingly
occurs through the apparatus of the nonprofit. My final claim here is that
the nonprofit production, regulation, and materialization of queer community serves as a hinge between affect, the "promise project" of homonormativity, and the biopolitical management of queer living and dying.

In the above article, the specter of the "gangbanger," mobilized by the
center's ED, is a discursive category through which both aspects of biopolitical power flow—the power to make live *and* let die. The most apparent
biopolitical function of the "gangbanger" is to give pretext to the technologies of surveillance that target, monitor, and give over to state discipline
young queer people of color. Jasbir Puar argues that homonormativity, the

"queer incorporation into the domains of consumer markets and social recognition,"[44] has allowed particular queer bodies to become folded into the biopolitical optimization of life. Puar writes, however, that

> The cultivation of these homosexual subjects folded into life, enabled through "market virility" and "regenerative reproductivity," is racially demarcated and paralleled by the rise in the targeting of queerly raced bodies for dying.[45]

The "gangbanger" is a discursive construction through which normalizing power also flows. The "gangbanger" is related to the "terrorist," the "criminal," and other racialized categories which evoke not just threat, but a particular gendered and sexualized threat. In this context, the gangbanger produces not just those who are outside "the community," troublemakers who must be policed, but also "the community" itself, those who are threatened: in this case a white(ned), (homo)normative subject. This subject has the resources and desire to participate in the center's programs, the menu of state and foundation-funded programs, working to produce and perfect the normalized capitalist subject: self-supporting, employed, having particular kinds of sex in particular kinds of arrangements (meaning "safe," monogamous, unpaid), and on a track toward, if not true social and political empowerment, at least limited and seemingly voluntary mobility within unquestioned constraints of continued racism, classism, and heterosexism.

These young people who are part of the desired and deserving community of the community center must "feel safe there," but also "respect others who are using the building and live in the neighborhood." This seemingly benign entreaty masks a much more complex dynamic of power. Located as it is in a nearly all white neighborhood, in a brand new "green" (read: fancy and expensive) building which rents space to a Whole Foods frequented by the residents of this gentrified neighborhood (increasingly young straight professionals with small children), demanding that the queer youth who access the center feel "safe" is a complex prerequisite for community membership. Clearly, gender-nonconforming homeless youth of color who experience violence and racism on the street and within the social service spaces they must engage with (shelters, public aid, food pantries, drop-in programs such as the Broadway Youth Center, and others), and are heavily profiled and targeted by the police, are unlikely to feel "safe" in such a space. One imagines that they are less likely to "respect" the shoppers at Whole Foods who treat gender non-conforming youth of color like aliens dropped from Mars, or the white gay "community members" who report that the black young people are too "loud" and "intimidating." These subjects—the *actual* young people who occupy Boystown due to the particular political economy of racism, poverty, and queerness in Chicago—are *not* the "queer community" produced through this normalizing discourse. This discourse calls forth a particular "LGBT" community—a phantom—a mechanism for normalization, through which this surplus population is managed.

In an interview with Chicago activist Laila Harim, who is involved in Gender Just, an organization that is critical of the center but also uses the center's space for meetings, I asked about her observations of the effects of these policies. She reflected on her own experiences of simply *being* in the center, sitting in the tables Whole Foods provides for shoppers to eat their hot bar food in the lobby. She reflected:

> The minute youth entered they feel surveilled, so I've seen this a lot. So I sat there in the lobby and it's so overtly racist. So there was this group sitting at a table and sometimes it would get a little louder and immediately they were shushed. It's like they are constantly being trained.[46]

She went on to describe how youth in the public spaces of the center were policed—shushed, asked to leave—by security guards and center staff, in response to feelings of "intimidation" by white adult patrons. She reported hearing that the staff of the youth space were directed to call the local precinct any time a young person on a list of individuals with warrants, provided by the police, accessed the youth space. In addition, following instances of "rowdy" behavior and youth "intimidating" clients on their way to therapy, security guards were hired to police the center. These security guards, in addition to policing what are clearly highly racialized complaints, routinely wake up and exit homeless youth who are sleeping on the very expensive furniture of the center in violation of a "no sleeping" policy. Harim described how the center's gendered bathrooms are patrolled by staff of the center, and that on numerous occasions the staff of the Whole Foods has called the police because of young people stealing food and customer complaints about people in the "wrong" bathroom. Further, she described the various policies used by the center to make homeless youth less welcome to access the space, including "no sleeping" rules. In particular, youth were coming to Gender Just complaining that they were asked to leave the center, or removed from the youth program for some specified period of time, through an opaque decision-making process and with no recourse. She said:

> It has a very top down structure, [with] a ton of different programs with constantly changing people, and it is constantly devising new programs. There is a huge amount of turnover. . . . This is why we [Gender Just] got involved in Restorative Justice stuff, because people can be reported and there is no process and people have no recourse. And there is always a new person they have to deal with, and they don't have up to date resources.[47]

Here the surveillance and policing is coupled with the same institutional instability found in the organization's early history—high turnover, little stability of programs, opaque or absent systems and policies, and lack of transparency or clarity about decision making.

Taking Back Community

In the years following the changes instituted at the center to weed out "troublemakers," and position themselves as weeding out "troublemakers," the furor surrounding supposed youth crime, loitering, and violence only intensified, particularly each summer. The center increasingly became branded as the locus of this intensifying uproar. In the summer of 2011, two separate instances of violence brought these issues to a head. The first, in June, involved a young white gay man mugged at knife-point who suffered minor stab wounds to the chest. The second involved a fight among a group of young queer people of color that resulted in stab wounds to the back and chest of a young African American individual. That incident, which took place outside a gay bar directly across the street from the center, was recorded by a nearby homeowner from his condo balcony.[48] That video went "viral," both on a local and, to some degree, national scale. In the weeks that followed, coverage of these events in the local press, on social media sites like Facebook and YouTube, and at a series of community meetings held by Alderman Tim Tunney and the Twenty-Third Precinct

Chicago Alternative Policing Strategy (CAPS) revealed the degree to which this was really a conflict over the relationship between the neighborhood and the "community," who constituted "the community," who was a threat to it and why, and the role of "community" organizations like the center in causing, facilitating, and managing such issues.

The video of the second incident was posted on YouTube with this description: *"This is exactly the types of violence that we have been bringing to light and complaining about.* The victim received multiple stab wounds to the chest and back, but is currently in stable/good condition. Hopefully this event will bring some increased awareness to the residents and patrons of the neighborhood who are concerned for everyone's safety."[49] This description suggests a vindicated homeowner, someone who had been "complaining" about these "types of violence" fruitlessly, but now hopes to be taken seriously. That individual was also part of a group of Boystown residents and business owners that came together that summer, calling themselves "Take Back Boystown." The breathless urgency with which this incident was described evinces the affective nature of narratives about criminality: fear, indignation, entitlement, a sense that a "way of life" to which one is entitled is being endangered. This feeling moves: it moves money, it moves policy, it moves bodies.

Take Back Boystown was principally a Facebook presence, although it organized events like "positive loitering" and various community meetings. Their presence was primarily felt in terms of how they organized and framed the conversation. For instance, one of their first posts after opening their Facebook account included a blurry photo of a group of young people of color, some apparently gender-nonconforming, with a CPD officer facing away from the camera in the foreground. The caption reads "A mob of Boystown residents?? I don't think so . . . and an injured officer as the result of it?"[50] The first commenter agrees, writing "Definitely not Boystown residents."[51] They framed the "problem" as one of young people from the South and West Side coming up to "their" neighborhood. In Chicago this means African American youth, both in terms of the actual segregation of space and because of discourses about "the South Side" and "West Side."

The site administrators adopted a hands-off approach to the comments they received, which ranged from barely coded racist stereotypes to explicit racial slurs. In the comments following the video of the incident posted on Take Back Boystown's Facebook page, one commenter suggested that "let's focus on the real problem: the violent criminals themselves. . . .

The problem is with the type of people that are coming into the neighborhood!"[52] Fundamentally, according to this logic, the "problem" is that "outsiders" are coming to Boystown. Not just any "outsider," either, but a certain "type of person" who is a violent criminal. Another comment makes the racial coding even clearer:

> Part of the problem is people are so PC. Look its fairly obvious walking down Halsted street at night who belongs and who doesn't. In this case the thugs are black. I would not care if they are black, white, latino or otherwise. If they are trouble they don't belong here. Yes your right I'm hostile and pissed. BTW crime dropped 53 percent in NYC when the Guardian Angels patrolled, so that argument does not work. What do u suggest we do? Stay inside? Build them a rec center? Move away? Pray for them? Fuck that I'm fighting for me for my friends and for my neighborhood.[53]

Posts frequently refer to "ghetto thugs" or "homey g's" and a number refer to such "criminals" as "fucking animals" and "savages." Despite this racial coding and frequent use of racist slurs, the site and frequent posters adopt a certain colorblind victimization when they are called out by other posters for racism. The site administrator writes:

> This page has come under allot of scrutiny lately. A lot of criticism is given because we refuse to accept crime and violence to be an integral part of embracing diversity. To our critics please understand by believing these kids can be in the neighborhood and NOT rob, fight or destroy public property, I think we are showing a less judgmental attitude than those of you who say we are racist because we don't believe they have to live that way. Shame on you. No one is on this page for fun. Trust me, we would all love to be able to NOT have to talk about a war being played out on our streets.[54]

Despite the overt racism of the response, those who named that racism were framed as "judgmental" "PC-ers" who are in denial about the "war being played out on our streets."[55]

In much of the commentary the actual events recede and it is renarrated as an antigay hate crime. One commenter asked, "This man, was attacked because of being gay?" The next commenter replied: "White

COMMUNITY AND ITS OTHERS · 101

stabbed and beaten, by a mob of black racist youths. Police call it a fight and not a hate crime."[56] Perhaps conflating this incident with the previous, in which the victim was white, this commenter fed a narrative framing these young people as not only not *really* of the community, but motivated by homophobia as well. Christina Hanhardt describes the prevalence of this narrative framing in gay responses to violence where "in the activist imagination, homophobia and a (racialized) culture of poverty were understood to share the same origins."[57]

In the comments section on the Take Back Boystown page as well as on coverage of the event in other news sources, the connection being made between this "wave" of "youth crime" and the center is abundantly clear. One commenter writes: "Start complaining to the Center on Halsted about ALL of the ghetto thugs, who are "playing" at being gay, that the Center INVITES to the neighborhood."[58] Notice the similar rhetoric of this commenter to that of the center's very own executive director discussed in the previous section. In both figurations these "thugs" and "gangbangers" could never be a *real* part of the LGBT community, even if they have same-sex sexual practices—they could only ever "play" gay. Another commenter writes simply: "Close the Center on Halsted."[59] The Center on Halsted, more so than the Broadway Youth Center, was blamed throughout social media and press coverage of the event, in part because of the center's physical space and superior branding. In an interview with one center staff member, she described the narrative put forth by Take Back Boystown: "basically any violence that happens within Boystown is blamed on the Center if it happens by young Black people. . . . To the point where people want to close the center."[60]

After the initial framing had been set on social media and in the comments section on gay press coverage, the story began to receive wider attention. The following excerpt from a *Chicago Tribune* article offers a clear picture of the dominant narrative produced about these events:

Jim Ludwig, who owns Roscoe's Tavern, a local gay bar, is the president of Triangle Neighbors and a board member of the Northalsted Business Alliance. Some gay patrons have also complained about the youth. . . . "It's not a race thing, it's a cultural adaption thing," Ludwig told me. "It's a youth rebellion thing. We're at a loss trying to figure out what's a good thing for these kids to be doing other than congregating on the corner. Sometimes there are 50 kids. But it's only a handful that doesn't have the social skills regarding side-walk etiquette, so it intimidates customers and residents."

What complicates this further, he said, is that the neighborhood does have to fend off a criminal element, including sex traffickers and those dealing drugs.

"There's a whole bunch of kids who aren't causing trouble," Ludwig said. "But they are an unknowing shield for others who do come here to commit crimes. Some residents can't or don't distin-guish between the two groups."

For its part, the Center is trying to be a good neighbor. While programming used to end at 9 p.m., it now ends at 7 p.m. Youth are instructed daily not to loiter and to be on their best behavior. The center also has hired additional security guards between the peak loitering hours of 4 and 8 p.m., to protect neighbors from distur-bances, but also to protect the youth.[61]

In this framing, the white bar owner is presented as perfectly reason-able, and the inability of white Boystown residents and "rightful" visitors (who, while they may be from the suburbs, are "really" gay and so there-fore rightfully in Boystown) to distinguish between "criminals" and the culturally maladapted but otherwise noncriminal youth is, apparently, ap-propriate. In this discourse, the responses of the center to crack down on all youth who attend their programs and receive services through limit-ing those services, increasing surveillance, and paternalistic policing, is being "neighborly." These responses on the part of the center, as well as the dominant explanatory narrative for the violence, clearly identified the real "community" and those who pose a threat to it.

In the context of this discursive framing, the Twenty-Third Precinct held a CAPS meeting that upwards of one thousand people attended.[62] By this point young people, especially young queer and trans people of color, were being targeted wholesale by local homeowners and business owners. The Northalsted Business Alliance had even hired private security to patrol the streets. In a video of the July 7 meeting posted on YouTube, one white man stands up and shouts, "We spent 30 million dollars to build the LGBT Community Center. Of. My. Money!!"[63] This man articulates the perspective held by many white Boystown residents and center donors. Their identity and donations *should* rightfully allow them a say in center services, policies, and programs, and their proprietary affect toward the center is and should be reciprocated. In other words, they claim the center as *theirs*, and the center should claim them and only them in return. As we have seen over and over in this book, the affect of donors is nearly always reciprocated. Organizations who rely on community members for donations must always be who those donors imagine them to be since it is that imaginary organization those donors fund.

But young person after young person stood up and named the larger issues at work. One such person, who from the film appears to be a gender-nonconforming African American young person, says: "There's a reason why the youth is lashing out at everybody, there's a reason why the youth is looking down to everybody in here, because y'all look down to us!"[64] At that point her words are obscured by boos and "come on's" and grumbling. When she can be heard again she goes on to say "as somebody who was homeless when I came up here, where was I supposed to go but to Belmont, but to walk the streets on Belmont?"[65] According to this and many other young people and adult allies, the real issues—the issues that preceded, and, in many respects, caused the violence—are the violences of racism, homelessness, poverty, gentrification, homophobia, and segregation. According to this narrative, the very "culture of poverty" discourses that framed the conversation—and the "tough on crime" neoliberal policies that followed—were to blame. The collapse of the social safety net that exacerbated poverty among people of color and the concomitant expansion of police powers, especially the focus on economic and "quality of life" crime, both of which intensified housing instability and homelessness, were named by these young people as root causes.

Despite this analysis by the very young people participating in the center's programs, the response of the center was decidedly in-line with that of their white donors. In an interview with one of the reporters from the local gay press covering the conflict, she characterized the center's response as "walking the line." She went on to say, "They tried to stay out of it, they invited people to tour the center, started a task force on crime, and tried not to engage."[66] Creating a task force on crime certainly sounds like engaging the narrative, however. In fact, the other changes she reports contradict this supposed stance of nonengagement. She described how "the security guards are carrying guns now. They're off-duty police guards. [The Center] switched security firms in April or May of last year, [because] they said they wanted to bring in more LGBT or ally guards, but they have guns now."[67] Furthermore, the center has "really cracked down on the no sleeping rule, [and] they won't let people charge their phones there. If you steal from Whole Foods you are banned from the Center. Also, I've heard that the youth program gets lists of people with warrants from the 23rd precinct and calls them when a youth with a warrant comes in."[68] Despite the analysis advanced by youth members, the response of the Center endorsed, however tacitly, is the racist narrative of Take Back Boystown. Perhaps more importantly, it actively contributed to the policing of youth of color, providing a very clear reminder about the biopolitical scope of community. Those that are figured as other to community, as threats, are directly exposed to violence, to surveillance, and to incarceration.

Of course, given its funding model, the center could hardly do otherwise. To do so would have been to jeopardize the meager program offerings directed at young people, as well as the rest of its programs. Such is the power wielded by donors—donors that the center intentionally cultivated to constitute its community.

Producing the "Sex-Trafficked Victim" and Its Others

The center actually has its own in-house antiviolence organization, which in the context of this outcry about youth violence, could have been expected to get involved. Although a program of the Center on Halsted, the Center's LGBT Anti-Violence Program (AVP) is also affiliated with a larger national coalition of antiviolence programs, some of which are housed in community centers and some of which are independent. I asked the coordinator of that program what its response had been, and she mused, "It's been very reactionary. Let's put out safety tips, blah blah, because most of that violence doesn't fit our [grant] scopes." Instead, the funding of the AVP demanded focus on another project.

At first glance it seems an odd alignment. The center's LGBT Anti-Violence Program accepted an anti-human trafficking grant from the Illinois State's Attorney's office to work alongside the Salvation Army's PROMISE program—the Partnership to Rescue our Minors from Sexual Exploitation. In announcing the new program, the community center reflected that "The Cook County State's Attorney, in offering this partnership, became the first law-enforcement agency in the nation to specifically address sexual trafficking of LGBT minors."[69]

I would like to explore this seemingly odd alignment in a couple of ways. First, I am interested in the frames of knowledge mobilized by this collaboration and the work it does in producing the gay "child victim," as well as Others who cannot be made worthy of life through that figure. Second, I would like to explore the ways that this collaboration is, in fact, not so odd. Instead I will analyze it as an extension of already existing collaborations between gay nonprofits and the state. Throughout, I am interested in the affective and political economies of this discourse—the ways that such alignments are invited by the structure of the nonprofit itself, reworking the charity's historic disciplinary technologies for determining life-worthiness, now deployed through the neoliberal register of community. I contend that through interventions which mobilize such figures as the gay "child victim" and the juvenile prostitute, gay nonprofits serve as key apparatuses for directing some bodies toward life and life-worthiness and other bodies toward policing, incarceration, and shortened life. In the first two sites of conflict, youth of color are clearly cast outside of community; this example shows the complicated routes by which nonprofits are also sites of the mediated and precarious reentry of *some* youth into community, albeit according to racialized scripts of "deservingness." Here, some youth can be redeemed, transformed from criminals into victims, but only at the cost of reinscribing the terms of criminality that render some youth permanently irredeemable.

Through this anti-human trafficking grant, with funds provided by the Department of Justice through the Cook County State's Attorney's office, the center is contracted to "expand services to victims of sexual exploitation," and works with the Salvation Army to expand its PROMISE training to be inclusive of LGBT victims of sex trafficking.[70] This grant is part of the Illinois Safe Children Act, which was spearheaded by the Cook County State's Attorney's office, and is intended to "enhance protections for juveniles caught in the sex trade and provide new legal tools to police and prosecutors to target those who prostitute children."[71] This law is similar to the Safe Harbor Act passed in New York State in 2008—both are envisioned to provide protection to minors by discursively transforming them from criminal "juvenile prostitutes," as the criminal code used to refer to them, into "child victims." A key provision of the law "provides for the transfer of jurisdiction over children who are arrested for prostitution from the criminal system to the child protection system, with special provisions to facilitate their placement in temporary protective custody if necessary."[72] Furthermore, it seeks to provide additional support systems for these newly-created child victims in order to facilitate more successful prosecution of "pimps." The community center's collaboration with the State's Attorney's office and the Salvation Army reflects a new trend in how criminal-legal and social service systems approach juveniles arrested for prostitution. Whereas before, minors involved in the sex trade faced jail time and criminal records, the law now seeks to provide counseling, child welfare, and even protective custody. We would be deceived, however, if we believe that the purpose of the law is to increase the options available to young people and thereby increase their access to safety.

Many activists argue that, like the Safe Harbor Act, both laws actually endanger queer and trans youth involved in the sex trade in a number of ways. First, both laws often mandate that youth be put into the child welfare system, a space of violence for many—and often a system that has already failed them in the past and is frequently a key reason they are trading sex in the first place. Similarly, youth are often court-mandated into homophobic, racist, and transphobic social services. The law relies on social services which often do not exist, and when they do, as a recent study of youth involved in the sex trade points out, such services are often perpetrators of violence against queer youth rather than "saviors" from it.[73]

A Chicago affiliate of Incite! Women of Color Against Violence released a statement critiquing this new wave of sex trafficking legislation and funding, and the overwhelmingly positive narratives that have been produced about it—even, and especially, from within progressive or feminist circles. In response to an article in the magazine *Colorlines* which positioned such laws as much needed "simple solutions" to the issue of sex trafficking, they argue instead that

> The Safe Harbor Act, along with initiatives like it that . . . are [being] promoted across the country, are NOT simple or solutions for most of us. First, they don't stop arrests of young people for prostitution-related offenses, or the police abuses of young people in the sex trades, including police trading sex in exchange for promises of dropping charges. They also don't stop arrests of young people in the sex trades that involve "charging up," i.e. charging young people with weapons or drug-related offenses which may be easier to prove. Second, while they may stop criminal prosecutions of young people for prostitution-related offenses, these laws do not eliminate detention and punishment of young people involved in the sex trades, they just shift young people from the jurisdiction of

the criminal courts to family court systems, where they can remain entangled until the age of 21. And, in the end, only a very narrow group of people can benefit from these laws.[74]

The authors of the piece go on to note the ways that LGBT youth are made invisible under the frames of knowledge produced by this kind of legislation, despite the active participation of programs like the Center on Halsted. They document the disproportionate numbers of LGBT youth experiencing homelessness, and the degree to which supportive services actually exacerbate youth homelessness, leading to a greater number of LGBT youth on the streets rather than in homeless shelters and foster care. Given the intensified policing of economic crimes under neoliberal "tough on crime" policies, LGBT youth of color are overrepresented in the criminal legal system, and therefore very rarely meet the criterion that differentiate the juvenile prostitutes from the child victims—such as no prior criminal or family court cases or no additional charges like weapons or drugs.

Given the critiques leveled against the legislation, even from within other LGBT Anti-Violence Programs, I was interested in why the Chicago AVP would choose to accept such funding. In an interview with the director of the anti-violence program, Michyl Hoffstead, I sought to clarify what the expressed goals of the program are:

> MB: What has the actual process been like? A young person gets connected to you . . . ?
>
> MH: It's been 100% stupidly frustrating. The reality is that most of what the young people need is housing, and, 'oh it's unavailable!' You're a young male or queer person and you're not finding one of the 118 beds available. It's very very long term and that's what's so frustrating. The long term stuff is the task, it's the work. . . . And the law stuff is only for people under 18, so that doesn't mean bupkis for the majority of people . . . who are over 18. So again the people who want to support or say 'you're being exploited,' the systems stuff overlaps with the law until you're 18 and then after you're 18 you should know better.[75]

In a surprisingly candid assessment, Hoffstead acknowledges that the program, which is intended to provide supportive services to those involved in the sex trade, presumably to support their exit from the sex trade, is unable to actually provide any of the services that would offer a young person more or better options. It cannot intervene in a youth shelter system that is severely underfunded to begin with and inaccessible to most trans and gender-nonconforming people. It cannot offer any other viable economic opportunities or solve the crisis of youth unemployment. Hoffstead notes that, because the legislation focuses only on "child" victims, the State's Attorney's office seems to imply that the restricted choices of young people involved in the sex trade are unacceptable until they are eighteen, but after eighteen, as Hoffstead says, "they should know better."

What is interesting here is the seeming knowledge, by the person paid to implement the program, that it doesn't work—either for the legal system or for the nonprofit. In fact, when I asked the director why a young person would engage with this program, Hoffstead replied, "The only upside is for young people who are currently involved in court cases or want traditional counseling, which sucks for most young people."[76] If we are to imagine that the purpose of the law is to make young people involved in the sex trade safer and have more options, it is unsuccessful. From the perspective of the State's Attorney's office, the purpose of supportive services is to enable people to "come forward" without fearing prosecution, and avail themselves of the criminal legal system as victims rather than criminals. However the law neither makes the majority of young people safe from prosecution themselves due to their participation in other criminalized behavior, nor does it actually fund any supportive services. If the purpose for the community center is to offer services to those young people that would enable them to be safer and have more options, it is similarly unsuccessful. But that does not at all mean that the program doesn't "work" in other ways; the remainder of this section explores the ways the program does work—or, rather, the work that the program does.

A primary way this program *does* work is in the production of the child victim as a discursive and material category through the technical apparatus designed to "support" them. A National Institutes for Justice study found that only 8 percent of people trading sex in New York City had been forced into prostitution by a "pimp." Despite this, laws claiming to help youth who trade sex rely on a narrative of a trafficked child victim. They do more than just *rely* on that narrative, however—they produce the subject of the narrative, materializing the "trafficked child victim" through the interventions the laws prescribe. Hoffstead went on to say:

I don't know how many of these folks would want to trade sex if they were housed and had all of the resources they need. I don't know what they would do if they had all their needs met. [But they] want to prosecute johns, or want to prosecute pimps. So there's a big role in saying what people *think* sex trading or trafficking *is*. . . . All these people who think of a little girl being kidnapped and tied to a bed in someone's basement—that's not what it is for queer youth.[77]

Here Hoffstead is acknowledging the ways that this law is producing categories of knowledge—sex trafficking, and the child victim. Although Hoffstead does not say this, I would add that the law also reproduces another trope, that of the "juvenile prostitute" who is excluded from the narratives of childhood innocence and victimization and thus also excluded from any kind of protection the law might claim as its purpose. This public narrative of sex trafficking is fundamentally not describing a young queer or trans person of color who is making choices to survive—no, the little girl is passive, innocent, and acted upon, she is not an actor. It is this passivity that enables her to be brought out of the category of juvenile prostitute and redeemed as a child victim. This discursive—and material—transformation is not available to everyone.

Hoffstead describes one mechanism for the production of this discursive category: the second imperative of the funding, establishing "numbers." She described how "It's not all getting folks in for prosecution. They [the State's Attorney's office] would probably like it, . .but it's not all prosecution based. . . . The other piece is numbers, they want to be able to show that this [problem] exists and people should support [it]."[78] However, Hoffstead expressed frustration at this catch-22: no one accesses the program, because the program can't provide the kinds of services—housing, economic support, employment, systems advocacy—that would make a real impact on the availability of choices for young people. However, since no one accesses these nonexistent services, the program can't gather the numbers to prove that the services are needed. However, the State's Attorney's office and other funders involved in antitrafficking work remain focused on the importance of data and proof.

Despite this, when I asked Hoffstead why the grant was worth taking in the first place, she replied in what felt like a pat way: "The Center recognizes the impact of youth who are trading sex. So establishing the numbers is worth it. Funders always want you to say the numbers, this problem exists."[79] In that moment I experienced her shift from a shared recognition of the failures of the system with which she—and I—are engaged, and into the voice of the program she is paid to represent and must, therefore, to some degree invest in. What is important about this shift in register is that it turns our attention away from the individual complicities, choices, and ambivalences, and toward the broader—and historically established— relationships of power that structure the nonprofit system. The funders will always get their numbers—these narratives will be produced and reproduced—that is the power that funders have over nonprofits. They demand a certain kind of narrative—the sex-trafficked child victim—in order to provide funding. Nonprofits must produce that narrative, whether or not it has any actual referents in their work, if they would like to have their program funded. For the community center, despite the fact that the child victim narrative actively contributes to the criminalization and erasure of queer and trans young people of color trading sex, it is, nonetheless, what George Henderson calls a "socially necessary representation," useful for raising money.[80] He describes these representations as "identities with good cash value, . . . surrogates for the representations of identity they often silence, because they are less 'useful.'"[81] The center can literally capitalize on the gay child victim narrative, selling a narrative to their funders, while simultaneously erasing, and enacting violence upon, queer and trans youth of color trading sex—the real "targets" of the program.

Here I argue that gay nonprofits create, through collaboration with and investment in this discourse, the worthy and deserving—the gay child victim—who is worthy and deserving *because* of the violences inflicted on him or her. In making these kinds of violences visible, reparable, discreet, and isolated from systems like poverty, the homelessness industry, the child welfare and juvenile justice system, they create the Other of the child victim: the juvenile prostitute who is fundamentally criminal, abject, outside the boundaries of community—fundamentally not deserving of life. This is by no means a new phenomenon. In fact, producing racialized and gendered narratives of life-worthiness, and distributing resources accordingly, is a primary historical function of voluntary organizations in the United States. This example demonstrates the ways that existing surveillance and disciplinary technologies are deployed in new and expanded ways under the rubric of "community," through such "positive," life-affirming programming around safer sex, HIV prevention, resume writing, and other so-called "life skills." As Jasbir Puar has pointed out, however, this turn toward life relies on its Other, who must remain cathected to death. It is for this reason that I find it useful to consider these examples alongside of one another; it is not that the previous example of racist profiling is policing, and therefore bad, and this example redemptive, and therefore better. The larger point is that they are both part of the *same* system of management of surplus populations.

Here the bio- and necropolitical valences of this collaboration become clear. The child victim narrative is a discursive and material category through which life-worthiness is allocated. Although the narrative doesn't "fit" for actual queer and trans youth trading sex, it "works" nonetheless by discursively rescuing the white gay child victim from criminality. Through this redemption, the gay "community" of the community center is recoded. "We are not pedophiles, we are the victims of them, and the police will protect us." And importantly, to be worthy of life, you have to want to be rescued, to "desire the state's desire" as Judith Butler has so aptly said. *But of course if you've actually done anything to ensure your own survival—to rescue yourself—you are no longer worthy of survival.* The state produces subjects who are victims of something that—if they were to choose it— would make them criminals. And in doing so it casts those who choose to trade sex as irreparably criminal, and importantly, outside constructions of queer community.

In analyzing the work this narrative is doing, for whom it is working, and on whom it is working, I would like to turn briefly to the work of Sara Ahmed and Jin Haritaworn. The process of creating a child victim can be usefully thought of according to Ahmed's description of "sticking" signs to bodies. In particular, Ahmed looks at how "different 'figures' get stuck together, and how sticking is dependent on past histories of association that often 'work' through concealment."[82] The child victim narrative, despite the fact that it doesn't quite "fit," can be stuck to some queer bodies through existing frameworks and narratives. The framework that is most clearly at work here is the existing hate crimes narrative that has a long history within gay antiviolence work. As I have argued, this seemingly odd collaboration between the state and a gay antiviolence project is, upon closer inspection, not odd at all; it is simply the most recent in a long series of seemingly strange alliances.

There is already a victim narrative—the gay victim of hate violence— that can be grafted on the child victim narrative. And in addition to a ready-made narrative there is an already existing infrastructure, expertise, interventions—regimes of knowledge. And in both narratives the police become the savior, a liberal force for inclusion, protecting the emergent gay citizen and ushering him into the care and community of the nation.

In their work on the emergence of hate crimes discourse in Berlin and the way that it is used to produce and criminalize the "homophobic migrant Muslim," Jin Haritaworn describes the gay turn toward the criminal legal system. Haritaworn is worth quoting at some length here, as the parallels are quite informative:

> The move of LGBT activism into the penal state enables the police to reinvent themselves as protector, patron, and sponsor of minorities, at the very moment that their targeting of racialized populations and areas is reaching new levels. The criminal/sexual justice discourse thus diversifies a process that is really about homogenization: the policing of inner cities, the displacement of poor and nonwhite people from neighborhoods targeted for "revitalization" and the abandonment, forced assimilation, incarceration, and expulsion of those who no longer symbolize diversity, but rather a threat to a society that is colorful and diverse enough without people of color.[83]

The white gay child can be rescued from criminality, but the Other, the juvenile prostitute, is a danger, and must be policed. We see this in the policing of the neighborhood at large, the targeting of queer and trans youth of color as "pimps" and "gangbangers"—those who could never be understood as child victims. In the previous section, that Other was explicitly identified in the *Chicago Tribune* coverage of the Boystown stabbing as a "criminal element" coming to Boystown to traffic sex. And the center, figured as the locus of this supposed youth violence, explicitly turns to the police and prison system in response. Recall the press release with which I began the section and the way that the community center praised the State's Attorney's office for being the first in the nation to "address the sex trafficking of LGBT minors." The criminal legal system is figured as a progressive response that can enable safety and usher these nascent citizens into full belonging.

Christina Hanhardt describes this as the outcome of decades of queer antiviolence organizing in collaboration with the state, in which organizers discursively separate the "gay victim" from the "other" urban deviants and criminals through a strategy of space claiming and community policing. These two strategies dovetail perfectly with neoliberal strategies of law and order policing and gentrification. As white gay people create "gay space" and come to identify with property, they embrace the racialized targeting of "quality of life crimes" under a framework of "antiviolence." Economic crimes become an assault on gay neighborhoods and the more diffuse gay "community," thus ushering in more policing and more "community solutions."

This particular intervention is but one in a long process through which the police and criminal legal system increase their reach into black and brown spaces under the framework of increasing safety for gay people. In addition to intensifying and consolidating the technologies through which the state can access queer and trans people of color, it further solidifies the role of the community center in gathering up those bodies through the affective project and technical apparatus of "community."

My interview with Michyl Hoffstead ended on a somewhat resigned note; she lamented that although the program doesn't allow them to do anything that "would change anything for people, we have to have these numbers to show that something needs to be different in order to fund [projects that could get at the root causes]. But you can't show the numbers because it's framed for only under 18." And, Hoffstead finished, "the reality is it's a two year grant. It's hard to dream big if it's only ever a two-year thing that supports half a person." Despite all the apparent reasons to the contrary, however, the center believes that this funding was worth accepting—funding is almost always worth accepting for a nonprofit. Invisible in these calculations, however, is the cost borne by LGBT youth of color who are further imperiled when the regimes of knowledge surrounding the "child victim" go uncontested by an important institution that claims to work on their behalf. The collaboration with the state, while it may be understood as inconvenient or burdensome, is figured as ultimately redemptive, or at least a necessary step on the road to safety, inclusion, and community. Meanwhile the gay nonprofit provides the technical apparatus through which the Other of the child victim, the juvenile prostitute, as well as the pimp, thug, and gangbanger, are subjected to the necropolitical power of the prison.

Conclusion

In her book *Terrorist Assemblages: Homonationalism in Queer Times,* Jasbir Puar notes that for all of queer studies' engagement with Foucault, prior to the publication of her book few queer studies scholars had taken up that part of *The History of Sexuality* that addresses biopower, the regulatory power addressed to populations which buttresses disciplinary power over the body. Though this has shifted since that time, it is interesting to note that Foucault theorizes that it is with the emergence of biopower, which he describes as the power "to *foster* life or *disallow* it to the point of death,"[84] that racism becomes inscribed in the mechanisms of the state. Puar comments that while queer theorists were largely concerned with the repressive hypothesis, postcolonial and critical race theorists have taken up biopolitics: the racialized management of life and death—the "distribution of risk, possibility, mortality, life chances, health, environment, quality of living—the differential investment of and in the imperative to live."[85] As Puar invites, "by centering race and sexuality simultaneously in the [analysis of the] reproduction of living and dying," the biopolitical function of gay nonprofit articulations of community comes into focus.

Using a biopolitical lens, we can see something else at work. Despite the supposed retraction of the state as prophesied by many neoliberalism scholars, what we see here is, instead, an *expansion* of state power, albeit organized in new ways. Craig Willse, in his work on the homeless sheltering industry, contends that the decentralized, nodal, dispersed, and often contradictory nonprofit/state/corporate apparatus is actually much more powerful than a centralized state, allowing for adaptive surveillance technologies, disciplinary mechanisms that expand and contract, and the multiplication of subjects and subjects of knowledge. He writes, "Surveillance technologies in this context do not 'clamp down,' but rather let loose. They let loose a biopolitical register toward the proliferation of governance and its populations, which is to say, they free new objects of intervention that may not look like one individual, but of which the individual, in order to survive, must become a part."[86]

Based on these moments of conflict, and according to these theoretical frames, I draw a series of conclusions. First and most simply, community is biopolitical. Community is an expansive discursive technology that crafts and enfolds an imagined "real" gay person/LGBT people while simultaneously constructing threatening Others, exposing those threats to early death, and rationalizing that exposure in terms of the safety and freedom of the "community." That enunciation of community relies on and facilitates neoliberalism in a number of interrelated ways. The services provided by the center to its rightful constituents are understood as appropriately dispersed through a private nonprofit rather than through the state, in part because of the race and class conceptions of who constitutes "the community" and who relies on the state. These culture of poverty and tough on crime notions—narratives that don't always fully accord with one another, but, nonetheless, live alongside each other—contribute to a sense of racialized threat. Further, the organization, in responding to the threat posed to "the community" by these threatening Others endorses and demands increased policing and expanded police powers, while the limited social services offered by the center, services which in many ways replaced a centralized social welfare system, are blamed for the presence of threatening others.

Further, the structure of the nonprofit itself invites and enables this way of knowing community and constructs the technical apparatus that requires, facilitates, and manages it. The funding structure of nonprofits invites a logic of community that is white and propertied, since its community is traditionally comprised of those who can fund it. In this articulation of community, as in that of the organization I analyze in the next chapter, *space* is a particularly important analytic. Ultimately we see that claiming space through the white(ned), homonormative, corporatized, nonprofit apparatus using rhetorics of safety and threat is always both a productive as well as policing gesture, a bio-necro collaboration.

Finally, this biopolitical enunciation of community fortifies state power, in particular through its policing apparatus, which is refigured as a progressive force protecting "the community" from threatening others. And in turn, the state can enter into that reciprocal affective relationship with the community (center), where the center and the city become, for each other, funders, endorsers, allies, mascots. Despite this, however, young people continue to *choose* the center, to claim it, despite being only vaguely and marginally claimed in return. Further, in interrupting the narrative produced about them in this enunciation of community, those young people achieved a solidarity and politics about racism and gentrification that will arm and equip them for their own survival. And, somehow, despite their seeming accordance with the racist narrative of threat, the center does continue to provide the services and spaces that were so attacked. Did they "walk the line" between maintaining donor investment and their own ideas of service, as one interviewee suggested? Or is the faith and commitment of youth and staff another instance of the kind of cruel optimism that Lauren Berlant describes, in which their very belief contributes to the fist of the neoliberal state expanded through this biopolitical conception of community?

4
_____

Capital and Nonprofitization

At the Limits of "By and For"

In the fall of 2010, I received an email solicitation from a Minneapolis LGBT youth nonprofit, District 202, which began: "It's been said that the act of coming out is a political act. I disagree. Hardly a week goes by when a sports figure, actor, musician or another celebrity comes out with little fanfare. The political act has become a more personal act. What was once 'I am gay—deal with it' in 1988, has now become '*I am gay, and I am no different than you.*'"[1] The shift in queer politics so enthusiastically charted in this email, from oppositional—"I'm gay, get used to it"—to assimilationist—"I am no different from you"—marks a sea change, not just within this particular organization but as a broader change in queer social movement politics. This statement certainly illustrates the shift toward homonormativity, the neoliberal politics of domesticity and recognition that now dominates contemporary LGBT politics.[2] For District 202, that shift took the form of a two-decade-long organizational makeover—from a grassroots upstart with dreams of queer youth liberation to a corporate-funded "social entrepreneurship" organization working toward "mainstreaming." The shift undertaken at this organization was by no means unique, and in what follows I use transformation of this organization as a case study to explore how pressures of the nonprofit structure itself drive the shift toward homonormative politics.

Founded in 1990, District 202 provided a drop-in space, as well as various kinds of youth leadership development programming, street outreach to homeless youth, HIV prevention programming, and extremely popular drag shows and other social events organized by youth. The organization was envisioned as a "nonprofit youth community center committed to providing social, cultural, and educational opportunities *by and for* lesbian, gay, bisexual, transgender youth and their friends."[3] Early organization materials always led with the Audre Lorde quote, "Without community there is no liberation." By the mid-1990s, District 202 was an incredibly vibrant organization, making "in excess of 10,000 contacts [with youth] a year"[4] and regarded as a national model among what was then a relatively small number of organizations specifically working with LGBT youth. Taking a stand that would prove difficult to maintain and always somewhat contentious, District 202 was unique in that it did not provide social services, instead focusing on youth leadership development through their mission to be driven "by and for youth."

Despite its incredible popularity among queer youth in the mid-1990s and early 2000s, District 202 was also plagued by financial instability and protracted struggles over the political mission of the organization. In 2009, the board of directors fired the youth staff, followed by the executive director, closed its physical space, shut down for six months, and re-emerged as a "social entrepreneurship" organization for LGBT youth with a marketing professional as the new executive director. Two years later, facing a storm of community critique, and without the skills to manage a struggling nonprofit, the board of directors of District 202 officially closed the organization, giving up its nonprofit status entirely. Interestingly, an echo of District 202 remains, as a support group hosted by a large social service organization that continues to use the name and logo of the former organization, evoking a nostalgic affection through a kind of brand memory and political cachet.

This chapter charts District's rise and fall, and explores a central animating tension that enabled it to be a much-beloved youth center but also led to its ultimate closure: the tension between the empowerment of the young people who were participants of the center and the powerful and conservatizing demands of the business of running a nonprofit. When District 202 opened the doors, it did so with a mission to be "by and for" LGBT youth. The organization's founders were clearly invested in resisting the charity approach, in seeing queer youth as leaders and thinkers, as valuable, instead of "victims" to be "saved." They resisted the savior model— but, as this chapter demonstrates, they underestimated the power held by the very structure of the nonprofit form. In particular, it is the necessary allegiance of the nonprofit structure to neoliberal circuits of power and capital that simultaneously enabled its survival and also facilitated its shift toward a politics of homonormativity, respectability, and assimilation.

In what follows, I begin by contextualizing the two opposing forces this organization reckoned with for twenty years: first, the demands of capital faced by nonprofits, and second, the political stakes of their "by and for youth" mission. I then trace key snapshots—flashpoints—from District 202's twenty-year history that illuminate the structural forces at work in the nonprofit form that facilitated these shifts in the organization's form and politics. How did an organization that once called forth a vision of liberation articulated by Audre Lorde become a "social entrepreneurship organization" that seeks "mainstreaming" through "corporate partnerships?"[5] In the following snapshots we see over and over a conflict between the political mission of the organization and the exigencies of its operation, illuminating ways nonprofit structure within queer organizations, and specifically the allegiance to capital, drives organizations toward homonormative politics. We can also trace the way that this conflict played out affectively, through the feelings it elicited, and the various ways those feeling are valued within the nonprofit structure. Some feelings—excitement, community, connection—can be translated into cash through the stories the organization tells to donors. Others—frustration, betrayal, anger— these feelings not only don't fit the prescribed funding narrative, but actively work against it, and therefore must be explained away, squashed, hidden. This chapter traces these excess feelings as well as the feelings the nonprofit structure welcomes, produces, amplifies, and exchanges for cash.

Ultimately, at District 202, this conflict was irreconcilable; neither the structure of the nonprofit, nor the political mission won, in the end, and the organization was forced to close its doors. Despite the best intentions, creativity, commitment, massive effort, and even actual protest, the political mission of "by and for" was fully eroded over the twenty years of its operation. My intent here is not to show that such a political mission is impossible, but instead that it cannot be reconciled with nonprofit "business as usual." The orientation toward neoliberal capital that inheres in the nonprofit form exerts its own power, yes, but my intent here is also to demonstrate that its transformation was contingent, that it was never inevitable, and in doing so, locate queer nonprofits as a site of ongoing struggle.

The Business of Youth Empowerment

Key to understanding the dramatic organizational and political shifts at District 202 is an analysis of the conflict between its mission—in particular the role that youth would play in the leadership of the organization— and the pressures of capital: to conform and "succeed" according to the nonprofit model, to be "fundable," deserving, to tell the right stories to the right people. For nonprofits, the pressures of capital and the need to be "successful" and "fundable" are existential and nonnegotiable realities—without funding, without convincing some funders somewhere that this organization and these youth are deserving, there would be no organization at all.

In an interview with Paul, District 202's founder and first executive director, he described what the "by and for" was intended to mean when the organization was created. He said: "It meant that youth are gonna name the agency, youth are gonna help define what it looks like, so they were on hiring committees, so youth are gonna define hours of operations and programs." But, he noted, "What became difficult is that as you become bigger, there is the business end and defining the culture, and they aren't the same body."[6] Paul imagined that the "business end"—by which he presumably meant budgeting and fundraising, primarily—could operate independently from the "culture," from the life of the space, from the programs in which youth participated. From his descriptions of that early process at District 202, the power dynamics *embedded* in the nonprofit form were either underestimated or ignored. Paul's recollections about these early days reveal core assumptions about nonprofits themselves: that they are essentially "good" and of "the community." That they are the kind of places where power falls away and shared identity is paramount.

But it is worth dwelling on this "business end" that Paul mentions. He is referring to more than payroll and insurance; included in the "business" of nonprofits is the entire development and fundraising apparatus. The nonprofit sector is funded by charitable contributions, from individuals, from private foundations, from corporations, and directly from the state. Of those sources, individual contributions are by far the most significant. For instance, in 2013, the largest source of charitable giving in the United States came from individuals at $241.32 billion, or 72 percent of total giving.[7] This is followed by foundations, at $50.28 billion, bequests at $26.81 billion, and corporations at $16.76 billion. And, in fact, individual giving has increased every year since 1973, with the exception of 2008–2009, due to the impact of the financial collapse. This increase in private giving is due in part to the focus on narratives of charity and volunteerism popularized by the Reagan, Bush, and Clinton administrations as alternatives to the welfare state.

It is over this period that the "business end" of the nonprofit also developed and professionalized significantly into the highly complex technical apparatus that it is now. For instance, the Association of Fundraising Professionals, which began in 1960 with only 197 members, cites the 1980s as a period of "impressive growth and an increasing sense of professionalism" in the sector.[8] Further, in the 1990s, they write, "fundraising and the nonprofit profession became a critical part of the economy."[9] During this period, fundraising became a professional and decidedly technical endeavor. Gone are the days of passing the hat: fundraising professionals now utilize complex donor management databases to track a donor's history of giving as well as personal anecdotes about donors, enabling them to produce the effect of personal connection. Fundraising professionals can check the database to remind themselves of donor's hobbies, children, and interests, and can target their "ask" directly to a particular donor's motivation for giving, whether a specific issue, a general sense of community involvement, a desire for personal connection, or status. Development now entails "prospecting" for major donors, utilizing "high touch" donor cultivation, even buying lists of donors from other similar organizations in order to widen the net. There are multitudes of trainings available to teach one how to "target" an appeal letter, even how many bullet points or bolded phrases are necessary to keep a prospective donor's attention! Nonprofits create a development plan with a yearlong calendar of activities intended to raise money: events, strategic communication, and individual donor cultivation, as well as grant writing to foundations.

An organization like District 202 may have had only some of these capabilities, especially during its early years, but nevertheless the group existed within a discursive and material landscape that was oriented toward capital: "success" looked like more donors, more *major* donors, and a more robust system for cultivating and managing them. And this definition of success is not just rhetorical and can't simply be refused: the majority of nonprofits are engaged in an ongoing and increasingly precarious struggle for their very survival, a struggle that directly translates into paychecks and needed services. This is also due in part to the fact that donors increasingly expect this kind of system, to be "cultivated" in a certain way, as a mark of professionalism and respect. Donors also expect a particular narrative from an organization like District 202, an appeal that produces in them a particular affective response that cues them to give. Overwhelmingly that narrative is about compassion or community, often both. Donors either want to "help" the children, or experience themselves as part of a gay community by supporting a resource they wish they had when they were young. Teresa, a former grant writer for District, described how one of their main funding constituencies was "gay men, sometimes lesbians, who became donors, who definitely had a sense of identification with District around healing their own experiences of being young and gay."[10] District 202 thus learned to speak to and craft the particular narrative of identity, community, and compassion that would appeal to donors, a narrative that was often at odds with the "by and for" mission of youth political power.

As we will see below, one of the ways District 202 learned to navigate this funding atmosphere was by staffing its board of directors with members who possessed these skills, relationships, and affects. The composition of most nonprofit boards—including that of District 202—is perhaps the clearest indication of the primary orientation toward capital: in staffing its board of directors with individuals who possess specialized skills in financial oversight (preparing and reading profit and loss statements, for instance), or who have relationships among wealthy individuals or particular corporations who might give financially to the organization, or who are simply themselves wealthy, the nonprofit can increase its access to capital. This comes at a cost, of course, because these individuals also wield enormous power over the strategic direction and functional interpretation of the organization's mission. And individuals who possess these specialized skills and advantageous relationships—people who have succeeded financially in the context of neoliberal capitalism—often have done so on the basis of various kinds of privilege as well as ideas about their own merit, skill, and capacity. They often believe at some level the incredibly pervasive and foundational myth of American capitalism: that those with wealth have it because they are more capable and skilled than those who do not.

This paternalistic relationship is invited not just by the demands of capital accumulation, but in the framing of the legal responsibilities of boards. Nonprofits are legally owned by their boards of directors, a relationship that is governed in the tax code as well as state law. Board duties are governed by three primary responsibilities: first, "duty of care," which involves the active participation and sound judgment of each member in caring for the fiscal well-being of the organization; second, "duty of loyalty," which is intended to prevent conflicts of interest by mandating that a board member's first loyalty should be in the best interest of the organization; and third, the "duty of obedience" refers to the board's responsibility to ensure legal compliance and that acts in accordance with its mission.[11] It is interesting to note that these duties are conveyed through the *feelings* they evoke: care, obedience, and loyalty. These feelings are interesting to reflect on: they harken back to the kind of explicit benevolent paternalism of yesteryear but are now wedded to a fluency with neoliberal capitalism.

And of course the logical conclusion reached by many nonprofits with board members drawn from the corporate sector, looking to appear deserving to increasingly corporate funders, is to become ever more businesslike. This is the route taken by District 202, despite the radical imaginary of their mission.

The Limits of "By and For"

The heart of this story is the incompatibility of what Paul called "the business end" with their "by and for" mission, and the power of that structure to move the mission. By and for youth was—and still is—quite a radical vision in the context of youth-serving nonprofits that retain the "save the children" approach of charity in the United States. It is an explicit challenge to the compassion narrative on which so many social service organizations rely. Instead, District 202 was asserting that youth could be more than victims, more than objects in need of discipline, that they could identify their own needs and advocate for their own vision. At its founding, however, District 202 did not recognize the degree to which "by and for" would necessitate any fundamental transformation of the nonprofit structure itself.

In an interview with Yana, a former youth who became a board member, I asked, "What were the limits of 'by and for youth' in those early days?" She replied that "basically there were none." Or perhaps more accurately, no one knew what they were. As she commented: "It was an experiment."[12] Many interviewees pointed to one incident in particular as the first challenge to the "by and for" commitment. Interviewees described "the poem," with an assumption that I knew the events to which they were referring—indicating that this incident had become core to the unofficial memory of District 202, a memory much more fraught and contested than the sanitized history found in holiday appeal letters. This excerpt from my field notes details an interview with Jax Alder, District 202's program director from 2001–2004, in which we discussed how the story is circulated:

We spoke for a moment about "the poem:" Jax described how a young person, Joan, witnessing the turn toward corporate money and adult power, wrote a poem calling out adultism and the hypocrisy of the "by and for youth" mission. After the poem was put on the wall, the Executive Director at the time took some major donors through the space who "freaked out." The ED removed the poem in response, and there was a great deal of outcry among the "youth community." Jax added that the youth made a proposal at their community meeting to put the poem back up. The staff agreed, apparently—but instead of being put back up where it was, it was painted on the wall *outside* the space, in the stairwell on the way up. Jax described how the ED could usher major donors right past it on the way up to the space. So it sounds like a bit of a draw—youth made a proposal and got to put the poem back up, but adult staff limited their power and limited the impact of their intervention by pushing the poem outside the space.[13]

There are numerous aspects to this story that reveal both the contingency of the "by and for" youth model. At first glance it seems like a fairly straightforward incident in which a young person named and critiqued the dynamics of power at work in the space, hitting a little too close to home for adults in power to handle, and her intervention was, in turn, censored. The sensibilities of major donors, and their expectation that youth be grateful and appropriately "empowered" but not politicized, *did* prevail.

Yet this moment also reveals a great deal about how "by and for" youth was imagined to begin with, for whom, and its limits. Not only did a young person feel enough ownership over the space and investment in its purported mission to protest what she experienced as hypocrisy, but the adult staff acknowledged the legitimacy of the critique in their willingness to compromise—they too believed in some version of youth power. What this reveals is not that "by and for" youth was a lie—or a marketing ploy, as it later became—but instead the underlying and often faulty frameworks about youth at work at District 202: their expected gratefulness, what their empowerment would mean and look like, and the idea that their power and leadership would never interfere with the unspoken and largely invisible structure of the nonprofit itself—the board and their power, its fiscal management, fundraising, budgeting priorities, and, perhaps most importantly, its understanding of itself in relation to its object, youth.

In another interview, Yana offered important context about District 202's early years and the assumptions on which the organization's "by and for youth" mission were based. Describing the poem's author, she said:

> I think Joan would say this about herself, she was a kind of embittered youth, who came up in youth services, who used services provided to young people. She had been a part of Safe Harbors' empowerment program. She wrote a poem that critiqued youth workers who think they are saving youth. So youth were painting walls and she decided to paint the poem on one wall. Paul [the Executive Director] felt personally attacked, like it was an assault on . . . staff. So he ordered it covered up. . . . He was dismayed that a young person would jeopardize our standing with funders. That's where the first challenge of what "by and for" meant came up.[14]

Yana makes clear that for the staff there was an underlying assumption that the role of the funders and their sensibilities were not discordant with a "by and for youth" mission. Paul's "dismay" suggests that at least for him, part of "appropriate" youth empowerment meant developing allegiance to existing structures of capital and funding. Yana was also very clear in laying out what she felt were the underlying political questions at stake in debates over how the "by and for youth" mission should be implemented. "Those four words were debated again and again. Whole board meetings were devoted to it!" I asked what the terms of the conflict were. She explained:

> [It was the] classic savior, or I would say custodial, model. Like, "while youth were here doing their fun youth things at least there were still adults here who understood how the world really works." And "we like youth, but there need to be adults who understand what the world is like." So the crux of the conflict was around savior/custodial versus a radical vision of youth liberation.[15]

Fundamentally, the concept of "by and for" is a profound challenge in this context because the nonprofit structure is designed to *manage* particular populations, based on the assumption that poverty is an individual moral failing rather than a systemic one, and, therefore, that wealthy benefactors are the moral and intellectual betters of those living in poverty. This means that the target population of a nonprofit—in this case youth, but this would also apply to homeless people, to immigrants, to incarcerated people, whomever—aren't expected to know how to help themselves, let alone to shape the organization intended to "serve" them. They are supposed to be instructed, to be lifted up, to be acted upon—and to be grateful for it.

At its founding, District 202 might have thought of itself as a new and unique kind of nonprofit building on the energy of an emergent social movement with a liberatory mission—but in its "not-profitness" it was always already tied to the uplift narrative of "proper" citizenship that is sutured into the nonprofit. Thus for social movement actors, activists who invest an enormous amount of emotional and political belief and energy in these organizations, this dynamic ensures that nonprofits create what Lauren Berlant calls "cruel optimism": that which you desire is actually an obstacle to your flourishing.[16] This cruel orientation is a function of the circuits of capital on which nonprofits rely, and the power of the moral economies of that relationship of dependence. The historical function of nongovernmental organizations in the United States—managing the "deviance" of poor people and immigrants, and "educating" them as to the ways of middle-class citizenship, while serving as a more punitive and less redistributive alternative to a welfare state—this does not disappear simply because nonprofits have been discursively recoded under neoliberal antiwelfare-state narratives as spaces of community.

The primary reason this orientation has not, and cannot, simply disappear is that it was always more than simply a set of feelings about poverty; it was, and is, a structural relationship between those with wealth and those without it—a relationship built on policing, surveillance, and control, a relationship facilitated by nonprofits through their use of, and reliance on, private funding. That reliance demands that organizations appeal to major donors, private foundations, and corporations, all of which have a vested interest in maintaining the present system to which they owe their wealth. Foundations are fundamentally tax shelters for families and corporations—they are required to give much less money in the form of grants than they would otherwise pay in taxes. These foundations can choose to support whichever cause is most "deserving," maintaining a centuries old relationship of dependence in which those with wealth determine how best to use their money to remake society in a way that benefits them and reflects back to them their merit and power, positioning poverty as a personal failing rather than a byproduct of the same system of capitalism that made them rich. Despite this cruel relation, actors on all sides of the nonprofit nexus remain attached to the nonprofit form as part of what Berlant calls "the good life"—that moral/intimate/economic fantasy that keeps people invested in institutions, political systems, and markets even when evidence of their fragility, ineffectiveness, or outright failure is apparent.

To be clear, I am not arguing that this structure of power within nonprofits is inescapable. On the contrary, District 202 is a clear example of the ways that the power of the wealthy board members, foundations, and corporate donors is *not* absolute, and the power can be mediated and interrupted by the very people they see as their objects of intervention. Instead, what District 202 reveals is that the problem lies in letting this relationship of power go unmarked, understanding it as ordinary, which is very different than *necessary.*

"Corporate Networks of Gays and Money": The Capital Campaign

In 1997, after six years of operation, District 202 moved from a small storefront space into a new home, renting a renovated loft space in a trendy neighborhood on the edge of downtown Minneapolis. Despite the hype evident in the District 202 archives, and the important attachment that many people—youth and staff—have for that space, this move emerged in interviews as a critical period of organizational transformation, a major driver of the political shift that later ensued. Yana described the buildup to the move:

> [District 202] was growing, had hired more adult staff. . . . Then
> the idea of expansion was raised, because of the numbers coming
> through the door and that three to four adult staff sharing one of-
> fice was untenable. With growth came more nonprofit structure. To
> me this is one of those turning points. When we moved to the new
> space there was a huge capital campaign, a lot of money invested,
> and the Board had been changing—less youth workers, more
> corporate—people who had ties to corporate networks of gays and
> money. Paul [the first ED] worked that really well as a cute gay
> white man can do. He was able to elevate and get District 202 to a
> place financially of stability and . . . desirability. People *wanted* to
> fund District 202! There was a volunteer backlog! When they did
> their first mailing—you always lose money on those things, but

they made money, which is practically unheard of when you're buying a list. What I really loved about District 202 at that point, it must have been . . . what was it '98? '97? Everybody loved District 202, [saying] "I want to put my money, I support this vision."[17]

What Yana captures here is the *excitement*, the feeling of community and possibility that District 202 offered and on which it was literally able to capitalize, a set of feelings that they could translate into cash value. Given this general environment, the capital campaign happened, by all accounts, fairly swiftly for a nonprofit, and District 202 moved into its newly renovated seven thousand square foot space in 1997. In interviews, the capital campaign and move to the new space emerged again and again as a pivotal moment of change. I want to highlight just a few aspects of this important transformation: the changing relationship to space itself and the ways that District 202's discursive representations of itself altered as it shifted its orientation toward capital.

Yana shared that in the new space the power dynamics that had been less visible in the original space emerged in stark relief. She remembered:

So with the move to the new space there was a desire for respectability, a desire for structure. It wasn't the rundown storefront so people had to take care of the space differently. There was a new conference space, new ED office, a new Development Director office. Space became an issue for the first time. . . . You had a doorway to offices [for the first time], and you heard the first grumblings about feeling like there were spaces where youth couldn't go.[18]

Implicit in Yana's description are the ways that unspoken, and presumably even unconscious, ideas about the way respectable nonprofits are "supposed" to look were incorporated into the new space. Importantly, the poem was written on the walls of the *new* space, which is critical to understanding how it emerged as such a flashpoint. It made explicit the ways that the "by and for youth" mission stood in marked contrast to the slick, sanitized world of "corporate networks of gays and money" that had been called upon to fund the new space. In counterpoint to the removal of the poem, Teresa, who later became a grant writer but at that time volunteered at District 202 leading a writing group, recalled that in the new space, painted over the doorway between the youth space and the staff offices, were the names of the major donors who had given money to the capital campaign. When donors would be given tours of the new space, she recalled, they would look for their names on that doorway. Moreover, when she began working in development, she remembers that the painted names over that doorway were "part of how she learned about who the 'gay elite' major donors were in town."[19] The space was literally remade in order to appeal to major donors, while the possibilities of youth power were diminished.

I want to briefly highlight one additional aspect of this moment of change: the ways that District 202's infrastructure—particularly its board of directors—shifted as the organization shifted its orientation toward capital, and the impact those changes had on the possibility of youth power. Yana characterized the early board as fairly naïve to the power traditionally held by boards of directors of nonprofits. Comprised largely of youth workers with political investments in youth liberation, "the Board was practically irrelevant. The Board had no idea. I don't think the youth really even knew they were there."[20] At this early stage, Yana emphasized, when the board was made up primarily of people who had *worked* in nonprofits, rather than gay and lesbian individuals with wealth, the board did not occupy the role of limiting youth power to nearly the same degree as they later would.

The board underwent a profound transformation during the capital campaign to move to the new space, however. To meet the increased fundraising demands, individuals with deeper pockets and wealthier friends replaced the youth workers on the board. Additionally, Yana said, the board, in the wake of the "the poem" incident, became more resistant to youth representation on the board. Though Yana and other advocates for increased youth leadership prevailed, and two youth members were eventually allowed to sit on the board, these youth members were not accorded voting rights, as the board didn't feel youth could take fiscal responsibility for the organization and were worried about unspecified "liability issues."

Yana characterized this change: "At some point their concern with the bottom line became more important than the young people and their day-to-day lives. That's what's shameful—you can see the connections. How do we explain that to the youth?"[21] Paul had a somewhat less damning characterization. "I think as you grow, and as you get formal structures of funding, your funders ask for more credentials and you look for experience and skill sets that aren't common among youth." Furthermore, as the board became ultimately responsible for raising more and more money, they also became more attuned to the needs and desires of donors. This is at the core of the relationship of dependence: District was reliant on its donors and had to please them to retain them, and youth were reliant on District 202 and felt pressure, therefore, to be pleasing.

Despite this seemingly successful capital campaign, the organization's financial stress only increased. In fact, underlying all of the structural transformations—and youth resistance to those changes—was a fundamentally unsustainable relationship to funds and fundraising. Jaime, who became the program director following Jax's departure in 2004, felt that after the move to the new space, District 202 never again regained its financial footing. In fact, ten years later, this fiscal instability was cited as the primary impetus for the organization to give up its nonprofit status and merge with a large social service. The fiscal unsustainability experienced by District 202 ever since the capital campaign and move highlights the difficulty of reliance on the kind of affect-based "good feelings" funding that Yana described. Such capital campaigns rely on the excitement of people to support new and innovative programs; individuals are invited to live out their feeling of community, feel a part of something that matters. However, this is understood and experienced as a one-time gift—anything more than that begins to feel uncomfortably like dependence, which of course it is, given that the entire nonprofit sector relies on the largesse of those with wealth.

Such one-time gifts that are the hallmark of capital campaigns cover the initial cost of a building or move, but once the organization is housed in this larger, more expensive space, the financial needs intensify even though the grant-based income and annual individual donor gifts often do not. This invites a widely observed cycle in which organizations chase grant funding to make up this budget gap, whether or not the program it would fund directly relates to the core mission of the organization. Nonprofit professionals call this phenomenon "mission drift." Although consultants make a living touting various solutions, its underlying cause is the untenable funding structure on which the nonprofit sector at large relies. This sector-wide precarity tends to produce a crisis-like atmosphere that in some ways mirrors and intensifies the crisis experienced by the organization's participants.

The Implications of "By and For"

Ten years after the founding of District 202, this new and more corporate board of directors undertook a strategic planning process that illustrates the degree to which, even after a full decade of operation, "by and for youth" remained an ambiguous and elusive idea, and one fraught with tension and uneven power dynamics. Further, the continuing conflict over this idea demonstrates the degree to which it challenged fundamental structural constraints imposed by the nonprofit form: the pressures of budgeting, funding, and fundraising, the types of narratives that are fundable, board ownership and the pressure to staff the board with adults with access to resources or particular financial skills.

In 2000, a consultant from the community was hired to run the strategic planning process, in the course of which she interviewed seventy stakeholders, including youth participants, every staff member, board members, local funders, and other, primarily youth-serving, community organizations. In interviews and focus groups the consultant asked: "District 202 was created to be a center 'by and for GLBT youth.' What does the phrase 'by and for GLBT youth' mean to you?"[22] In a report presented to the board in August of 2001 that compiles the responses to these interviews, the wildly inconsistent—even diametrically opposed—answers to this question are starkly revealing. Many respondents seem to imagine a significant role for adults, especially in offering mentorship, guidance, and skills: "There has to be a balanced input from youth, but run by adults. Need to show good adult leadership, role models, mentoring. 'Not youth empowerment run amok'"[23] The direct quote is informative: youth empowerment, this respondent believes, has the potential for danger, disorder, perhaps even leading to the collapse of the organization. Another respondent goes even further: "In this day and age, you have a real problem raising money if you use this approach. Not due to anything inherent in the 'by and for' mission, but organizations that adopt this approach typically lack formality."[24] The "lack of formality" that this respondent warns of *is*, actually, inherent in the "by and for" mission, if by "formality" the respondent involves the complex financial systems of most traditional nonprofits. These skills sets are not often possessed by young people, an issue that does indeed make youth-led organizations more difficult to fund, since these are systems expected, even demanded, by funders.

Another respondent addresses this issue head on, suggesting that "youth

lead where they have the skills and tools and adults provide the infrastructure and the tools where youth lack them."[25] It is not entirely clear if
this respondent imagines a vision of "by and for" in which adults intentionally share the skills that are necessary to run a nonprofit with young
people, or a vision more closely aligned with the first executive director,
Paul's: youth direct the programming and adults run "the business side."

However for one respondent, who, one can assume based on the comments, is a youth participant, "by and for" means just that:

> GLBT youth and their friends are the ones who run the center. I
> feel that they should be able to make decisions to run the center
> and I think that whatever direction the youth feel that District
> should go it should go and its not really up to anyone else besides
> us. I don't think adults have a huge place in the center. I under-
> stand there is a need for them to be here, but not to sound bel-
> ligerent or rude, but they should know their place, whether it's the
> ED, adult volunteers, adult staff, board members, etc. They should
> know their place as supporter and nothing else.[26]

It is an interesting turn of phrase for a young person to suggest that adult
participants should "know their place," an idea often implied in the reverse
by the various constraints placed by adult staff and board members on
youth leadership. But this young person's response, while articulating a
very logical definition of the phrase "by and for," also suggests that youth
participants at District 202 have a fairly hazy idea about how nonprofits
actually operate, where the money comes from, what is necessary to get
it, and what skills would be necessary to manage it. This hazy-ness is instructive: it reveals the degree to which the "nonprofitness" of District,
meaning the systems and structures through which it reproduces itself,
are imagined to be neutral, outside the purview of youth leadership. This
is the split between programming and "the business side" that Paul, the
founding director, described. District 202 imagined that there was a way to
offer young people the opportunity to direct programming while leaving
budgeting, fundraising, and financial management in the hands of adults.

This fundamental conflict plays out again in response to the subsequent question, "What advice do you have for District 202 as it embarks
on strategic planning?" One respondent replies, "Don't get too bureaucratic. Don't get too mainstream."[27] This respondent seems to recognize

the degree to which the bureaucracy of nonprofitization would weaken the organization's commitment to true youth leadership. Another respondent, however, suggests the opposite: "Start thinking like a business. Many nonprofits don't know how to manage themselves. 202 needs a solid management structure. Have a plan for growth. Be able to explain financial statements. The Executive Director and Board must stay involved."[28] While young people certainly can explain financial statements when offered the same opportunities for skill development as do adults in order to do such tasks, this response demonstrates the external pressures faced by District 202, pressures that would have almost certainly been internalized by those in leadership positions: success looks corporate, glossy, top-down, and neat, the kind of success easily recognized as such by nonprofit professionals and funders alike.

This corporate vision of success was not universally held, however. One stakeholder group comprised of former board members was asked what the phrase "by and for" meant to them. One response in particular stuck out: "The heart of it was to push ourselves to be uncomfortable."[29] This former board member recognized that "by and for" would indeed be difficult, since the structures of the nonprofit are designed otherwise, and that it would make many adults uncomfortable, since its measures of success would differ drastically from that of traditional nonprofits, let alone businesses. Further, it would require nontraditional systems, and implementation would be necessarily messy and uneven. Unfortunately we never get to see what "by and for" would have "successfully" looked like at District 202, since, instead of exploring new and alternative means of funding and management consistent with their mission, District eventually shifted its mission away from "by and for."

This strategic plan reveals an additional nuance in the debates over the mission, one echoed by many interviewees: conflict over *which* youth would be included in the youth community. For instance, in response to a question about areas upon which District 202 could improve, one respondent replied: "racial segregation within the center—it's a very good resource for queer youth, and better for queer youth who are non-minority."[30] And alongside the dynamic of racism and segregation is class; in a question about the effectiveness of District 202 in meeting its mission, there were a significant number of responses dealing with the increasing number of homeless youth accessing the space. One respondent felt that "the place is really clicky [sic]. I talked to a lot of suburban kids who used to come here and don't anymore because of the homeless kids."[31] And another articulating the same sentiment: "Rank it as one because at one point in time it was a cultural and educational experience; now it feels like I'm in a drop in for homeless youth that is decorated with LGBT things."[32] Another response, presumably from an adult staff member frames it in this way: "I think we need to address the fact that we have a lot of homeless youth and the problem isn't dying down."[33] The increasing number of homeless young people accessing the space and the racial segregation within the space, and the degree to which those issues overlap, is an important dynamic in the conflict over "by and for." Many interviewees suggested that as the community of youth became less white and less suburban, adults—both staff and Board—became less able to imagine them as agents and leaders. Instead those youth were thought of as the targets of "life skills" and "empowerment" programs that focused on their economic self-sufficiency.

"Moments of Insurrection"

In the years following this strategic plan, District 202 increasingly adopted the language of "empowerment," a framework that seems to have been employed to manage the conflict between the youth power suggested by the phrase "by and for" and the traditional nonprofit hierarchies that it nonetheless maintained. Empowerment programs had the potential to *feel* like "by and for" to youth, as if their leadership, opinions, and insights were solicited, cultivated, and valued. Empowerment is also *fundable.* Empowerment is legible, even desirable, for philanthropies and corporate foundations, whereas "by and for" seems risky and informal. For adults invested in traditional nonprofit hierarchies, empowerment programs could give the impression of being reassuringly corporate, controlled, and neat. This was an unwieldy compromise, however, as the malleability and opacity that allowed empowerment to flourish as a compromise framework invited inevitable conflict over its meaning and practice. The following example highlights the possibilities created within nonprofit spaces for those "objects" of empowerment to exceed the discourses about them, to turn their "empowerment" back on the organization itself.

In an interview, Jax described how only a couple of years after this strategic plan was completed, in 2004, the ongoing conflict between the real transformative possibilities of "by and for youth" came into direct and explosive conflict with the limited vision of "empowerment" solidified by the capital campaign and subsequent move. Once again, structure won out over mission.

Jax Alder was hired to develop and implement the empowerment-based "Youth Leadership Development Program" in 2001. Jax, a black genderqueer person who used gender neutral pronouns, had previously been working at an HIV/AIDS organization for men of color. When Jax was hired at District 202, they described putting together youth leadership programming that dealt directly with issues of difference and oppression, and that encouraged youth participants to assert their power in impacting the space itself. Jax expanded the existing youth employment program into a comprehensive, "empowerment-based leadership development program that coupled job skills training with political awareness."[34] It was a multitiered program that allowed young people facing various kinds of barriers—housing instability, heavy policing, poverty, for example—to engage as workers in the space in whatever way was accessible to them. So some youth could develop their job skills working as baristas at the coffee bar in the youth space while others, who had been there longer and begun to develop more leadership skills, could organize events, emcee, work security, or staff the drop-in space. Jax described how a core group of youth, many of whom had been youth staff for more than two years, became increasingly aware of the pay discrepancy between youth and adult staff. Possibly more important was their growing recognition that, as youth staff, they were understood to be targets of empowerment, not "real" staff who had the actual power to influence the organization itself. In response, youth began to openly discuss and strategize about the issue of pay discrepancy. Jax supported their work, bringing in a financial expert to help them learn to read budgets, and as they learned they became more and more frustrated that youth who had worked there "from the beginning," who worked all day to staff the center, were paid on a completely different pay scale than the "professional staff."

After some months of conversation, the youth staff brought the issue to the youth community meeting, the official "voice" of youth in the center in which the "by and for youth" mission was most closely approximated. The actual power of the community meeting was always fairly vague. For instance, the community meeting made a proposal that the poem be replaced on the wall and it was, but not in a prominent location. On another occasion the community meeting voted to ban smoking in the center and it was henceforth banned.[35] Youth were under the impression that what the youth decide at the community meeting, goes. But paradoxically, their "demands" were put forth in the form of "proposals," although to whom the proposals were directed was, again, vague. Adult staff were the most likely target of such proposals from the perspective of youth participants, although in the overall structure of nonprofit organizations the power of the staff is limited by the board, in this case wealthy gay and lesbian individuals who wanted to "help" the youth. Once again, the invisibility of the underlying structures of power within nonprofits limits the kinds of politics that can be enacted from within them.

In the instance that Jax described, the outcome of the proposal offered by the youth made clear the limits of their power, and in so doing, the limits of the "by and for youth" mission itself. After the youth staff described their concerns at the community meeting and shared the research that they had compiled on the budget of District 202, the youth voted to make a proposal to equalize pay throughout the entire organization. Jax recounted that when the proposal was presented to the board they, unsurprisingly, "said no way in hell."[36] In many ways, it is remarkable that there was enough buy-in from staff that the proposal even went to the board. The vagueness around the extent of the power of the youth council is fascinating in this way. It offers clear evidence of the paternalistic understanding of what "youth leadership" would mean—that it would be directed outward, at becoming "successful" citizens, not at transforming the hierarchies of power within District 202. On the other hand, the language around "by and for" invited youth and staff alike to believe its promises. This again reveals the messiness of nonprofits, especially as stand-ins for social movements: spaces of policing, yes, but also the production of intense aspiration and resistance.

Interestingly, the board did not quash the proposal outright, but asked the youth representatives to rework the proposal numerous times, while Jax, who was the staff person held responsible for letting the youth get so "empowered," was increasingly shut out of meetings and cut out of key communications, until, after a few months, Jax's position was terminated as a cost-cutting measure. Subsequent to my interviews with Jax, I found that the archival record left by board members from that time shows that the financial distress offered as rationale for Jax's termination was indeed real. Board meeting minutes from September 2004 show that in response to an anticipated budget shortfall, the executive director would take a

$5,232 pay cut, the formerly full-time development director's position was cut to thirty-five hours, two staff members had their medical and dental coverage eliminated, and the webmaster's contract was eliminated entirely, for a total savings of $77,564. Though the financial distress was real, for youth members who were not involved in the ongoing conversations about the financial situation of the organization, this must have felt like a convenient excuse. Ultimately the position of program director was not permanently cut, and soon after Jax was terminated, the position was filled by Jaime, a white former youth participant who had gone on to get a degree in social work.

The ultimate denial of the youth council's proposal and Jax's subsequent termination caused a firestorm among youth. Their first action was to create a very detailed list of grievances, and they presented it to the board in a format that clearly appeals to the aesthetics and style of the nonprofit: a spreadsheet with three columns, one listing their "concerns," the second organizing those concerns by "theme," and the third offering "possible solutions."[37] The amount of work and preparation that went into this document is clear. The first of seventeen concerns listed is the termination of Jax's position. Subsequent concerns include: "[Jax] was the person who provided youth with the opportunity to empower themselves."[38] It went on: "Youth were not involved in the decision making and when youth were included in parts of the process it was too late."[39] The young people who prepared this document offer a thorough indictment of District 202's failure to implement its "by and for mission." They identify instances in which young people's ideas are simply disregarded, when they are told not to worry about fundraising when they want to get involved in "the business side" but are then expected to show up and participate in the fundraising ideas of adults, the lack of youth involvement in hiring practices, and the absence of formal youth involvement in leadership, which results in young people being told "this isn't the place/time" when they share their ideas for the center.[40] Another concern sums this up: "The decision making power of the Board versus the decision making power of the youth community is not well articulated in policy. This has resulted in the Board making decisions that the youth community has been outspokenly against and the youth community having no recourse after the decision has been made."[41]

The solutions to these issues proposed in the document are ingenious and impressively practical: make sure the composition of the board is half youth; involve youth in all stages of programming, including budgeting, rather than just implementation; include youth in hiring committees and on the board nominating committee; and finally, "decision making power regarding changes in center operations and the termination of positions should be *equally* shared between youth and adults."[42] Though there is no available record of the board discussion of these concerns and proposed solutions, the rapidly escalating youth response suggests that their response did *not* involve the immediate implementation of these solutions.

In a marked change in tone from the very formal and professional spreadsheet of concerns, the next step taken by young people involved direct action. The youth staged a "lock-in" in which only Jax and another former youth staff were allowed into the center. Youth clearly recognized the denial of their proposal as an insult and offense to the organization's purported belief in "by and for youth"—a belief that had been shared by Jax, who, when I asked whether they really thought that such a change in the hierarchy was possible, replied that they truly did. Jax believed that "by and for youth" meant just that. Among the material saved from this time by a former board member was a document that listed a series of consequences that would be imposed if the concerns identified by the young people were not remedied. "The following," they wrote, "WILL happen with or without your consent": "1) The center will be closed to all adult staff and Board members until concerns are addressed and remedied. 2) ALL adult staff with keys will turn their keys in immediately (upon completion keys will be returned to their perspective [*sic*] parties)."[43] The document ended with a note: "If by any chance the above stipulations are broken in any way shape or form the person will be required to have a mediation with the YLDP [Youth Leadership Development Program] and upon completion the youth in YLDP will determine whether the infraction was warranted, if it fact was not [*sic*], that staff will be terminated effective on date of incident."[44] This is a remarkable document. The sense of anger and betrayal held by young people is palpable, though I also imagine that this action was felt as a betrayal by staff and the all-volunteer board of directors. The means by which young people would take staff member's keys, for instance, or terminate employment, isn't clear. And one wonders if that was beside the point; perhaps more important was simply controlling, physically and discursively, the space in which young people were otherwise objects of control, for however short a period.

The feelings here—betrayal, anger, frustration, disloyalty—are instructive. How could an organization end up in this situation despite the shared belief by people at all levels in the value and importance of queer youth to a vision of social change? The youth certainly forced clarity about what District would not do, which was to change governance structure. Even after the youth tried using direct action, turning social movement tactics back on the organization itself, the power structure of the nonprofit remained entrenched.

Meanwhile, the board simply waited for the firestorm to quiet and for youth to get back to the business of becoming *appropriately* empowered. The realities of young people's lives, and their profound need for and investment in a space like District 202 almost guaranteed that young people would return and, although angry, would continue to invest in a vision of "by and for youth" that was discursively encouraged but structurally prohibited. Ultimately, there was no infrastructure in place at District 202 that would have enabled true youth decision-making and power over the space. Youth were never more than tokens in fundraising, in strategic planning, in hiring and firing, or in board recruitment. They were the *objects* of such work, the targets of empowerment.

In her book *Logics of Empowerment,* Aradhana Sharma writes "these questions get to the heart of the 'dangers' and murkiness that empowerment presents."[45] Building on the work of Barbara Cruikshank, she goes on to describe the "messy interplay between depoliticization and repoliticization, surveillance and subversion, and regulation and unruliness" inherent in empowerment programs.[46] As Sharma and Cruikshank contend, there are reasons that corporate funders like Target and General Mills supported District 202's capital campaign and responded to "empowerment" and "leadership" programs targeting "at risk" youth—such models function under neoliberalism as tools of governance. Empowerment dovetails nicely with the "personal responsibility" logic of neoliberalism, producing self-governing subjects, oriented toward the market, who understand "freedom" to be connected to certain kinds of self-management. However, as Sharma and Cruikshank also show, empowerment and leadership-based programs are also inherently political and unwieldy, in which subjects can and do exceed the governance tools—they actually become *empowered.* And, as such, they speak back to and challenge the organizations that seek to manage and direct that power.

On Community in Late Capitalism, or Off the Streets and onto the Web

In 2007, District 202 was at a crossroads. After years of inaction, the fiscal situation had become dire, and the numbers of youth participants had begun to wane. In response, the interim executive director championed another strategic planning process, packaged in language appealing to the largely corporate board. In an interview with one of the consultants hired to conduct the assessment, she described the way they intentionally proposed this assessment to the board "from a 'change management' perspective" that they felt would appeal to the business sensibilities of most and the progressive politics of a few.[47] Among the staff and consultants this was a strategic review intended to address the failure of the organization to live up to its social justice "by youth for youth" mission, for board members it was intended to figure out how to reduce costs and address the fiscal crisis. The consultants hired to facilitate this process, both of whom are local progressive queer activists, engaged a wide array of key stakeholders, especially youth, and produced a report that described the current conflicts and recommendations for moving toward a truly "by and for" model.[48] These recommendations included moving to a smaller space, developing key relationships with other grassroots organizations to ensure that the homeless queer youth continued to have their basic needs met, and working to move away from a services framework and toward the leadership of young people at every level, including management and fundraising. It is worth noting that many of these suggestions were not new; some had previously been put forward by youth participants during the 2004 lockout, and even prior to that, many had been made during the 2001 round of strategic planning.

Nonetheless, following this review and the development of these recommendations based on community feedback, the board instead hired, and then fired due to mismanagement, a new executive director whose approach to these recommendations, according to interviewees, varied between hostile and indifferent. The organization then fired all of its youth staff, ended programs targeting trans and homeless youth, and ultimately closed its physical site and went into a "cocooning phase" of reevaluation.

After being closed for six months, District 202 reemerged as a web-only presence—a "mobile delivery system"[49]—with a new narrative and marketing strategy. They announced that *another* executive director had been hired, this time a marketing professional with no experience working in nonprofits. This new executive director, Carl Dunn, author of the email in the chapter's opening suggesting that coming out is no longer political, had formerly been chair of the board of directors at District. In an interview with an online LGBT news blog, Dunn detailed major changes to the structure, mission, and programs of District 202 and proclaimed, "We're shifting the organization from being a social justice organization to being a social entrepreneurship organization."[50] Although this rhetoric of "social entrepreneurship" quickly became the defining language on District 202's website, Facebook page, and newsletters, there was little explanation for this transition. Perhaps the new leadership of District 202 believed such a change would be self-explanatory, as this seemingly abrupt departure, in fact, reflects an increasingly powerful set of symbolic and material shifts that are central to the changing imagination of contemporary queer social movements in the United States.

The language and framework of "social entrepreneurship," which seems to be antithetical to the history and mission of District 202, or at the very least, to queer social movements, mirrors a much broader shift in the nonprofit sector. Particularly in the past ten years, there has been a notable and explicit turn toward neoliberal corporate "business" models of efficiency, flexibility, and value within the nonprofit sector at large.[51] So when District 202 describes turning toward "social entrepreneurship" and "building better relationships with the corporate community in Minnesota," they are echoing a larger neoliberal transformation, a marketization of the nonprofit sector. Social entrepreneurship relies on discourses of individual ingenuity, "entrepreneurs" who recognize a social "problem" and utilize business models in order to make social change. A well-known example of this strategy—micro loans—seeks to "develop cultural capital" in individuals in order to ameliorate persistent poverty, rather than movements of people that act together to contest capitalism. Under this logic, the non-profit/state/foundation nexus becomes transformed into a wholly corporate remaking of the social according to market logics of "value," including what kinds of bodies are "valuable" and which are expendable. This then begs a troubling question, and one that is especially significant in analyzing the shifts that took place at District 202: how can market logics solve the problems they have created? At least in the case of District 202, they couldn't. Of course to facilitate homonormative politics that centralize identity rather that inequality, and seek access to wealth and corporate power rather than critique it, social entrepreneurship makes perfect sense for a queer youth organization.

In *Social Entrepreneurship: New Models of Sustainable Social Change*, which editor Alex Nicholls intends to be a "research primer" for the field, Nicholls describes a sea change in approaches to social change. Driven by what Nicholls characterizes as the "failure of the social market" to alleviate "problems" like persistent poverty, the lack of affordable housing, climate change, and a host of other social issues, this response is informed by the "outstanding success" of the multinational corporate framework of Walmart and other corporations. These corporations offer examples of "how to scale operations internationally and to maximize value creation through innovation and technology."[52] Relying on the logic of financial markets, as well as its rhetoric—flexibility, deliverables, metrics—this model also imagines that social "problems" exist simply because no one with enough ingenuity and creativity has come along to solve them. These kinds of "problems" can be solved through the actions of a business hero, the "entrepreneur" who is variously characterized throughout the text as an "innovator," and an "unrelenting, disruptive change-agent," who can "move easily across sectors, often diversifying from their core mission to expand overall social impact and increase resource flows."[53]

This logic has been widely adopted by nonprofits, individualizing systemic inequality and transforming justice as the goal of social movements into "social value" as the goal of the "social economy." This illustrates one key mechanism in which the existing disciplinary technologies and logics of the welfare state, already at work in nonprofits, are wedded to neoliberal biopolitics in which the social is remade through the production of "valuable" bodies, subjects, and subjects of knowledge. The transition to a fully corporate rationale of "value" production—even within organizations that are funded in part by the state—fundamentally transforms the kind of social world and political imaginary enabled and produced through nonprofits. Despite the rhetoric of innovation, creativity and social change, such logics are fundamentally not intended to reduce the inequities caused by capitalism or significantly redistribute wealth and resources. Instead such logics represent a tool of management, a technology for the discursive and material supervision, policing, and control of populations made surplus by capitalism.

"I Am Gay and I Am No Different Than You"

The shift toward social entrepreneurship further required a restructuring of District 202's approach to queer politics. In the narrative District 202 has produced detailing its shift toward social entrepreneurship, it repeatedly called on a narrative of progress, of acceptance, of "mainstreaming."[54] And they pursued this homonormative turn with a vengeance. In its new life without a physical space, District 202 existed primarily on the web, as a "lean, tech savvy" social media tool. But it also "partnered" with other organizations to create "mobile safe space"—basically subcontracting actual programming to other organizations that wanted to be "queer friendly" and using the District 202 brand as a substitute for safe space— anything with their logo became, apparently, "safe space." Now, instead of a safe space where they could express political realities of their lives through drag shows or attempt to exercise youth power through community meetings, youth could attend yoga classes and resume writing workshops, provided, of course, that they could access the various suburban locations in which these programs were held. As an example, consider this email sent to members of the District 202 donor database in 2010. Notice the tone; no longer is District 202 raising awareness about an issue or a program intended to address an issue—nor are they even soliciting contributions to address an issue facing queer young people. Instead they are advertising the services of one of their "collaborative partners." The text of the email read: "District 202 Makes January Hot! Yoga Begins January 23. The yoga kickoff workshop starts this weekend! It's a great time to meet new people and get started on your yoga classes. By attending the workshop you will receive 10 free coupons for yoga . . . . Normally these classes cost $150!"[55] The targeted audience for such a program is primarily interested in networking and getting a good deal on a luxury product—a fair distance from the kinds of emails donors would have received just a few years before.

In transforming its mission and closing the physical space, District 202 dramatically shifted away from serving youth who were homeless, involved in street economies, or just plain poor—youth for whom a physical place to go was paramount. This also meant that the organization dramatically shifted away from serving trans/genderqueer youth and youth of color. In Minneapolis, and nationally, the majority of homeless queer youth are people of color. Instead, District 202 reoriented their programming toward suburban youth, youth with access to computers, youth who had their basic needs met. Again, this meant a whiter, wealthier group of young people. In this context, District's appeal to "mainstreaming" *produced* "the community" of LGBT youth itself, in this case a white(ned), (homo)normative subject. This subject has the resources and desire to participate in District 202's online and outsourced programs, working to produce and perfect the normalized capitalist subject: self-supporting, employed, having particular kinds of sex in particular kinds of arrangements, and on track for some level of mobility within the unquestioned constraints of neoliberal capitalism. This is, of course, a central aspect of the homonormative shift of District 202 as well because, as Kwame Holmes has reminded us, "homonormativity is a racial formation."

In analyzing the shifts undertaken by District 202, as well as the stories told about those shifts, this racializing project of homormativity becomes clear. "Mainstreaming," as Carl Dunn terms it, is clearly only accessible for those queer young people with a certain amount of privilege—often white, gender-normative, and experiencing some level of class privilege. It is these young people who can disaggregate LGBT identity from queerness, from marginality, policing and discipline.[56] Those young people who can "mainstream" according to a homonormative project of inclusion, "equality," and privatization, are folded into and oriented toward life. For those who are not invited into the "mainstream," but continue to be policed as a threat to it, District 202 is part of an apparatus of regulation and discipline that orients those bodies toward incarceration, poverty, and shortened life.

It is not surprising, then, that the narrative District 202 produced about itself in this new incarnation—its official history—had telling absences. Gone was any mention of race, of course, but also homelessness, poverty, or even homophobia—except in the past tense. For District 202 in this new homonormative age, queerness was no longer cathected to oppression—it had become a vehicle through which certain subjects, conversely, become folded into life. It was only within this context that Dunn, as the ED of District 202, could claim that coming out is no longer political—as he did in the email with which this chapter opened. District 202 now saw itself as a social media marketing tool for those youth and corporate donors for whom LGBT identity is no longer political, instead of working to change the systems that make coming out for *some* youth always political, because they are policed due to their sexual identification, kicked out for it, or broke because they can't "hide" it. This progress narrative—which District 202 was certainly not alone in embracing—is a ghost story, haunted by those who are fundamentally outside such a "mainstream," threatening Others who cannot be folded into life. For District, it was also haunted by the specter of the space itself and the struggles over youth power and social justice undertaken within it.

Conclusion

After its "cocooning" and reemergence, District 202 existed for two years in this "mainstreaming through social entrepreneurship" format. In this incarnation, the organization was barely more than a web-only trace, although it invoked the *idea* of youth power and physical space—almost as if the space had become its brand. All of the gimmicks they employed online to produce the effect of "youth voice" and to mobilize the affective project of "youth empowerment" had no referents in real life—they were phantoms intended to be bought and sold. For instance, on the District 202 website, there was a tab entitled "youth voice" that led to a blog that adult staff updated. The website flipped through photos that intermix old quotes about "youth empowerment" and "safe space" with new narratives about "marketable skills to actualize their potential in the world."[57]

Importantly, District 202 used the *idea* of youth voice and youth power—which did at one time exist at District 202, however partially, and which was intentionally and forcefully silenced—in order to raise money. Their website prominently displayed a slideshow of black and white photos of former youth and youth staff with quotes superimposed over the images that said things like: "District 202 is an organization that works hard to understand youth empowerment.—Supporter," and "It's a safe space where many young people can relax and be themselves.—Amy, donor." These voices were youth staff members who were fired, young people who lost access to a space and community, being used as props to raise money. Of course, right next to these photos was the icon "Click here to support District 202."

Although this shift felt like the final word on the question of the limits of "by and for youth"—and, perhaps, on the larger question of the relationship between nonprofits and social movements—this story has an interesting coda. In 2011, following a truly offensive fundraising appeal in which

District 202 exploited the recent suicides of gay teens in order to raise money, an anonymous group of individuals circulated a letter and online petition calling for Dunn's resignation.[58] People found a way to speak back through Facebook, blogs, and email, forcing District 202 to confront the conflict between the narrative it was selling and the work the organization was actually doing. In a searing indictment, this letter exposed the way that the new organizational structure, what the authors termed a "hollow marketing scheme," disproportionately impacted poor queer and trans youth of color. They wrote: "The new structure of District 202 is inherently classist: by forcing queer youth to access District 202 via internet only, you have made the organization's limited services utterly inaccessible to poor queer youth."[59] And Dunn did indeed step down, and following a yearlong process of evaluation, District 202 gave up its 501(c)(3) status and became a program of a large social service organization, The Family Partnership.

Now housed within an organization founded more than one hundred years ago as a social service charity, District 202 has made quite the circuit: from youth liberation to social entrepreneurship to charity. That "by and for" mission, a direct critique of the savior model of charity, now subsumed within a charity, co-opted and used as a way to refresh the disciplinary function of charity in the new neoliberal age of empowerment and community.

Despite the best intentions of many liberation-oriented activists, including those at District 202, the nonprofit structure wields its own power, and it tends toward maintaining existing systems of inequality. While this is certainly not inevitable, this power must not, nonetheless, be ignored. For queer organizations, the convergence of the power structure built into nonprofits with the neoliberal equality politics of homonormativity is acutely debilitating. In particular, maintaining a critique of capitalism—a critique that is necessary in order to combat the structural causes of racialized poverty—is very difficult when your continued existence is dependent on those who benefit from the system, whether individual donors, corporations, or private foundations.

In particular, the transformation of District 202 is particularly illustrative of the power of *capital*, and the orientation toward capital, that inheres in the nonprofit structure. This organization further demonstrates that this orientation toward capital is both normalized and obscured by affect. In particular, this is a story about the transformation of feelings into value. The nonprofit structure takes, harnesses, amplifies, and capitalizes on some affective orientations and renders others unvaluable—without cash value. In this case, the feelings that are more valuable for the nonprofit are those that can be exchanged for cash, feelings that tug on the heart strings of donors, or inspire the confidence of foundation funders—those feelings are amplified. Other, less valuable feelings—frustration, anger, even the joy and solidarity found in resistance, are less translatable into cash. Nonprofits are saturated with affect: feeling motivates staff, it keeps board members working even when there are no monetary rewards, and it is directly transformed into cash through the mobilization of a good affective narrative that inspires donors. Importantly, however, not only are our good feelings not enough to resist the power that is wielded by the nonprofit structure's inherent orientation toward capital, those good feelings often obscure or even normalize that power.

5

Navigating the Crisis of Neoliberalism

A Stance of Undefeated Despair

The stance of undefeated despair is "that familiarity . . . with every sort of rubble, including the rubble of words," that grief over cruelty and injustice, which is "without fear, without resignation, without a sense of defeat," and that "stance towards the world," which is the basis for the carrying-on-regardless that the struggle for emancipation and happiness requires. The stance of undefeated despair is a position from which to carve out a livable life when everything is organized to prevent you from doing so.

Avery Gordon, "The Prisoner's Curse," Towards a Sociology of the Trace

Trauma is a frozen state—a hold—[and] non-profits are post-traumatic stress institutions, which is why we hold on to them so hard. Most non-profits are visionary responses that intend to right a wrong, but they come out of trauma, and play out the shit that happened the first time.

Nora, Interview with the Author

Actress Laverne Cox, famous for her role in *Orange is the New Black,* gave the 2014 keynote address at the annual National Gay and Lesbian Task Force (NGLTF) Creating Change conference. In that speech, she described meeting and working with CeCe McDonald, who had, just weeks before, been released from prison after serving nineteen months of a forty-one-month sentence. In June of 2011 CeCe, an African American trans woman, and a group of her friends, also African American, were accosted outside a bar in South Minneapolis by a group spouting racist and transphobic slurs. In the fight that ensued, one of the assailants, Dean Schmitz, was killed. Despite having been slashed across the face with a broken beer bottle, CeCe was the only one of the group to be arrested that night, and following a court battle in which it became clear that CeCe would never be seen by a jury as someone who had the right to defend her life, who had the right to live, CeCe accepted a guilty plea. As Laverne Cox said in her speech, "trans women of color are not supposed to survive. So often, so often, people seem to prefer us to be dead."[1]

Cox went on to describe meeting not only CeCe, but also a group of activists in Minneapolis who supported CeCe throughout her trial and incarceration. She named some of the leaders of that group by name and also called out TYSN, the Trans Youth Support Network.

She said:

> And CeCe survived. And there are so many survivors out there, but CeCe's survival and her resilience was made possible because— because she was brilliant and she was amazing and she led her support team in an amazing way. But it was also possible because of the work of grassroots activists in Minneapolis, Minnesota. If it were not for those activists, we would—the story of CeCe McDonald would be what mainstream media wanted to tell us about her. They made sure we knew the real story. They made sure that we knew that CeCe was attacked because she was Black, because she was trans, because she was a woman. And that she was railroaded by the criminal justice system because of all those things. They're doing amazing work in Minneapolis, but it's with very few resources. They can use some resources in Minneapolis, Minnesota.[2]

I was not present at the conference, but I listened to her speech the following day with the other members of the TYSN board. TYSN's staff member, Vienna Stanton, had just come from a television studio downtown where she and CeCe McDonald had filmed a segment for the Melissa Harris Perry show on MSNBC. We were listening to Cox's speech in the context of a weekend-long strategic planning session, the second of three long weekends in which we discussed the future of TYSN. Our facilitator for that session asked us to listen to Cox's speech and reminded us that we were on a national stage now, that people would want to support our work, that the work TYSN was doing was important, necessary work. When Laverne Cox said, "They could use some resources in Minneapolis!" we listened as the audience of thousands cheered. It was an essential reminder, and a timely one, because we were, as a group, very tired.

Over the previous six months, we had thought it might be necessary to close the doors. Perhaps the cost was simply too high. We had attempted a new leadership development program that left youth feeling patronized and frustrated, and then welcomed the youth who stuck it out onto a board where they felt dismissed and tokenized. We were trying to transform an organization created by mostly white adults into an organization led by trans youth of color. Everyone in the room shared a similar vision for what they would like to see in TYSN: a youth-led space where trans youth, especially trans youth of color, could share resources and knowledge, come into their power, and work together toward a more just world. Despite that shared vision, though, the path to achieving it remained murky and fraught with frustration and unintended betrayal.

My involvement with TYSN began in 2008 when I moved to Minneapolis to begin graduate school. When I entered the Minneapolis scene of queer youth workers, nonprofiteers, genderqueer folks, and trans activists, District 202 had begun its slow death and people were frustrated and sad and lonely for each other and missed the promise that had been made to them through and in the idea of queer youth power at District 202. In that same year, TYSN, an organization created by youth workers at District and a couple of other youth organizations in the Twin Cities over the period of 2005–2007, began to announce itself, in part through hiring a new director who had been a fierce youth advocate at District 202 and who believed in the vision of youth power once dangled there and jerked away. Having the good fortune of being close friends with that person, and at that time only months removed from my life as a youth worker, I began organizing with TYSN, on the edges, with hope that all of my work on the nonprofit industrial complex could be put to good use by this organization that was attempting to chart a different path.

TYSN is an interesting example for this project because, through both intention and intentional inaction, it did *not* become a formal nonprofit. It did not have its own 501(c)(3) tax-exempt designation, but was instead fiscally sponsored by another organization that is a 501(c)(3) and through which funding flowed. Fiscal sponsorship is often a step fledgling organizations take on their way to nonprofit status. It is a way to begin raising money, and have that money be tax-exempt for the donors, without having achieved tax-exempt status. A small minority of organizations, ones that are explicitly critical of the NPIC, use fiscal sponsorship as a way to side-step the legal restrictions placed on 501(c)(3) organizations, specifically those around board composition, bylaws, and other process requirements.

TYSN's decision to remain fiscally sponsored was due to both of those reasons: capacity and critique. In practice this status meant that donations made to TYSN came through the fiscal agent, and legally the fiscal agent's board was the board of directors with fiduciary responsibility for TYSN. TYSN, though, had its own board, the board on which I served. It was technically an advisory board, although in practice it dealt with the budget, with fundraising, with staff supervision, with programming, with strategic planning, and with setting organizational priorities. TYSN was, oddly, also lucky to have a fairly indifferent fiscal agent. Its simultaneous distance from and proximity to the nonprofit structure makes TYSN particularly illustrative as a case study. It existed in what Ruth Wilson Gilmore refers to as "the shadow of the shadow state," and while not a nonprofit itself, certainly operated within the NPIC.[3]

Now years later, my relationship with TYSN deepened and intensified and the stakes were much higher—high enough to leave me feeling weak, grasping, frustrated, defeated, and, sometimes, hopeful. Sometimes proud. Over those years, TYSN worked toward shifting from an organization of youth workers focused on making social services more accessible to trans youth to becoming an organization fully led by trans youth, and focused on their power rather than on the services they must sometimes access. Though trans youth rely on these services at disproportionate rates, which makes the accessibility of social services a life-or-death issue, TYSN organizers were critical of the compassion narrative, recognizing that they would never be seen as "deserving" enough. At the time of this writing the project of transformation remained unfinished and has not and would not come without cost. In fits and starts, in moments of solidarity and distance, frustration and connection, a shared vision of youth leadership was articulated, although the map from here to there remains fuzzy and blocked by barriers both seen and unseen.

For what follows I gathered together my fellow travelers, former and current TYSN youth and adult board members, youth and adult staff, grant writers, and supporters of various stripes, and asked them to consider their experiences with TYSN, with movements for justice, with violence and fear and solidarity. Why, I asked, if everyone involved in the organization believes in youth leadership, have we been unable to become a youth-led organization? Why was it so hard? Why, despite that, were we all still there? In writing this book, I had originally imagined that TYSN would offer a counterpoint to the three previous case studies, an example of how to do it all differently, to resist the co-optation of the nonprofit in-dustrial complex. It doesn't, exactly. What follows is an attempt to reckon with what it *does* offer.

I begin by analyzing how the violence out of which TYSN emerged, and which structured the lives of its youth constituency, impacted its un-derstanding of itself as an organization. In the section that follows I ex-amine how TYSN positioned itself in relationship to the social services on which its youth participants relied, services that are necessary if trans youth of color are ever to occupy full power within the organization, but which seemed simultaneously to prevent the entire project of youth lead-ership itself. I then turn to the question of funding through three related but distinct moments in which TYSN grappled with the dynamics of in-corporation, mainstreaming, and the impossibility of representing trans women of color through the single-issue lens of homonormativity. I close with a discussion of how these various issues came to bear on the ques-tion of nonprofit status as TYSN considered whether to pursue 501(c)(3) status. My intention in this chapter is to explore the forces that make the nonprofit form particularly inhospitable to young trans women of color, as well as to document the strategies that those trans young people have used to take and wield what one board member calls "the devil's tool," the nonprofit structure.

The Feeling of Crisis

In this chapter, I explore these questions through the affective register of *crisis*, most acutely felt in the form of precarity. TYSN is by no means unique in the degree to which all relationality—both structural and interpersonal—was experienced through the prism of crisis. Many of the informants at the nonprofits I analyze speak about their own feelings of crisis, that of their clients, the fiscal crisis of their organizations, and the larger social and economic crisis that is the backdrop to their work. Crisis is, in fact, a necessary precondition for compassion, the structure of feeling at the heart of the social safety net in the United States, an arrangement that Loïc Wacquant calls the "charitable state."[4] Unless and until people are in acute crisis they are not seen as deserving of care or worthy of do-nations. Or perhaps, given the proactive way that many highly resourced white communities are cared for, a more accurate depiction is this: crisis seems to be the only state that transforms otherwise "undeserving" people

into communities and individuals deserving of care and resources. Charitable giving in the United States is marked, in fact, by massive outpour-
ing of donations following a natural disaster or other such crisis event,
but donations wane as the sense of crisis fades. While perhaps this disaster response is appropriate, the affective requirement of crisis in order to
produce compassion makes it difficult to gather the funds necessary for
ongoing day-to-day work in the face of the unending social disaster of
neoliberalism. This kind of crisis response does not fund services for pro-
longed homelessness, healthcare for the uninsured, formerly incarcerated
people, and others who are locked out of job markets, for example. And
certainly it doesn't fund organizations that are working, over the course of
years or generations, to transform the systems that produce this inequality.
This means that structurally the nonprofit must produce and perform crisis in order to access funding, a clear example of which is Howard Brown's
lifeline appeal analyzed in chapter 2. This performance is aided by the fact
that nonprofits are often actually *in* crisis, whether financially or otherwise. Though this is a feature of the sector as a whole, TYSN offers us a
window onto the cost of crisis as a mode, as a structure of feeling, where
the feeling of precarity in the lives of young people is amplified by the precarity of the organization itself, both of which exist within the larger social
and economic crisis of neoliberalism. For TYSN, where the life possibility
of the youth members was so curtailed, and the pressure of funding so
acute, the feeling that there was simultaneously no way through and no
way out was a constitutive and omnipresent affective orientation.

Lauren Berlant describes precarity as a structure of feeling that operates on two primary registers: on the one hand precarity is shared, as we
are all vulnerable, contingent beings. On the other hand, precarity is an
"ongoing (structurally) economic problem" caused by an economic system, namely capitalism, which requires, produces, and thrives on instability. Precarity is therefore differentially distributed across the population.[5]
Judith Butler, in conversation with Lauren Berlant, reflects on this uneven
distribution: "every political effort to manage populations involves a tactical distribution of precarity, . . . one that depends on dominant norms
regarding whose life is grievable and worth protecting, and whose life is
ungrievable, or marginally or episodically grievable—a life that is, in that
sense, already lost in part or in whole, and thus less worthy of protection
and sustenance."[6] For Butler, the first register—the shared experience of
vulnerability—should be political grounds from which to address the sec-

ond, to "refute these normative operations, pervasively racist, that decide in advance who counts as human and who does not."[7] This politics, what Berlant calls "an idiom of care," is at the heart of social movement organizing, perhaps: a recognition that our precarious hold on life is both fundamentally shared and unfairly determined by our relationship to powerful systems and institutions.[8]

Though this sense of shared precarity animates social movement organizing, the nonprofit form largely works against such a politics. This is the case because the nonprofit structure is itself a primary vector for the uneven distribution of precarity, one which operates according to the "normative operations, pervasively racist," that determine life-worthiness. Time and again, this structural orientation of nonprofits triumphs despite the best efforts of those activists working within them to draw on or even center a principled understanding of shared vulnerability. TYSN offers us a window onto this scene of crisis.

Present Absence and Traces of Violence

TYSN was created by a small group of youth workers from District 202, YouthLink, a homeless youth organization in Minneapolis, and Face2Face, another homeless youth organization located in St. Paul. TYSN wasn't a project of these organizations, but a project of these youth workers. They were responding to what they understood to be a crisis, a war being waged against the youth they served. The story TYSN tells about its creation is this: in 2004 (perhaps) there was a series of instances of violence against trans women of color in the community, and a group of youth workers and youth (although the bit about youth participation is perhaps apocryphal, and perhaps we all knew that all along) came together to challenge local social service providers to be more accessible to trans youth, so that those youth could be safer and get their basic needs met. In my 2014 conversations with the TYSN community, the actual events were fairly hazy. When did it happen? One youth member thought late 2007. One thought 2004. Another was sure 2005. Or maybe early 2006? I was told that there had been sensationalized and awful newspaper coverage, so I could find out the details that way. I searched the local news media during that time frame for "transgender," "transsexual," "shot," "shooting," any of the most sensationalized terms I could think of, all to no avail. Later I found out that, as for so many other trans victims and survivors of violence, the story itself was made invisible through the press's use of the victim's legal name rather than her preferred name, thus erasing her trans identity.

As I spoke with my comrades, the degree of violence, the story of violence, the cost of violence constantly rippled underneath our conversations. That TYSN was created as a response to violence against trans women of color, that we entered the national stage years later through a story of violence against another trans woman of color, CeCe McDonald, that in the interim so many young trans women had both come to and left TYSN because of violence, that our progress toward becoming an organization led by trans youth of color was marked and blocked by violence—violence emerged as a key aspect in understanding how TYSN was always haunted. The story of this originary violence, the trauma out of which TYSN emerged, was an example of what Herman Gray and Macarena Gómez-Barris call a "social trace," the "excess in the collision between structural projects and social experience."[9] As a social trace, it "leaves few material and social historical registers."[10]

One of the founders of TYSN shared with me his memory of the story, the incident of violence that precipitated TYSN's founding, but he was unable to share any names or details because he had been a youth worker and she had been one of the youth with whom he worked. To have shared her story would have been unethical. He put me in touch with a former youth member of District 202 who had been friends with one of the victims of violence, and she described what happened:

> The morning of Veronica getting shot . . . I ran into a mutual friend and neither of us knew what happened. And I called the hospital and she was in the hospital and so me and my little sister caught the bus back to Minneapolis and we ended up sitting in the waiting room and we saw her get rolled past and I knew it was her. She got shot nine times and he basically left her for dead. One of the bullets ricocheted into her eye so she lost an eye. And he really wanted her dead—he had people who was trying to kill her. So it got serious in the neighborhoods where we stayed and hung out. During that time, things really changed around District and just around the neighborhood because we started hanging around in packs.
>
> We tried to embrace Veronica and embrace each other 'cause a lot of us were afraid to really go out and were looking over our

shoulders. Some girls did walk around with knives and mace and they had to use them. They had to do what they had to do.[11]

Two young people I interviewed described the would-be murderer as her "boyfriend" or "secret lover"; the adults described him as a john. All agreed that he found out about her trans identity and tried to kill her. The interviewees who had been youth workers at the time at local nonprofits like District 202 and YouthLink shared that this was just one among a series of instances of violence directed at trans and gender-nonconforming people, though it was the most serious, and the one that galvanized the community. Following her shooting, youth and adults at District 202 organized a candlelight vigil and a march from District 202 to the Hennepin County Medical Center where Veronica was a patient.

Duke, one of the board members who was and still is a youth worker narrates this origin story:

> It was a response to violence that was happening to youth I was working with. There were lots of things happening to trans women of color on the street, violence stuff. And the formation came out of that, through District 202. The conversations were being held about how as organizations we could help support these women better. What could I, as a YouthLink employee, do to support these folks better? What were we not doing? For me it felt like it was outside conversations I was already having within the organizations, so it felt like a youth worker response. [There were] some young people. *It felt like it was something, and nothing else was happening.* No other institutions or groups of people were responding, [though] certainly in community, [in] trans women's communities they were gathering.[12]

"It felt like it was something, and nothing else was happening," he says. Why this, though? One question that emerged for me in my interviews was "why emulate a nonprofit?" Why was the impulse, following these instances of violence, to create a new organization? Vienna, a white trans woman who was a young person at that time and who eventually became the executive director of TYSN, reflects that "it was what they were rooted in. From my perspective I don't know that they questioned it. This is what you do."[13] Further, she said, "I don't think that anyone was surprised, to the point of not even questioning it, that the organizational structure was modeled after nonprofits." Given the social location of these youth workers the appropriateness, the utility, the *right*-ness of the nonprofit structure *just made sense.*

Another adult board member, who had also been a youth worker during that period, offers a counterpoint. For Randy, TYSN was created out of fear. Whose fear, I asked?

> [That] fear was way more about the adults [than the youth], because [the youth] were pretty used to it. "We have to *do* something!" There was also some knowledge that—you know how in nonprofits there are waves of people that come in and out? A wave of people came in and were like "Oh my God, these youth are doing sex work, and you guys all know about it and what are you doing?!"[14]

For whatever constellation of reasons, the violence that is ever-present in the lives of young trans women of color was newly seen by the adult youth workers with whom they worked—as well it should have been—and it was brought forward by those youth workers, people who have access to such spaces and such registers, as a problem to be addressed through the nonprofit structure.

In her afterword to Herman Gray and Macarena Gómez-Barris's anthology on "social traces," Sara Banet-Weiser offers critical insight for thinking through this originary violence. "Social landscapes," she writes, "are emptied and filled with new meaning, memories refashioned in the 'name' of unity, and identities crafted as stand-ins for violence—all leave a trace of not only what they 'are' in current manifestations, but also what they could be, what they might have been, and what they have been historically."[15] In the wake of this violence, violence that was erased even as it happened by the same social forces of racism, capitalism, and transphobia that engendered it, a memory about that violence was crafted by those in proximity to it—not the trans youth of color themselves—but the adult youth workers with marginally more access, more social power. Over the years of my involvement with TYSN I witnessed all of us grapple with that memory, be haunted by it, and craft identities as stand-ins for that violence.

But the scene of violence—both the particular instances of violence and the ongoing structural violence—out of which TYSN emerged, posed a profound problem for its institutionalization, for it as an organization. Despite having been created as a response to violence faced by young trans women of color, trans women of color were the group of youth *least* able to participate in TYSN in a lasting and meaningful way over the years I was involved. While many young trans women of color were involved in various ways at various moments, organizational leadership was still held almost exclusively by a multiracial group of trans-masculine people and by white trans women. Young trans women of color, faced as they are with constant threat, with overwhelming exclusion from legal employment, with having to erase themselves and their identities in order to access shelter, or having their identities forcibly stripped through exclusionary policies and constant policing—the trans women TYSN was created *for* occupy a category Lisa Marie Cacho calls "ineligible for personhood."[16] Cacho describes those categories of people who are always already criminal "as populations subjected to laws but refused the legal means to contest those laws as well as denied both the political legitimacy and moral credibility necessary to question them."[17] The denial of CeCe McDonald's right to fight for her life, her "audacity to survive," is confirmation of this ineligibility; CeCe accepted a plea because she knew she could never have been seen by a jury as a person with a life worthy of defense, especially not if that defense cost the life of the individual attempting to kill her. For Cacho, "to be ineligible for personhood is a form of social death; it not only defines who does not matter, it also makes mattering meaningful."[18] In a compulsorily gendered context, trans people exist outside social membership, of precarious legal status, and for trans people of color especially, perilously unworthy of life: this is indeed a form of "social death." I would like to complicate Cacho's formulation somewhat, though, as nonprofitization can be one avenue for social reanimation for marginalized communities, though the terms for this social life remain heavily constrained. As we will see later in the chapter, trans people and issues are newly becoming subjects of interest to funders. This interest is both welcome—the potential of funding more spaces in which trans people can exist with self-determination—and risky—constraining the terms by which *some* trans people can access that self-determination to the exclusion of other, less "worthy" trans people. The example of TYSN's trans youth organizers illustrates the precarity of social reanimation through nonprofitization.

The difficulty of the social exclusion faced by the youth that TYSN was created to serve, but *by* whom it actually would have liked to be *led*, is more than the obvious difficulty of doing anything—staying alive and eating and being housed—while occupying a precariously close proximity to social death. As I have argued throughout the book, nonprofits are structures intended to uphold and police the systems that produce the differential conditions of social life. This function is *built into* the structure of the nonprofit system, and it does not go away even when occupied by those it is intended to police. This impossibility is one we grappled with often within TYSN. In one conversation I asked one of my fellow board members, Logan, another white trans-masculine adult, to reflect on why the work of TYSN was so hard, so frustrating, and why, despite wide agreement that we would like to shift toward a youth-led structure, we had been unable to make that shift over so many years. He replied:

> Racism and classism make it really hard. The two people who had the idea [for TYSN] are both white people with class privilege, although neither of them always had class privilege. So this is another example of an organization started by people who had the capacity to do that, who could get a grant. *But when the mission is to subvert the very institutions that made it possible to get a grant, it has to be hard, because you're using a tool that is designed to maintain a structure that you're trying to dismantle. So there's a tension between money and resources and doing the work.*[19]

Here Logan names the fundamental paradox of the nonprofit system: the impossibility of subverting the structure the organization relies upon to exist. But Logan went on to describe what this impossibility *feels* like, how it is experienced on a day-to-day basis. He said:

> But [actually] what I mean is interpersonally, between advisory Board members, . . . *We are really trying to bring communities together who are not supposed to be together.* I want for TYSN to be a space where individuals work that out and build together, but that's the behind the scenes work, and then there's the face of TYSN that we need to get a grant. [There's also] transportation challenges and who has eaten today and who has to work at the last minute and who can make meetings. Some people come to the Board without their basic needs met and some people have access to excess and that is really hard to set aside to make a decision about Board process.[20]

It is not just hard, I would argue, but impossible to set aside this profound imbalance of resources—even though it is the systems that produce these very imbalances that TYSN challenges. This imbalance has very different costs for youth members. One youth member, Sophia, who at the time of our interview was the only trans woman of color on the board, described what this imbalance meant in practice:

> From a youth perspective, it's trans youth support network. There's a clothing closet, there's a leadership academy, there's a speakers bureau to get you a little side cash, but there comes a place where people get invited to programs, but there's no conversation about what you are sacrificing to be there. Should I eat or get transportation? Should I get make-up to make myself passable? They're brought in to agencies and told they can help out but there's no conversation about your needs, about what you need to be here, what you need to better yourself to move up the ladder to stability.[21]

I remember very clearly Sophia expressing this in a board meeting, and thinking with frustration—and a significant degree of shame at my own frustration—"doesn't she know we all knew that?" But Kevin, another youth member, expressed the same frustration:

> That's why that's been hard these past two years, we've provided bus tokens and expected that to make transportation less of an issue, but we have to consider that we're giving people two bus tokens, [one] to get home and [another] to get back, but we haven't considered that in the past seven days, you've had to get to work, to pick up a prescription, to get out of a bad situation—that you don't have the token to get to the leadership academy [anymore]. Trans folks are so under-resourced.

The difficulty then is twofold. Clearly the level of social exclusion, and the lack of resources provided by TYSN to combat that exclusion, presented real barriers for trans women of color especially, making their sustained participation in TYSN impossible. The second problem was much trickier: *we all already knew about it and couldn't figure out what to do.* It wasn't as if any of us didn't know this would be a problem or that when Sophia or

Kevin described the dynamic it was surprising to anyone involved. It is this problem, then, to which I turn.

The Question of Services

TYSN was created to hold social services accountable for providing the very services that might provide at least some measure of possibility for trans women to participate in TYSN. The mechanism through which this was supposed to happen was the Network Collaborative, a group of willing and interested social services—shelters, clinics, and advocacy organizations, primarily—that would meet quarterly and work toward accessibility. Concrete changes to paperwork, policies, and positions were expected, and over the years, while there were some successes—one free clinic, for instance, successfully lobbied their executive leadership and began offering hormone prescriptions—little substantive change occurred. But, nonetheless, social services *loved* the network collaborative. It was generally a group filled with progressive social workers, many of them white queer folks—similar, in fact, to the youth workers who started TYSN—who wished their organizations were more radical, less punitive, more expansive, less *social-service-y.* Through the Network Collaborative, TYSN gave training after training after training after training. And despite this, youth continued to be kicked out of shelters, given impossible hoops to jump through to retain access to their services, have demeaning interactions with school social workers, and be so heavily policed that just being out in the world was a war to be waged. Eventually, we decided we would no longer give any trainings that weren't paid trainings, so at least youth members could get some benefit. The fundamental problem, of course, was that the social service system itself is not designed to actually end poverty, *but rather to manage and discipline those who experience it.* And still, despite this, reliance on inadequate and dehumanizing social services was one common feature that the vast majority of youth that TYSN worked with experienced on a daily basis.

This paradox made TYSN's approach to providing, or even working with, social services especially fraught. In 2014, as it focused on its transition to youth leadership, especially through the new leadership academy, TYSN put the Network Collaborative on hold. Nonetheless, the frenzied requests from case managers, school social workers, teachers, youth workers, and many others continued to roll in—at a rate far beyond what TYSN could ever respond to, even if it was the only thing the organization did. The desperation people have for *something*, for some *help*, is similar to the affective response that led to the creation of TYSN in the first place. As Duke noted, *"it was something, [when] nothing else was happening."*

Harrison, another of the four of us white trans-masculine adults on the board, expressed his position with regards to social services—the position that most closely mirrored my own. He said:

> Social services are meant to stabilize the social situation we're in now and provide band-aid solutions for folks that are being structurally hurt by the system. We want to get to the root causes of the violence and poverty. We see that social services are a necessary stop gap but they're never going to be a solution, and they are so often really premised on breaking down people's dignity and taking away people's self-determination—that's structurally how those systems are built.[22]

But other people, especially youth members, saw more possibility, or at least necessity. Malik, an African American trans-masculine young person said: "If I had it my way, we would [provide services]. I just think it's really necessary. I'd love to see a queer YouthLink, where you can just go and get all the resources. 'Cause YouthLink is horrible but queer youth still need all the stuff, someone to help them get food stamps."[23]

I dreamt of this too; perhaps finding a space where the downstairs was a meeting and drop-in space and upstairs we had a few apartments that were available for emergencies or as part of the compensation for youth staff? That would solve so many problems! But then I was always reminded what social services are actually like, how punitive they are, where youth become "clients" to be managed instead of peers. Sophia expressed that perspective, thinking out loud:

> What is the paperwork required? Do we have to report runaway youth? Are there quotas? What does it entangle [*sic*]? Just thinking about Avenues [for Homeless Youth] and YouthLink, just thinking about there, they walk on eggshells around youth: "I want to help you but I have to help you within these guidelines, and if I can't I'll just take you to the clothing closet to pacify you." Because that's state money, they're very "dot the I's and cross the T's."[24]

In previous chapters I have discussed at length the power dynamics embedded in the social service model. Everyone involved in TYSN, youth workers and young folks alike, knew this model intimately, had participated in it to some degree, and even recognized that they couldn't simply "refuse" it. The power dynamic of social services, functioning as it does through racialized bodies, operates even in the absence of those services, simply through racialized bodies in proximity to one another, each having very different needs and very different access to the resources to meet those needs. Xavier, a former TYSN board member, reminds us why this is: "The nonprofit sector developed out of missionary work, which developed out of genocide and conquest. The only way to achieve 'success' then is to conform to the standard of those missionaries trying to teach 'skills.'"[25] The twofold mission of TYSN, to hold social service providers accountable through the Network Collaborative and to foster youth leadership through programming like the leadership academy, was an attempt to navigate this dynamic.

For Duke, the reality was that "TYSN has been offering social service the entire time off the record, off the books. I don't think you can do youth work without offering services. It's hard for me to see someone struggling and not offer support."[26] The critical difference, many of us felt, lay in recognizing and intentionally resisting the paternalistic gaze. As Duke expressed, "It's a community thing, it's about holding each other. We've been doing it for years and not getting funded or paid or recognized for it. 'Cause we're working with young people who are in survival mode."[27] Duke's sentiment harkens back to Butler's hope that this sense of shared precarity could be the basis for political organizing.

The same day that the TYSN advisory board listened to Laverne Cox remind us of the necessity of this work, the revolutionary value there is in loving other trans people, we as a board clarified the values that informed our approach to social services and the vision of TYSN's work in the world. "Survive, dream, build," we said. This is, in fact, an approach that Dean Spade has advocated and one that most closely matched TYSN's values. We decided TYSN's work was to support trans folks in *surviving* the systems with which they must engage, create the space necessary to *dream* of another world, and then gather the resources and power necessary to *build* it. What this vision would look like in practice was as yet unknown—intentionally. We all believed that it must be youth themselves who decided how to navigate this social service dynamic. Duke believed "the answer . . . is to not have people like me there, [but] to have young people there, to chat with [youth who need services], to [have them] be in charge and to let them decide."[28]

For Vienna, the outgoing executive director, in reflecting on the impact this dynamic had on her as a young person coming into a staff leadership position, the social service model is about much more than services: it is about how we are slotted into the project of nonprofitization. For her, through "exposure to social workers and social services through trainings, or just being a person who relies on social services, there are all these professional expectations that keep you either *scared* or *angry*—scared you aren't enough, or angry you aren't given opportunities."[29] Vienna's reflection points to the ways that proximity to the social service system is pedagogical: it teaches us each how to relate to bodies with more than or less than us, how to naturalize that difference, how to grasp, how to be grateful, what expectations to have of those living in poverty or of those who "help." This is a function of power.

For Avery Gordon, "the idiom of social death speaks of the captive, but it only partially addresses him or her."[30] According to Orlando Patterson, the idiom of social death teaches "how ordinary people should relate to the living who are dead."[31] Compassion, I maintain, is one such relation, taught to us, in part, by the social service system. As I illustrate in chapter 1, compassion, the affective stance of the social service system, is a mode of governmentality, one that buttresses and stabilizes the more overtly policing modes of power analyzed so effectively by Gordon and Cacho. Although the affective response of TYSN's founders to the violence experienced by trans women of color—horror—is one that I share, and the practice of that affect—the creation of a nonprofit—was likely one I would have wholeheartedly participated in, and one, on the balance, I am grateful was undertaken, it did nonetheless emerge from a project of compassion. I am not arguing that the crisis perceived by those individuals who witnessed such violence and the compassion response that compelled them to action was misplaced. I am, however, instead aware that both crisis and compassion themselves are imbricated in the mechanics of maintaining a neoliberal social and economic order, an order stabilized by a social service system that is, by design, inadequate to the need.

As I noted earlier, that TYSN's main constituency is precariously situated in terms of personhood posed a problem not just for the internal project of crafting an organization in which trans women of color could actually participate. It also constrained TYSN's ability to pass in the non-profit system, its ability to get funded, or at least funded to create the kinds of infrastructures that would be necessary for trans youth of color to take leadership in the organization. This was due, in large part, to the discordance of TYSN's work and constituency with the project of homo-normativity, and the degree to which even the presence of organizations like TYSN and its members is disruptive to the mood and materiality of homonormative capitalism.

Funding as a Technology of Control

As each of the case studies has demonstrated in its own way, the nonprofit system as a whole relies on a fundamentally unsustainable relationship to capital, both materially and discursively. As an alternative to the welfare state, nonprofits must never seem too dependent, too needy, and so must constantly promise to solve the "problem" they seek to confront within one grant cycle and must woo donors with the promise that their one financial contribution will fix broad social inequalities. TYSN, despite never having tax-exempt status, was nonetheless *not* exempt from this dynamic. In this section I explore TYSN's relationship with funding in order to contextu-alize how its location "in the shadow of the shadow state" impacted its political project.

One of the first acts the small group of youth workers who created TYSN undertook was submitting a grant to the Minneapolis Foundation to hire a full-time staff member. They received that grant, and from that time forward, with a salary to maintain, TYSN was reliant on grant fund-ing to survive. Although much effort was put into cultivating a grassroots individual donor base to offset this dependence, TYSN was always un-able to retain its staff and run its programs without grant funding. When I began organizing with TYSN, the sole staff member wrote all the grants personally, and as such had little time to develop programming, build rela-tionships with new young people, or grow the organization toward youth leadership, despite his desire to do so. When he left the organization, a former youth member was hired as the interim and then permanent ED, and she was clear when she was hired that grant writing and fundraising were not her areas of expertise. As a working-class white trans woman who had experienced homelessness and come up through social services, Vienna spoke many times about not only doubting her abilities in this area and how seriously she would be taken by funders as the representative of TYSN, but also having a great deal of disdain for the entire project, for dealing with wealthy donors and for jumping through funder hoops. To enable her to focus on building youth leadership programming, TYSN hired Harrison, one of the white trans-masculine board members, for the grand sum of $2,000 per year, to write grants. Harrison remembers:

> I came in with very little grant writing experience—with formal education and pretty groomed by life to do that work, but without formal training. And Vienna, similarly, had pretty minimal experience dealing with funders and fundraising. We were making it up a lot of the time. We had some amazing people in the community who had been grant writers or who were in the foundation world who helped us, so I think we were way better resourced than many . . . Most of our [financial] support came from small social justice community foundations doing gen[eral] op[erating] support who wanted to hear our vision. While those really felt like a challenge at the time, those were super sympathetic funders and a lot of that was that we were pretty young and just coming out of being the new org and people were excited.[32]

Between them they were able to create a fairly sustainable fiscal arrangement for TYSN. And due to Vienna's work in building relationships in the community, she doubled our individual donor revenue from $8,000 to $16,000 in 2012. But still it never felt like enough. There was always more to do than could ever be done, and we really wanted to be able to *pay* youth to attend programming, something we recognized was necessary in order for those most impacted by racism, transphobia, and capitalism to access TYSN. Eventually we wanted to hire full-time youth staff, enough staff so that we really could work on holding social services accountable at the same time as we offered meaningful youth leadership programming.

After years of applying to national funders and major local private foundations with little success, TYSN received word that we had been approved for a grant from the Progressive Center Foundation for $100,000 over three years.[33] This would enable us to hire a part-time program director and two youth staff. The experience of actually getting the Progressive Center check in the door, however, was instructive.

With the tagline "Change. Not Charity." one would think that this particular funder would be a great fit for TYSN. That was, unfortunately, not the case. Harrison described how "as we were trying to make the jump to bigger or national funding we didn't understand the difference between a goal, a strategy, an outcome, and a deliverable."[34] Which, according to foundations, are apparently *vastly* different things, and aren't you just a charming country rube if you think an outcome is in *any* way similar to a deliverable. For Vienna, it was "gratifying to be seen by a national foundation after spending so long being unseen or misunderstood, but then we were right back with the same old bullshit using language that meant nothing to us. And we still are trying to translate it, no matter how many times I try to explain it I just don't think it will ever make sense. . . . We went through four drafts [of their required work plan], until finally they accepted it and they gave us the money."[35] The foundation literally withheld the committed grant money until TYSN submitted a work plan that correctly used their framing. I would clarify these terms here for the reader, but the difference between an outcome and a deliverable remains opaque to me, even after all these years. I asked Harrison and Vienna to explain exactly what it was that the foundation wanted from us that we couldn't provide. Harrison explained:

> And you know, I think though they have pretty clear social justice values and we are an organization it makes a great deal of sense for them to fund—we are doing queer youth organizing. But what they needed from us, like what our work plan looked like, what they needed from us in terms of deliverables, was so far outside our [scope]. We were trying to live our values, we were being led by someone who had come up through the ranks, but she didn't know—and none of us did—how to do it, and no one had the time to figure it out. They wanted a work plan that . . . promised clear deliverables in a certain way. Our tension was that we wanted to leave ourselves space, 'cause we're trying to transition into youth leadership so we can't say what our programs are going to be [over time], and none of us had the savvy because of who was in the organization.[36]

The foundation demanded a three-year plan with clear numbers and outcomes, certainly not leaving room for youth to completely rework the entire organization! And, in fact, the work of trying to force our program ideas into their framework *did* have an immediate impact. I clearly remember a discussion at a board meeting about youth frustrations with the leadership academy and pushing back against that frustration by saying "This program was what youth developed last year!" But one young person replied, "This is *not* what we created." Vienna reflected:

> There's something about the rigidity of it, in part the language. We need to see a, b, and c. And we're like "well, we don't entirely know what's next." They want our three-year plan and we're figuring out the three-month plan. . . . What's an outcome mean to this foundation? What's a measurable outcome to this foundation? And what's it mean to us? Nothing.[37]

Somehow in the translation process something key had been lost. Youth felt that their vision was mangled by the attempt to fit it into the constraints of funders, while Harrison and Vienna struggled to get even this now-compromised vision past the foundation censors.

As Harrison recounts, this kind of rigidity is not confined just to the Progressive Center Foundation but is a sectorwide phenomenon. In fact, he argues, this feature of foundation funding is tremendously damaging to social movements, preventing organizations from doing the deep internal work necessary to truly build trust across differences and craft long-term strategies, and instead pushing them toward short-term campaigns. He elaborated:

> I just think of the depth of the work, and how it's so slow—the internal work that TYSN is trying to do to reshape our organization and it's so slow and so deep. It's not the *only* kind of work that's necessary, but it *is* necessary to get us to where we need to be as movements. That's what we've been trying to do for a while, but that's just not what anyone wants to fund. People want to fund an organization that's robust and deep rooted, but they don't want to fund how much work it takes to get there.[38]

Foundations simply do not want to fund process, to fund the slow-moving relationship building and infrastructure development that is necessary for real sustainability. Instead, they demand quantifiable results. Even grants that explicitly fund "base-building" or "movement-building" still demand quantifiable outcomes within the one- or two-year grant cycle: a certain number of contacts, a certain number of summits, and the development of a platform, perhaps.

This feature of foundation funding is, ultimately, a market logic. Foundations, built as they are on corporate profits, were key engines of the discursive neoliberalization of the nonprofit sector. Foundations exert profound discursive and material power by simply demanding that nonprofits adopt their frameworks of knowledge for measuring risk, success— even value itself. In the case of the Progressive Center grant, the incredible rigidity of their work plan was intended to standardize information and thereby monitor the exposure to risk of their "investment." This, like the example of social entrepreneurship in the previous chapter, illustrates the significant degree to which market logics have come to dominate even progressive grassroots organizing.

This dynamic is even more important as major national funders like the Ford Foundation get into the business of funding LGBT issues.[39] The demands placed on organizations seeking this funding will only increase, and smaller organizations, for whom sophisticated tracking and evaluation software is out of reach, will be locked out. Those organizations that *do* receive such funding might find themselves, as TYSN did, having their vision distorted by the professionalization, adultism, class privilege, and savvy demanded by that funding.

Foundation funding was not, however, the only aspect of the nonprofit system with which TYSN grappled. In the next section I closely analyze one instance in which the stakes of mainstreaming were laid bare.

Proximate Danger, Exceptionality, and the Philanthropic Stance

In the fall of 2011, TYSN was invited to speak on the topic of "community" at the annual National Coming Out Day luncheon held by Quorum, the Minneapolis LGBT chamber of commerce. What followed offers an interesting encapsulation of many of the pressures TYSN faced as it navigated wealthy donors, a mainstreaming and corporatizing LGBT community, and a rigidly single issue political climate. These many pressures were, perhaps, not at the forefront of Vienna's mind when she walked into a room of attendees ready to accord her "exceptional transsexual" status, hoping that she would articulate a vision of incorporation that could dovetail with the kind of corporate homonormativity that brought them together. As she later reflected in a blog post on the progressive queer website The Bilerico Project, Vienna chose to demand solidarity instead of quietly asking for charity.

Without perhaps as much intentionality as she later wished for, Vienna accepted the invitation and gave a speech very similar to one she had previously given at the state capitol on Lobby Day, an event organized by Out-Front Minnesota, the statewide LGBT rights organization. In the Lobby Day speech, Vienna critiqued the push for marriage—which had brought much of the assembled audience to the capitol that day—and urged them to instead embrace a broader movement for justice recognizing that for trans youth, issues of poverty, homelessness, and policing were much more pressing than marriage. In that Lobby Day speech on the steps of the statehouse, Vienna said:

> Your equality is linked strongly with my liberation as a queer trans woman. And I need your solidarity in demanding justice for my community. When you ask for your marriage to be legally recognized, remember to ask for incarcerated young trans women of color's healthcare needs to be legally recognized. Make the connection clear in your mind, because if you achieve equality with this racist, transphobic ruling class, you have assimilated into my enemy. You have left a sea of bodies in your hurried wake.[40]

On that day, the wildly positive audience and viral social media response elevated TYSN's profile and cemented Vienna's reputation as a speaker who often pushed a mainstream LGBT crowd just to the edge of comfort, allowing them to feel connected to and a part of more radical work. Perhaps thinking that this would be more of the same, Vienna prepared a very similar speech for the Quorum luncheon. In it, instead of imploring the assembled crowd to connect marriage equality to issues of homelessness and policing, she again called for "solidarity," asking that they connect their advocacy for employee nondiscrimination policies in the workplace to a similar project to address the disproportionate impact of the prison "workhouse" on trans people, and further to fight for those who are locked out of above-ground economies and heavily policed for their participation in or proximity to underground economies.

Perhaps if she had left it there, the audience—much more mainstream, much more corporate—could have left with a sort of patronizing indulgence for the young radical. However, Vienna went on in her speech to connect these issues with the corporate practices of the audience's main funding sponsor, the Minneapolis-based multinational food and agriculture conglomerate Cargill. Vienna cited examples of Cargill's antiworker policies, their reliance on trafficked child labor, and the devastating forest loss their palm oil extraction practices have caused in Indonesia. "Our struggles are bound together," she told them.[41] She said:

> To an audience full of economic privilege, do I ask for charity to pass on to trans and gender non-conforming youth, who are in much need of their resources? Or do I ask for their solidarity, with trans youth and our greater community? In asking for their charity, I must encourage a relaxed atmosphere and affinity. In asking for solidarity, I must ask us all to reflect on our privileges and place within these systems of oppression.[42]

Vienna reflected on the oft-critiqued dynamic in which the Human Rights Campaign's corporate equality index uses a rigidly single-issue framework for evaluating corporate "gay-friendliness" while ignoring their abuses of people—of all sexualities—in the global south. Speaking to an audience of gays and lesbians who were granted access to corporate "success," who have become cheerleaders for the corporations for which they work, and who have translated that corporate access into nonprofit board positions, major donor status, and community praise, Vienna's speech was experienced as a slap in the face.

The fallout was swift and fierce. Immediately, TYSN received calls for Vienna's resignation and for a formal apology to Quorum. One letter we received stated:

> Though I have not been involved with your organization, I had heard some good things about TYSN. Upon completion of my transition, this is exactly the kind of organization I was looking to support by taking an active role. Further I brought with me to the National Coming Out Day luncheon those from my company who are responsible for financially supporting organizations such as yours. I think it's safe to say they will NOT be supporting TYSN anytime soon.[43]

She concluded by calling for Vienna's ouster: "I hope you are replaced and TYSN is able to repair its reputation."[44] Quorum issued a public apology to their attendees and to Cargill, distancing itself from TYSN. They wrote:

> A very anti-business speech was delivered at the National Coming Out Day luncheon that attacked not only our presenting sponsor, Cargill, but also all corporations, . . . and those who work in business in general. This speech was not only completely against the spirit of the luncheon but also against the principles of inclusion that Quorum as an organization believes in. . . . Going forward we will not only use a strengthened and enhanced vetting process for all event speakers, including the requirement of a signed contract, we will also be more thoughtful with our community involvement. We hope that you can accept our sincerest apologies for not appropriately and effectively representing our membership and the spirit of NCOD.[45]

The TYSN board posted a response to this letter, supporting Vienna's speech, reinforcing that Vienna represented TYSN's values and mission to fight for racial, social, and economic justice, but internally there was considerable discussion—not about the content of the speech itself, but about the strategy of waging this conflict. Randy recalls:

> People all over the community were freaking out about it. I remember having a profound sense of pride that someone in our community was willing to say fuck it I don't need your money, and this is the principle on which I stand. And I remember thinking that if every non-profit did that it would be like if every accused criminal refused to cop a plea—it would just bring the system down. And at the same time, as someone [who is] a part of an organization with the word trans in the title it caused people to not want to do business. And so on my Board, for the organization I work for, they were like "we shouldn't work with TYSN." One Board member said: "I don't even know why we are trusting you right now" and I felt like that was a direct pushback because I am brown skinned, I am lower income, and I have a direct affiliation with TYSN, and with Vienna.[46]

Throughout the ensuing conversations, everyone involved with TYSN shared Vienna's analysis, shared her anticapitalist critique, and supported her personally. I remember reading the text of her speech and thinking, "Right on. I'm so proud to be working alongside this person." There were a number of questions that this raised for the board, however: first, could we have been more intentional in taking this on? Why did Vienna even accept the invitation? Why are we as trans people so grateful to be asked to speak anywhere that we agree to speak at an event that in no way matches up with our mission? In our conversations we reflected on the internalized transphobia and trauma that has caused us as an organization, and many of us personally, to agree to share our stories with all sorts of people and spaces that actually do us harm—whether giving workshops to medical students or social workers, or agreeing to speak to groups who only want us to share our "personal stories," but not give a training and have to acknowledge us as experts. We reflected on how we participated in our own exploitation by allowing ourselves to be devalued, by repeatedly providing trainings for organizations that had no intentions of actually changing their exclusionary policies but want to say they had "a training" on these issues. We further discussed the differential way the trauma of these trainings and speaking engagements is felt; I as a white trans-masculine academic am often asked to speak as an expert on trans issues, despite the fact that it is not actually my area of research, whereas young trans people of color, especially trans-feminine people, are asked to share their personal stories, as if they are oddities to be understood, or to share their "wisdom"—which is very different than expertise.

The second question we discussed had to do with our own reliance on corporate money. Although many of the angry letters threatened to withhold some promise of future funding, the reality was that TYSN, given its political commitments, had never and would never be funded by any of the wealthy patrons in that room. We were, however, proximate to that funding, funded by people and organizations that profited from that wealth. One of our most longstanding funders, and certainly the one with whom we had the closest relationship, did benefit from numerous ties to corporate wealth. PFund Foundation, the local LGBT community foundation, had funded TYSN at the level of $5,000 to $10,000 nearly every year since its inception. A community foundation, as opposed to a family or corporate foundation that has an endowment, PFund had to raise all of the money it gave away in the form of grants, which made it uniquely reliant on wealthy gay donors and corporate sponsors. To my knowledge they never had Cargill as an event sponsor, although they did have Target, Wells Fargo, Medtronic, General Mills, RBC Wealth Management, and other, equally culpable, corporate sponsors. I would further imagine that if they could have landed Cargill as a sponsor, they would not have turned them away. And we absolutely relied on that $10,000 to pay Vienna's salary each year.

While TYSN fielded its share of angry emails, that anger did not translate into a direct financial impact, since it wasn't actually funded by those individuals in the first place. But an interview with Nora, PFund's executive director at that time, puts this instance into a broader context. She described how "one of the very first conversations I had with a major donor when I started with PFund, was straight-up, 'why is PFund giving grants to transsexuals, because that has nothing to do with gay communities?'"[47] She went on, "It shocked the shit out of me, but over time, I became aware of the tokenizing of the T, and for white gay men—and to some degree white lesbians—who had successfully navigated the straight world in terms of passing, economic success, social power, anything connected to the T made them too faggot-y."[48] Here she named the degree to which proximity to trans bodies and issues threatens the project of mainstreaming and, relatedly, to the philanthropic stance itself—a key issue to which I will return.

Nora went on to describe the immediate impact the speech had on their funding base:

> The first call we got was within the first week, from a donor, who called to ask if we did indeed fund TYSN, and they wanted to lodge a complaint because they felt that the speech was disrespectful to the hosts, it set the movement back decades and it had taken Quorum years to build a relationship with Cargill and she had spit in their face. . . . There was a mix of phone calls and emails, not that many people who were directly furious, although a few who were really livid. Just rage. Most of it is "I'm no longer in alignment with PFund's values if they fund TYSN." Some people were trying to be rational, saying, "You know TYSN is never going to get funding from any of the people in that room." We lost a lot of donors. Well, I'm not sure a lot, two donors who were major donors, one of our founders, and one who was in the process of setting up a scholarship.[49]

Vienna's speech was more than simply a critique of the corporatizing of the LGBT movement, it challenged the philanthropic system on which the entire nonprofit system rests, and further, the social "good-ness" of wealthy donors. Cargill is a *major* local funder in the Twin Cities. It is the largest privately held company in the United States in terms of revenue, leaving enormous wealth in the hands of the Cargill family.[50] Their personal and corporate wealth has meant that they are often the white whale of local funding; having Cargill as the funding sponsor for the NCOD luncheon was presumably a major coup for Quorum, the product of years of donor cultivation. At last the vast Cargill wealth would finally be turned toward LGBT issues.

For Vienna, however, the tokenism and erasure of the space of the NCOD luncheon was galling. And further, in the context of that time period, in which enormous amounts of money had begun to flow into the campaign to legalize gay marriage in Minnesota—a sum that eventually totaled more than $10 million—the profound impact of that sort of single-issue politics on trans communities of color could not go unremarked upon. She reflected,

> When I got to the Hilton, I got that I was about to be the asshole. . . .
> I could have just walked out, but I felt really strongly about how
> those dynamics have played out over my lifetime and how horrible
> it is to go from not having enough [then] into a banquet room.
> Banquet rooms are just a really triggering space for me because . . .
> I've never been in a space like that without being a token: the
> token homeless youth, the token trans person, it just never felt
> authentic. . . . I'm sick of sitting in the corner filling my pockets
> with bread rolls, I'm gonna get on stage and tell the enemy, or who
> I perceived as the enemy as I got more and more standoffish, . . .
> 'cause that feels worth it.[51]

In our conversations about the letter we would write in response to Quorum's demand for an apology, we discussed Quorum's expectation that TYSN would have been so grateful for the invitation and so desirous of the money in the pockets of the audience members that Vienna would have comported herself exactly as she clearly had done in the past, metaphorically, if not literally, "filling her pockets with bread rolls." Many in the group who had come up through social services, including Vienna, described their experiences being trotted out to share their stories at the yearly gala of whatever shelter or social service they relied upon. They described being dressed in borrowed clothing, watching other attendees gorge on catered meals and open bars, while they went back to the shelter for their dinner. This dynamic, which is intended to make wealthy donors feel good about how they are "saving the children" and thus encourage them to donate even more, comes at a cost. While it certainly raises money, it also is pedagogical; it entrenches and performs the relationship of power that the social service system relies upon and enforces.

That moment of truth-telling came at an immediate cost, however. When we met as a board to respond to the emails following the event, Vienna was clearly concerned we would be angry, perhaps even that we would follow the advice in those emails and ask for her resignation. She recalls,

> In the moment, especially when Quorum called for my resignation, I thought "I've pushed too hard with the wrong people, and I've jeopardized the sustainability of our organization." I was freaking the fuck out because here was this group of people who could have squashed us, especially because I didn't feel like we had a party line about economic justice, so I took on Goliath but I left my slingshot in my other pants.[52]

She notes here that TYSN, at that time, did not have a clear approach to its economic justice work. It was absolutely a shared value, but there was little clarity about what that value meant in practice and how it informed decisions about organizational partnerships, what funding to pursue, or even how we would hire consultants and grant writers. Vienna went on to reflect that, if not for the NCOD speech, "We would have and could have built a lot of inroads with employee groups at major corporations. So one of the consequences is that we can't get funding from those folks. And it does stand out, given our funding, that we don't get money from employee groups."[53]

This episode is a revealing one. It illustrates the lack of capacity and seat-of-the-pants organizing that characterized TYSN, both for good and for ill. But it also teaches us larger lessons about trans individuals' proximity to funding wealth and the impact of that proximity on those individuals, as well as on the philanthropic stance itself. Trans peoples of color are threatening to the project of mainstreaming, bringing with them, as they do, the specters of poverty and homelessness, policing and criminalization. TYSN understood itself to be a response to the war waged against trans women of color in the United States, and on that basis it carried the violence, the fear, and the anger with it. The single-issue politics of homonormativity could perhaps incorporate Vienna as the exceptional white transsexual, the kind of homonationalist subject Jasbir Puar describes. The proximity to Cargill, the possibility of funding from employee groups was what Ana Agathange-lou, Morgan Bassichis, and Tamara Spira refer to as the "promise project" of homonormativity. "It is precisely these affective economies," they argue, "that are playing out as gay and lesbian leaders celebrate their own new-found equality only through the naturalization of those who truly belong in the grasp of state captivity, those whose civic redemption from the category of sodomite or criminal has not been promised/offered."[54] As trans issues increasingly receive mainstream coverage, the pressure to adapt to this homonationalist narrative will only increase.

The Trans Funding Vanguard

This struggle over the incorporation of trans people and issues into the project of mainstreaming is aptly illustrated by the 2013 announcement of, and then backlash against, a call for proposals offered by UCLA's Palm Center to study trans military service. This initiative was funded by a $1.35 million grant from Col. Jennifer Natalya Pritzker, an heir to the Hyatt hotel fortune, through her personal foundation, the Tawani Fund. Reaction was mixed; while this was the largest single philanthropic gift to date to support trans issues, many activists were frustrated that it would support something that benefits so few trans people, people who might name rampant criminalization, exclusion from legal employment, and poverty as much more pressing issues.

In a recent interview on this new funding, scholar and activist Dean Spade noted that "military service is [not] the most pressing concern facing trans populations or the thing trans people want most. It is because one very wealthy individual has picked this issue and is funding advocacy about it—putting more money toward trans military inclusion than is currently devoted to any other trans issue."[55] Spade goes on to say that it is not only a waste of money, it is actually a danger to trans movements for justice that have been working for years on the local and national level. Instead, he states, "as the Pritzker money pushes a national conversation on trans military service, all the red herrings used against trans people will play out in the national media."[56] Spade foresaw a sensationalized national debate over "how trans people use bathrooms and showers, whether government money should pay for gender-related health care, and whether and when we have to report our genital statuses."[57] This debate, he argued, will set back efforts to increase access in shelters, schools, and much needed services, and will have a disproportionate effect on trans folks of color for whom those services are a much needed, and yet still inadequate, safety net. Spade's warning was prescient; the spate of legislative efforts to limit transgender people's access to bathrooms, beginning with House Bill 2 in North Carolina, confirm that Spade was certainly correct in his predictions.[58]

As trans issues began to become the new vanguard of homonormativity, the project of TYSN became even more precarious. In our interview, Harrison reflected on the pressures the faddishness of trans funding was placing on TYSN's organizing. He said:

> We've benefitted from people wanting to fund something trans and looking around and seeing we're the only option in the Midwest. . . . We've been swept up in that wave as everyone wants something from us and it's been hard to say "no, we're doing this [instead]." That trajectory is a mainstreaming one, [and so there's been] this big political tension about who do we train. Do we train cops? Prison guards? Do our work internally to know what our values are? Because we're always going to be hustling for resources and that puts us at a disadvantage, [which makes it harder to] not get pulled by this growing tide of trans mainstreaming. That's great but let's talk about racism and not safer cages for trans folks.[59]

Harrison names the difficulty of charting a path based on political values—or even getting the resources necessary to come together to articulate those values—within a funding system that encourages a much more ameliorative, rights-based politics. Following the 2013 national media coverage of CeCe's incarceration, TYSN was contacted numerous times about providing trainings to various prisons—one of which was the very prison at which CeCe was incarcerated. In fact, TYSN was approached to provide cultural competency trainings on behalf of the U.S. Department of Justice (DOJ) Community Relations Service.

TYSN's stance against offering the DOJ trainings was due in large part to how "cultural competence" is used as a pretext to expand policing and incarceration. In their work on the Free CeCe campaign, Vienna and other TYSN members experienced this firsthand, with the prosecutor arguing that a single two-hour training session five years ago made his office perfectly able to prosecute a trans woman "fairly." That same year, TYSN was approached by the National Center for Transgender Equality (NCTE) about collaborating on trans "cultural competence" training for the Department of Justice Community Relations Service (CRS). In an email response to NCTE describing TYSN's reasons for declining to participate in the DOJ trainings, Vienna wrote:

> I've been giving the CRS the cold shoulder for months now on this issue. Partly because it's been unclear to me what the broader strategy is behind the DOJ wanting to "respect trans people culturally" while incarcerating them, and partly because I personally am very distrusting of federal agents. The ways the Matthew Shepard Hate Crimes bill is talked about in this TDOR [Transgender Day of Remembrance] release from the White House sums up for me some of my concerns. The hate crimes bill has so far increased the power of the state, particularly to continue incarcerating people of color and has done little to address the root causes of the violence against our community. More than anything it's felt like a pink washing of a legal system build to enslave people of color. I worry that we're stepping into a similar trap with this new curriculum.[60]

Vienna went on to describe the surprisingly reformist sentiment she saw among those being elevated as national trans leaders. For instance, she wrote, at the recent National Transgender Advocacy Convening held by the Arcus Foundation she heard one participant arguing that "the best way for us to support incarcerated trans people was to expand prisons to reduce overcrowding."[61] She couched this refusal as an attempt to "give [NCTE] some perspective on how it's played out for me in the past and ask the question—what's the broader strategy? Is this adding to the agenda of prison reform and expansion or is it adding to the agenda of prison abolition?"[62] As trans issues become the next big thing, the next vanguard of homonormative incorporation, TYSN having the resources and space to intentionally craft the practice of its vision becomes even more critical.

In the context of this increasing pressure toward what we might term transnormative incorporation, one key issue with which TYSN struggled mightily was whether to become a formal nonprofit. In what follows I explore the dynamics of proximity to the nonprofit structure and the factors that weighed on TYSN's decision whether to pursue 501(c)(3) status.

"The Devil's Tools": Negotiating Nonprofit Status

In the years I was involved with TYSN we never made a definitive decision about whether to pursue nonprofit status. We had the conversation, in fits and starts, but set it aside as more immediate concerns pressed in around us. It felt important that youth have access to as much information as they needed to make an informed decision about this question, rather than adults who had experience in nonprofits and access to the critique of the NPIC pushing the conversation. In interviewing my compatriots on the board about this issue in 2014, I discovered there was a great deal more consensus than I had imagined, based on the limited conversations we had over the years. There was a strong shared distrust of the nonprofit structure, although some disagreement about the degree to which we are already implicated in its structure of power even as a fiscally sponsored organization. As I trace the contours of this conversation within TYSN I do so with an eye for the lessons it can offer about the possibility of resisting the co-optation of the NPIC more broadly.

For Kevin, one of the youth board members, his position was clear: "I don't think we should. I have a skeptical feeling about nonprofits, because nonprofits are not created for grassroots organizations. It's about the stipulations that are put on us. Nonprofits are motivated by money, grassroots organizations are motivated by the shitty things that happen in community."[63] Duke, one of the white trans-masculine adult board members who had worked for years as a youth worker, shared Kevin's assessment. In Duke's experience, nonprofits "just get too big, they lose their mission, their vision, they chase money, and young people get lost."[64] "I guess I'm biased," Kevin went on, "it just feels tainted." What exactly feels tainted, I asked? "The whole process, because we have to almost suck cock to get the money anyway, and a lot of the money has been raised by individuals and weird little events, letters that go out at the end of the year. That just feels better to me." Duke acknowledged, however, "There's no security in that though."[65]

The idea of security was raised also by Vienna, who had been perhaps the strongest voice in favor of pursuing tax-exempt status, although she certainly did so with a healthy critique of the NPIC. For Vienna, the decision was about strategy. Vienna was involved with TYSN when it went through the arduous process of separating from its former fiscal sponsor, District 202. Due to the lack of a clear, legally binding contract, District 202 believed TYSN to be its program and wanted the former director to work shifts in the drop-in. During the separation approximately $20,000 came under contention, with each organization believing the money was intended for them. As the fiscal agent, District 202 was able to keep the money. Since then, for Vienna, even though "things are hunky dory with our current fiscal sponsor, I can't help feeling like the other shoe is going to drop."[66] Vienna expressed that in her estimation, both from her position as a youth member during the separation from District, and from her current position as staff, "Ideally I'd like to see those of us who are most connected to the work have legal and financial power."[67] Though, she added, "If there is a fiscal sponsor, [I think it's important] that we have much deeper understanding so that there's less risk of it becoming adversarial."[68] Our fiscal sponsor at that time was a small nonprofit with whom we had little in common. AMAZE creates antibias curriculum for schools and community groups. To date, it had been a pleasant relationship, with little oversight. On the few occasions when AMAZE has been contacted with complaints regarding TYSN—notably following Vienna's speech at the NCOD luncheon and due to TYSN's public support for CeCe McDonald—AMAZE offered their support. To Vienna, however, the question went beyond security. The nonprofit status itself had some allure: "I want to look a little deeper behind the curtain—does it give us more power? Could we adapt those tools? There's danger that we can't adapt the tools, we just become a cog in the machine."[69] Despite being the strongest voice in favor of pursuing 501(c)(3) status, Vienna clearly recognized the dangers of co-optation.

For Harrison, it was the recognition of that danger itself that was the most important factor. "My gut," Harrison reflected, "is that I think I would like us to be fiscally sponsored by someone else and not be a nonprofit. The reality is that many of the things that would be binds [if we were a nonprofit] we're already in as a fiscally sponsored organization. I really don't think that it's important to become a nonprofit for its own sake."[70] There is an option other than nonprofit status or remaining fiscally sponsored, however. One option that was always on the table was to create even more distance between us and the constraints of the NPIC by giving up our fiscal sponsorship, thus giving up our ability to receive foundation funding, and become entirely volunteer run. For Harrison, though "[While] there are times I've thought we should consider that just to free us up from how we're getting pulled around by doing that dance, . . . I don't actually think that it would be possible for TYSN to be out of the nonprofit realm, not getting foundation funding, not having paid staff, just opting out."

For Harrison, like for Logan and Randy, the way forward lay in reckoning with the constraints, recognizing them, and building that awareness into the structure of the organization itself. Harrison articulated this vision:

> I think just knowing the traps to look out for. What are the directions
> it is trying to pull you? Like resisting professionalizing, . . . sharing
> skills, avoiding non-profity shit around martyrdom and churning
> around at a pace that's about a two- or three-year grant cycle and
> not a multi-generational change movement. [Resisting] the mo-
> mentum around having the end goal being getting the work done
> you said you'd get done and staying open as opposed to being ready
> to radically pivot or change shape if you're not getting the kind of
> change done that you want to. Because non-profits are built to be
> open stay open and TYSN is built to make deep change in the world,
> and those are conflicting goals.[71]

This approach dovetails with the vision expressed by Nora in our interview, in which she offered a vision in which our organizations are simply containers, "assumed to be temporary." "Rather than big metal and plastic things," she says, "instead, terra cotta jars that naturally erode based on the conditions around them."[72] In this way, TYSN's approach to the question of nonprofit status was deeply strategic. The organization was facing many, if not all, of the constraints faced by nonprofits already, simply through its reliance on foundation funding. As a group, we were aware that perhaps there might be additional financial and legal security in the nonprofit status, but perhaps not. Though we may not have had the language to express it in these terms, we all certainly felt that it would have further bound us up in a discursive and material world that is not conducive to the project of sustained, long-term change organizing.

Conclusion: Futurity, Fellowship, and a "Stance of Undefeated Despair"

At the conclusion of my conversations with my fellow board members and compatriots, I often asked them to reflect on why, despite the frustration and the emotional toll, they stayed. I was especially interested in the experiences of youth members, as I understood that like myself, other adult board members felt strongly that to step away from TYSN during what seemed like a constant period of transition would impose an unfair burden on youth leaders when the organizational structure did not yet fully incorporate and foster their power. But youth members experienced such profound disappointment and frustration with the slow pace of change, a pace that demanded such material sacrifices and was, in many ways, a betrayal of the values we said we shared. Why, despite this, did youth continue to show up, to invest their time, and even more importantly, invest their personhood, their hearts?

For Sophie, exchange and connections were a key survival strategy. In her experience with District 202, Sophie observed that "when youth get closer to age out they tend to disappear. Maybe it's not a bad thing, but there's no bridge to [close the] gap [between] youth and adults, and get youth who have aged out back in the agency to mentor youth. So the cycle just renews over and over. *What's learned isn't transferred.*"[73] Sophie clearly craved a space where the vital information-trading that trans women already engage in to keep one another alive was fostered, was supported with the resources that would enable it to become more than a survival strategy, but a life-building strategy, even a movement-building strategy. For the youth of TYSN, this information trading was vital, a method of staying attached to life when the social forces intending to shorten their life and expose them to death snapped at their heels.

Kevin described a similar attachment. Kevin began at TYSN by "going to open hours, and there were events that I went to, and chances to volunteer so I did. And I was like 'so there are words that express me!' So now I want to be around, because I want to vocalize these words that express me that I've never had before."[74] For Kevin the chance to feel connected to other trans people had a profound effect. "Just being around Randy and Vienna a lot, just everyday conversation, just normalized my internal life."[75] Kevin described how prior to coming to TYSN he had volunteered at other organizations but felt "really stupid and ignorant" for not understanding the terms that they used to describe their work. "I didn't know what the term campaign meant, or even organizing. I didn't understand having a set of demands. [I didn't understand] why I was angry with so many systems and not even realizing that they were systems."[76] There is power then in understanding oneself in relationship to others, to the systems that have kept trans youth in isolation, that have kept all of us apart from one another, because in our distance any one of us alone is unable to challenge the systems that make it so.

In my conversation with Kevin I struggled to articulate my final question. I asked "What does TYSN mean for you here," putting my hand on my chest. I didn't mean in his heart, exactly. I meant in his body, in his sense of himself, in all his vulnerability and strength. He replied, "A sense of community and belonging: that we all struggle, that we all need support, and that when I'm struggling someone is supporting me and when someone else is struggling I'm supporting them."[77]

Avery Gordon suggests that a "stance of undefeated despair," is, in addition to being the "carrying-on-regardless" in the face of profound loss and constant threat, also "a standpoint that guides political movements."[78] Gordon reflects that the fate of those who are imprisoned, or, I would add, socially dead, are bound up with the fates of those of us "not yet captured."[79] It is fellowship, Gordon argues, that keeps us all, both the captured and the not-yet-captured, from "possessing and being possessed by social death."[80] This kind of fellowship is profoundly different from the uncritical fetishization of "community" that so many LGBT nonprofits embrace. Instead of the progressive narrative of community, a stance of undefeated despair is a posture that recognizes the cruelty of nonprofits, the power embedded within them, the degree to which they discipline us and our movements—and, critically, the necessity of carrying on regardless.

Coda

Even as I completed the interviews for this chapter, TYSN was taking a major—and, for me, both terrifying and exciting—step toward youth leadership. Vienna, after more than three years as TYSN's executive director, and after struggling mightily against burnout and exhaustion, had decided to step down. Although we on the board knew her decision was coming, and sincerely wanted for her to nurture her creativity and heal from the grueling pace and emotional toll of being the single staff of an underresourced organization, it still, nonetheless, threw us into a bit of a tailspin. Our various assumptions about success and failure, stability and risk, were immediately apparent. Right away I started thinking about messaging and who I would reach out to as we, *of course*, conducted a national search to hire a new executive director with youth work and fundraising experience, someone whose identity and politics would foster the kind of youth power we are working toward, over a period of a few years. Logan was right there with me, I think. For Malik, Sophia, and Kevin, however, this felt like the moment to put our money where our mouth was, literally. If we say we want to be youth-led, they said, then let's be led by youth, let's hire the young people we've been bringing through the leadership pipeline.

But what about the funders, I fretted? If we lost our funding because the foundations that fund us think TYSN is unstable and not "professional" enough, then hiring youth members is an empty gesture, I argued. Would it not be better to transition to youth leadership over a year or two, and have an interim director, one who conforms at least somewhat to funders' ideas of what a nonprofit executive director looks, sounds, and acts like? A person trusted by funders could introduce the idea of youth leadership and hand off those relationships with funders in an orderly and planned fashion, I thought. Malik was frustrated with me, with funders, with the pressure to conform to expectations. Are we willing to lose funding, Kevin asked? We discussed it as a group. We don't necessarily need to lose funding, I reminded myself. There are lots of small progressive foundations that would be excited to fund the first trans-specific youth-led organization, the only one, we thought. And individual donors, too, would be excited to support our vision. Maybe we could find more of those elusive rich radical lesbians? We would need to take advantage of the new national attention TYSN was getting, thanks to Laverne Cox and the Free CeCe campaign. We could use social media and put together a Kickstarter page, so even if we do lose some of our current funding, other people could make up that difference, right? It is worth doing, worth taking a risk, we decided. It is what we believe in. The mission we created together specified that we wanted to dream of a different world and get young folks the resources necessary to build it. So let's do it, we said. Kevin, Malik, Sophia, and DJ— all youth members—became TYSN's new leadership staff, each taking on a different core set of responsibilities: programming; fundraising and communications; finances and operations; and sustainability, accountability, and community relationships.

It still felt risky to me, but I was simultaneously aware that my sense of risk is a disciplining force, one that has been instilled in me over my years working in nonprofits, and it limits—just as much as losing funding—the radical potential of our movements. As I wrote the final paragraphs of this chapter, it felt fitting to conclude this project with TYSN's attempt to chart a new course, fraught though it was.

Conclusion

In my six years of involvement with the Trans Youth Support Network (TYSN), it always represented possibility, an alternative to the mainstream gay and lesbian organizations pushing a rights and equality agenda. TYSN also explicitly eschewed the charity model of benevolent caretakers and grateful, deserving recipients. TYSN understood that kind of charity as a part of the systemic violence experienced by poor trans people, especially trans people of color. Instead over those years, TYSN—the only trans-specific organization in the Midwest—worked to shift from an organization of adult youth workers focused on making social services more accessible to trans youth to becoming an organization fully led by trans youth, and focused on their power, rather than on the services they must sometimes access. TYSN believed in the power of trans youth to chart their own course and wanted to construct an organization run by trans youth, organizing with other trans youth to amplify their collective voice and power, rather than being "served" by adults. After a multiyear process toward that goal, TYSN announced that its adult staff had stepped down, the youth leaders stepped in as the new staff, and TYSN was officially youth-led and youth-run. It was both deeply exciting and profoundly nerve-wracking, defying expectations about what "success" and "professionalism" within a nonprofit must look like, with the livelihood of our youth organizers and the future of the organization on the line.

Less than one year after that announcement, however, TYSN released another statement. It read:

> We can't give a simple answer to explain why TYSN is closing. The short version is that we don't have the resources that we need to sustain our organization. Like most organizations that are youth-led, trans-led, or people of color-led (let alone all of the above!), we're struggling to balance our budget and navigate foundation funding. It also takes an enormous amount of work to get a

youth-led organization up and running. Last month, we came to the realization that our work had become unsustainable for us, personally and collectively. We made the difficult decision that it's time for TYSN, in its current form, to come to an end.[1]

The closure of TYSN offers an opportunity to think through our attachments to nonprofits, to a nonprofitized version of queer politics, and to our love for and belief in organizations that exist in a form that I argue ultimately polices us and our movements, and does so structurally, in such a way that we can't simply opt out. Despite this relation, in which the structural form of the nonprofit actually interrupts the queer potentiality of that work, we remain bound to these organizations, we love them, such that we grieve when they close.

In what follows, I would like to use the closure of TYSN to reflect on some of the lessons that the case studies in this book illustrate. I begin by taking a close look at the structural and concrete ways that organizations attempting to advance intersectional queer politics, a politics that contests the rights and equality agenda of the gay and lesbian mainstream, resist the co-optation of their mission through the demands of the nonprofit structure. I then reflect on the affective questions at stake in this book, especially what to make of the profound attachment we feel to queer nonprofits, despite the fact that the nonprofit form constrains queer politics. I end by reflecting on the lessons these case studies offer in this postmarriage moment, as the LGBT movement charts a course forward in the face of a Trump presidency.

Resisting the Logics of the Nonprofit Industrial Complex

When I began this project, I hoped that this research would lead me to a "solution" to the "problem" of nonprofitization. It didn't. It led me to a landscape of complexity, of longing, of frustration, of co-optation, and radical imagination. People are reworking the nonprofit structure in large and small ways to radical ends, *and* those attempts at charting a new course are fraught, partial, and often short-lived. Dylan Rodriguez argues that it is critical that we "fully comprehend the NPIC *as the institutionalization of a relation of dominance.*"[2] Although there are specific tactics that organizations are utilizing to resist the disciplining power of the nonprofit, some of which I will discuss below, at their core each strategy involves a reorientation away from capital, away from a neoliberal system of valuation and common sense that has been deeply incorporated into the nonprofit structure. This reorientation is based on a recognition of, and disciplined resistance to, the neoliberal values that promote the continued existence of *organizations* at the expense of *movements*, an infrastructure that prioritizes major donors over basebuilding, and that individualizes systemic crisis.

This is instructive for thinking through TYSN's closure. At a recent conference on the impact of the NPIC on queer movements organized by Dean Spade and Urvashi Vaid, one of the overarching themes was our overinvestment in, and overreliance on, particular organizations, rather than an investment in and reliance on the *movement*.[3] Again and again, attendees and panelists reiterated that organizations are *not* the movement. They can be tools or containers, but movements are made up of people, not organizations. There is a danger in conflating organizations with movements. Instead of building organizations, we need to focus on building movements, and to do that we must focus on building activists. When particular organizations have served their purpose, activists work in other spaces and with other tools. Even in the absence of TYSN, Kevin, Sophia, Malik, DJ, and all of the other trans young folks of color who came up through TYSN's political education programming will still *be* the movement, and the fellowship and solidarity they have with one another is, ultimately, more important than the particular organizational container.

I know this intellectually, but I still keenly felt the loss of *TYSN* specifically, and I felt deeply grieved by the loss that Kevin, Malik, Sophia, DJ, and the other youth leaders were experiencing. This is, in part, because when organizations fold, it is not usually because they have "served their purpose." It is almost always because they lost their funding, and their staff are left scrambling for another low-paying nonprofit job, and the people with whom they worked, the people who relied on that organization—whether for services or solidarity—are now more isolated and precarious. In the past couple of years, key movement organizations have folded, organizations like Queers for Economic Justice and the Young Women's Empowerment Project, central figures leading the left edge of queer movements. Neither had finished "serving their purpose," although they certainly served many purposes during their tenure and would have continued doing so were it not for the precarity of funding and the policing experienced by the members of both organizations, poor queer and trans people of color. Although certainly the activists who were a part of both of those organizations are infinitely stronger as organizers for their work in those spaces, the amount of energy invested in scrambling for, and often losing, funding is incalculable.

At the conference I mentioned above, aptly titled "Queer Dreams and Non-Profit Blues," Urvashi Vaid noted one of the structural reasons for these closures, one illustrated by each of the examples in this book: neoliberal policies have had a paradoxical effect, decreasing funding while simultaneously increasing demand. This precarity is disciplining not just to the people who rely on those services, but also on the movement organizers who must scramble to provide them. As I have argued, precarity is a key technology of neoliberal governance. When people are struggling with precarity, they are not struggling with the state, they do not have the time or the energy to make revolutionary demands. Dean Spade argues that the NPIC is a "containment strategy," a carrot to the stick of COINTELPRO, surveillance, police violence, and criminalization.[4]

Some activists argue that we must simply refuse the NPIC. That the nonprofit form is irredeemably damaging, rooted as it is in white supremacist capitalism. Those scholars and activists call for an autonomous grassroots movement, peopled wholly by volunteer activists, and sustained by anticapitalist collective economic communities. This, they imagine, could produce the kind of global solidarity that is currently missing on the left. Others, however, focus their critique on the profound power of private philanthropy and argue that instead of doling out paltry grants at a rate of 5 percent, those foundations should simply be taxed at the rate that individuals are taxed. Those billions of dollars in increased tax revenue could easily meet the basic needs of people living in poverty, freeing up progressive organizations to focus on social change. I believe this approach is shortsighted for at least two reasons: a) it ignores the fact that increased money would not necessarily be spent on creating a welfare state—a change of this magnitude would require the pressure of a social movement, and b) it romanticizes the history of the welfare state in the United States, which was not, even when it was somewhat robust, all that egalitarian. Given the political economic realities of contemporary capitalism, the nonprofit system is a tool we simply cannot afford to let go. But there are strategies to reduce its harm.

Some organizations, like Southerners on New Ground (SONG), which is committed to building a "multi-issue southern justice movement," use a membership structure in order to shift the power away from major donors and foundations and toward its actual constituency. At SONG, members give at least fifteen dollars annually, or provide some sort of in-kind donation or service in lieu of cash, and participate in political education and basebuilding work. SONG, "also look[s] to our members for more than money. We need folks to actively participate in stopping cycles of violence, oppression, deceit, and isolation. We look to our members to commit to the life-long process of being anti-racist, gender liberationists, truth-tellers and healers."[5] Membership-based structures are intended to reduce the power that foundations and wealthy donors have on the mission and programs of an organization by shifting the burden of funding from a few major sources to hundreds or thousands of small donors.

Other organizations operate according to nonhierarchical principles and structures. The Sylvia Rivera Law Project (SRLP) makes decisions using a collective structure, in which each area of the organization's work, from direct legal services to fundraising, is coordinated by a collective of community members. An advisory board of incarcerated people also guides their work in order to increase transparency and accountability. According to SRLP, their structure is intended to "support work that aims to redistribute power and wealth for a more just society. We also strongly believe that our community-based structure, which maximizes community involvement, will support the sustainability of our work and the accountability of SRLP to its constituency."[6] SRLP has also made their collective structure handbook available on their website so that other organizations can modify and replicate their structure to suit their own purposes.

Communities United Against Violence (CUAV) in San Francisco has also adopted a nonhierarchical model and has shifted their organizational structure to accommodate a flat pay scale across the organization, a move intended to resist the professionalization of antiviolence activism that overvalues skills like fundraising and administration. One of the country's first LGBT antiviolence organizations, founded in 1979, CUAV has had, for most of its history, a fairly traditional nonprofit structure and one that prioritized issues common to the mainstream LGBT antiviolence movement: hate crimes legislation, police sensitivity training, legal assistance, peer support, and a crisis hotline. In 2007, in response to pressure from queer and trans activists of color, the organization began a process to reevaluate its structure in order to enable intersectional politics and an analysis of systemic violence. They write: "At this powerful juncture in our history we transitioned to a shared leadership staff structure and integrated our long-standing support services with opportunities for LGBTQ survivors to develop their leadership and organize to address the root causes of violence."[7]

TYSN, as well as many other organizations nationally, including FIERCE in New York, recognize the necessity of crafting a board that is reflective of the community most impacted by the issues the organization addresses. For TYSN, this meant that the majority of the board must be trans people, young people, and people of color. This approach intentionally resists the pressure to have a board composed of those with greatest access to wealth.

Andrea Smith has called for activists in the United States to approach nonprofits similarly to the Zapatistas and other global south revolutionary movements: as a tool. "Elsewhere in the world," Smith argues, "organizers still use nonprofits, but they aren't 'the movement,' and they are accountable towards the movement."[8] Smith argues that nonprofits can be used strategically as mechanisms to funnel money toward grassroots movements. She critiques the "politics of purity" that rejects the nonprofit form entirely, arguing that there is no pure space outside of capitalism. These small decisions matter, the strategic approach is critical. It does not fully undermine the power of the state and private philanthropy, but it enables, at least to some degree, possibility.

Failing Queerly?

Ultimately, as critics of the NPIC have made clear, this institutional form that houses our movements for justice is actually one of the drivers of ongoing injustice. The voluntary sector in the United States has always existed to manage, pacify, and discipline populations surplus to capitalism. The nonprofit form has had a similar impact on social movements, as movement organizations increasingly incorporate through the nonprofit form, becoming beholden to foundation funders, corporate wealth, and individual donors. It is worth asking, why, if nonprofits are so imbricated in racialized capitalism, in maintaining rather than ameliorating the crisis of the present, do so many of us—organizers and activists savvy to the dangers of co-optation—still invest so much of ourselves in these spaces? It is this question that animates my interest in the grief experienced by so many in the wake of the closure of queer organizations.

In the wake of the closure of TYSN I gathered my fellow travelers and

comrades who had for so many years worked to make something different, never quite what funders and donors and volunteers imagined, something that at times seemed impossible—and, in the end, perhaps was. One
board member, Harrison, articulated one of the factors that contributed
to the decision to close: "There was just a terrible funding situation right
when we transitioned to being youth led—the biggest grant TYSN had
ever landed had a staff transition and pushed out their decision for a few
months and just never told us." For months TYSN was operating with no
cash flow, unsure of whether it would receive that all-important grant,
with the new youth staff working for no pay, and where they could, seeking second jobs at coffee shops and such. Harrison continued: "That sort
of precariousness TYSN didn't have the resources to handle." It was in that
moment of impossibility that the group decided to close the doors. Ironically, Harrison said, in the end—about a month after the press release announcing the closure—they were offered the grant.

Was this closure a failure? Kevin, a black trans-masculine youth staff
member reflected on the affective process of closing:

> My own personal feeling [was]: why are we open? We're sick;
> if this isn't a healthy thing for us then how are we going to cre-
> ate a healthy space for other youth. And to be honest I feel like, I
> feel like TYSN closing was my fault, or the initial idea. . . . Yeah,
> I brought it up and I feel like everyone was like "are you fucking
> kidding me right now! After we did all this?" I didn't propose the
> idea because I thought we had failed, but because I didn't want to
> continue to be part of this fucked-up cycle. All these people felt
> this deep connection and commitment so we would do whatever it
> takes to keep it alive, and that was . . . I'm not saying it didn't work,
> but it wasn't good. . . . But every day I think: should I have brought
> it up in the first place? I don't know.[9]

Here Kevin articulates that this wasn't a "failure," but a principled choice.
But is there some political utility in failure, can we understand it as the
kind of antinormative, antidisciplinary refusal that Jack Halberstam describes? He writes: "Under certain circumstances, failing, losing, forget-
ting, unmaking, undoing, unbecoming, not knowing may in fact offer
more creative, more cooperative, more surprising ways of being in the
world."[10] And further, "Failure allows us to escape the punishing norms

that discipline behavior and manage human development."[11] This certainly resonates with TYSN's choices: knowing that there was a real risk of loss of funding attached to a certain mode of organizing, one centered in services and advocacy, but moving toward transformational youth leadership anyway. Refusing a narrow transnormativity meant failure, meant closure.

For another board member, Logan, a white trans-masculine adult who had been involved with TYSN since its founding in 2006, there was no other choice if TYSN wanted to really enact the political vision it had built, even if that meant it would lose funding, so much funding that it would have to close. He reflected:

> I really believe we all did the best we could to make decisions that
> prioritized the youngest people and people of color in the room.
> Our process was solid and when it wasn't we called it out and went
> back and did it again. I wish more organizations could operate
> like this and we didn't have to focus so much on products and
> outcomes . . . because that shit isn't working. Racism isn't done yet,
> that shit isn't working. So for me, it was great.[12]

But as appealing as it is to think about failure as enabling a queer future, that future is differentially livable. Logan went on, "but now I'm thinking about my privilege in saying that, since two of the four are pretty precarious and unemployed." He refers to two of the four youth staff who were hired. One just recently got a job as a case manager with homeless queer youth, after nearly a year of spotty employment. But the other three are marginally employed, struggling to maintain stable housing, and one is grappling with addiction.

This example offers a perhaps more complex and less hopeful view of failure—not everything "fails forward," producing ever more queer organizations. I wish that TYSN's failure to accede to the terms of the NPIC made something else possible. Instead, it just meant that this mode of organizing was *im*possible. Nonetheless, by naming the toxicity, the cruelty of the nonprofit form, this "failure" did create a kind of queer future, though that does not make it a capacious and progressive future, or even necessarily a life enabling one.

And what does this conception of queer failure mean for those who "succeed" by choosing survival within a world of circumscribed choices, survival at the cost of acceding to the terms of funders, who choose to articulate the narrative demanded by donors and those with wealth? This is a failure of queerness, perhaps, but not a queer failure.

When queer nonprofits fail, however, queer relationality is often foreclosed rather than enabled—this is often the primary loss, in fact. Everyone I spoke to reflected on how, beyond their personal loss, it was a loss of a broader connection. Each reflected on the calls, the emails, the Facebook posts they received from youth from all over the region, all over the country, even internationally. The desperate questions, the isolation, the impossibility of navigating schools and shelters and families all seemingly hell bent on making trans lives impossible to live. Logan described this: "What we lost was a rallying point for broader community, a lifeline. . . . The thing that is impossible to measure is that . . . presence, even if it is just a facade, a Facebook page. People elsewhere who connected to TYSN in ways we couldn't see, people who never came to meetings, never used resources were the ones we heard from."[13]

This loss of community was also one of the primary losses named by Kevin:

> I think it was harder than my first real relationship breakup. But I'm glad we can still have conversations about how hard it was. But that healing process is deprived from the rest of the community—the community is deprived of that healing process. When we lose somebody to police violence in the street, we go to the street to grieve, we protest, we rally whatever, but its against something bigger, its against the police, something. An organization closes . . . we have no space to grieve. We've also lost something big, but we have no place to go, "Hey you did this thing." Because we have no place to put that grief in the non-profit world, loss is different.[14]

Kevin names a core feature of the nonprofit system, one that organizes life in nonprofit work, and apparently, the affective landscape produced by their closure: the privatization and individualization of systemic failures and harms. Despite the systemic nature of TYSN's impossibility—the combination of inhospitable funding and prioritizing the leadership of people who are grappling with homelessness and violence, addiction and trauma—the closure of that organization was felt as an individual loss and an individual failure.

So perhaps TYSN's closure could be read through the lens of failure, as an antinormative, future-enabling unmaking. This could be read as queer futurity, "failing queerly," but what does that mean—both for the people who "failed" as well as for those who have acceded to the terms of possibility laid forth by the NPIC and have therefore "succeeded?" What is the queer future that envisioning this as a queer failure enables? This is a failure of queer failure. "Failure" on all fronts: those who claim and embrace the terms of the NPIC, those who strategically align, as well as those who refuse, either through lack of capacity or principled refusal. This is true: none of the systems that TYSN refused to conform to are actually transformed by that refusal. Also none of the lives and livelihoods that TYSN supported are made more livable by that refusal.

Trans Mainstreaming

There is an additional piece of context here that I can't leave unremarked upon. The same year that *Time* magazine declared that we have reached the "trans tipping point," that Caitlyn Jenner graced the cover of *Vanity Fair* and video of Laverne Cox schooling Katie Couric became a Twitter sensation, this trans youth organization closed its doors. There is a seeming paradox presented by the fact that TYSN closed at the very moment that major funders like the Ford and Arcus Foundations "discovered" trans issues, that according to pop culture and social media it became newly fashionable to support trans people.[15] Though this paradox is not, in the end, so paradoxical, it is quite instructive: it is not despite, I argue, but *because of* this increased visibility that a project like TYSN's becomes less viable. We find ourselves at a dangerous moment of trans mainstreaming; it is a danger not simply because it advances a single issue transnormativity, but because—through funding and the nonprofit system—this mainstreaming forecloses other options and politics. The terms of intelligibility for such a mainstreaming project are capacious enough only to incorporate those bodies and narratives that do not fundamentally challenge the terms of neoliberal capitalism. These narrow and politically debilitating terms are then produced and articulated through queer and trans nonprofits, in large part because of their reliance on foundation funding, a source of funding that demands a particular narrative and logic in exchange for resources. The articulation of this mainstreaming through the nonprofit form will follow a similar path as the LGBT movement has, one that ultimately entrenches racialized capitalism. We can see this happening now as trans issues and bodies are increasingly framed through a rights framework—as the pervasive violence that trans people, especially poor trans people, are exposed to in public space becomes narrowed to a question of what bathroom it is legally permissible to use. This framing then will demand a focus on rights and antidiscrimination law, and that focus will be the project and narrative that can be funded. Multi-issue projects that take on poverty and police violence and what Dean Spade so aptly calls administrative violence experienced in shelters and social services will no longer be fundable, to the extent it ever was.

Considering these issues in the post-marriage context enables reflection on the consequences and outcomes of those forces on a large scale. For instance, many queer organizations now find themselves scrambling for funding, as donors believe the LGBT movement is "over" now that marriage equality has been achieved. In fact, contrary to what marriage activists have long argued—that marriage is simply a first step toward a broader vision of social justice—many of the donors that were excited to fund the gay marriage movement are uninterested or even threatened by the idea of a more robust antihegemonic queer movement. There is no longer the affective pull of normalization to draw in donors; queer liberation simply doesn't capture hearts, minds, and pocketbooks on anything near the scale at which gay marriage did! Although many laud the *Obergefell v. Hodges* decision as representing a moment of strength for the LGBT movement, in many ways it reveals its underlying weakness: its reliance on an institutional form that is incompatible with any "next steps" that move beyond assimilation into neoliberal capitalism. This moment demonstrates the tension illustrated in the book: the nonprofit structure is fundamentally antithetical to a multi-issue, anticapitalist politics—designed, as it is, to sustain and buttress capitalism. The turn toward marriage is a *result* rather than a cause of this institutional arrangement. This structural constraint facilitated the emergence of marriage as the eminently fundable, short-term issue around which nonprofits could mobilize and funders could coalesce—an issue which, as many scholars have noted, does not disrupt, but in fact further entrenches, neoliberal capitalism. The primacy of marriage in queer movement politics has simply exacerbated an already foundational tension with which the movement must contend: the nonprofit form's tendency to undercut antiracist, anticapitalist visions of justice. Therefore, as scholars and activists develop their critique of homonormativity and imagine a future of the movement that fundamentally challenges current arrangements of power, I contend that any critique of homonormativity that doesn't address the institutional structure of the movement is bound to fail. In other words, a critique of homonormativity *must* incorporate a critique of nonprofitization, as the two are bound together.

In this political moment, in which fear-based hysteria about trans people in public bathrooms will serve as potent ammunition to advance a terrifying rightward shift under a Trump regime, queer movements for justice must learn these lessons, and fast. We must resist the impulse to counter these moves with a palatable, *fundable*, trans narrative of acceptance and assimilation. Instead, let us look to the intersectional mass mobilization united under #Black Lives Matter, and the power that mobilization continues to have in shifting our conversations around not just racist police violence, but the project of policing and incarceration itself under white supremacy. As BLM grapples with questions of funding and fends off the many philanthropies that would like to fund, and thereby pacify, that movement, the viral, dispersed, decentered, and not entirely aligned nature of their power is revealing. This is the project, then: to build up a mass mobilization of people, not to replace our funded organizations, but to augment, push, and eventually surpass, their power.

Final Word

My initial impetus to study nonprofits came from my need to grapple with the desperate sadness I saw all around me in queer nonprofits, from participants and clients, but especially from staff. In interviews, however, I was reminded that it was not the sadness itself that was the issue—the sadness made perfect sense, in response to the pain we saw every day from people struggling to survive the wreckage of neoliberal capitalism, pain we could do nothing, truly, to mitigate. Instead, what was crazy-making, both for me and for the majority of those I interviewed, was the individualized narrative *about* that sadness that operates within nonprofits. We had trainings about how to manage "vicarious trauma," or my favorite, "*compassion fatigue.*" The solution was always more and better "self-care," as if the cause of our sadness was a failure to meditate and take soothing baths. This is, of course, a perfectly neoliberal response, but it illustrates an important lesson: the answer to the underlying paradox of nonprofitization lies not in happiness, or in connection, or even in *feeling better*. Again, I am brought back to the stance of undefeated despair. Jose Muñoz reminds us that for marginalized people, melancholia is not, as Freud has said, pathological. The refusal to let go of a loss is, for Muñoz, politically enabling.[16] For Muñoz, melancholia is a "mechanism that helps us (re)construct identity and take our dead with us to the various battles we must wage in their names—and in our names."[17] For Judith Butler, too, grief can be politically enabling; grief "furnishes a sense of political community of a complex order, and it does this first of all by bringing to the fore the relational ties that have implications for theorizing fundamental dependency and ethical responsibility."[18] Unlike compassion, which imagines suffering to be *over there*, and community, which beckons us to love the very systems that produce that suffering, a stance of undefeated despair recognizes that in response to the state of ongoing social crisis we must carry on regardless, making do, carving out a livable life and the possibility of something different.

Acknowledgments

This is fundamentally a shared project, and I write alongside and in solidarity with activists and organizers who are struggling in and with nonprofits. First and foremost I must thank the activists, direct service staff, volunteers, young people, and nonprofiteers who shared with me their experiences of frustration, of depression, of hope, of connection, and of struggle within LGBT nonprofits. Each of you bestowed on me a gift of trust; I hope this, as a contribution to the larger project of building movements for justice that engage more strategically with the NPIC, is worth that gift.

I am blessed to have scholarly work that grows directly out of the shared political project of my chosen family. That this project exists at all is because of that community: Katie Batza, Lara Brooks, Ryan Li Dahlstrom, Jai Dulani, Kellie Magnuson, Owen Marciano, Susan Raffo, Henry Schneiderman, and Rocki Simões. Each of you has taught me treasured lessons about living with purpose and integrity. Thank you.

As this project was developing as a dissertation I was lucky to be among a fabulous community of activists and compatriots in the Twin Cities: Jahleel Arcani, Kelly Brazil, Katie Burgess, Tayvon Caples, La'Niya Dixon, Shayden Gonzalez, Lex Horan, Omi Masika, Jakob Rumble, Lisa Sass-Zaragoza, and Claire Wilson, as well as Shira Hassan and Tony Alvarado-Rivera in Chicago, who helped me survive and think through what it means to do activist work in nonprofits. I am particularly lucky to have been able to work alongside my compatriots on the board of the Trans Youth Support Network and do the painful, hard work of building solidarity across the lines of difference that are intended to keep us separate from one another. I have learned so much from everyone involved at TYSN, especially the youth members who gave me the undeserved gift of their trust and who supported my growth as an organizer and ally to young people.

I'm also incredibly grateful to the group of activists and scholars advancing such a nuanced critique of the NPIC, and from whom I've learned so much: Caitlin Breedlove, Trishala Deb, Kenyon Farrow, Paulina

Helm-Hernandez, Amber Hollibough, Soniya Munshi, Cara Page, Andrea Ritchie, Dean Spade, and Urvashi Vaid, to name but a few.

This project was completed while at Virginia Commonwealth University, where Chris Cynn, Brandi Summers, Cristina Stanciu, and Jesse Goldstein generously read every chapter and offered keen insights and much needed encouragement. Students and colleagues in the Gender, Sexuality, and Women's Studies Department have been kind and convivial: Sandra Burke, Kimberly Brown, Liz Canfield, bee Coston, Chris Cynn, Matilde Moros, and Archana Pathak. Thanks to Kathy Ingram for working so diligently to safeguard time for writing. In addition to my fabulous colleagues, Dandy Dextrous, Nancy Johns, Lindsey and Nicole O-Pries, Julietta Singh, Nathan Snaza, and Penn Ward have made our life in Richmond warm and welcoming. At Colby College, Jay Sibara was a fabulous friend and ally.

Thank you to Danielle Kasprzak at the University of Minnesota Press, who has expertly shepherded this project through the publication process. Profound thanks also to Lisa Duggan, Christina Hanhardt, and Craig Willse, as well as to an anonymous reader, who each offered such generous, thought-provoking, and nuanced feedback as readers of the manuscript. The book is immeasurably better for their insights.

This project, in its incarnation as my doctoral dissertation, benefited enormously from an extraordinary group of scholars and mentors at the University of Minnesota. In particular, my advisors Kevin Murphy and Teresa Gowan modeled for me the kind of generosity, intellectual rigor, and kindness that I hope to embody as a teacher and scholar. Their excitement for this project and support for me personally has meant the world. Thanks also to Bianet Castellanos, Jigna Desai, Regina Kunzel, and Jennifer Pierce, for their generous and thoughtful contribution to the development of this project, and for the integrity, generosity, and kindness that they exhibited. I must also thank my brilliant adviser from Oberlin College, Meredith Raimondo, whose courses and conversation helped me see a way forward when I was struggling. It is thanks to her support and example that I went to graduate school at all. My compatriots in graduate school showed me incredible generosity, reading drafts, discussing ideas, and sharing tips and insights into the murky land of academia: Steve Dillon, Eli Vitulli, AJ Lewis, Karla Padrón, Tom Sarmiento, Alison Page, and Charlotte Albrecht. Thanks to the members of two incarnations of the gender and sexuality studies dissertation writing group who gave me much generative critique: René Esparza, Karisa Butler-Wall, Katie Mohrman,

Jesús Estrada Pérez, Mike Cheyne, Andrew McNally, Lars Mackenzie, Jess Petocz, Kong Pha, and Angela Carter. I am also especially appreciative for my comrades in Sociology: Erin Hoekstra, Madison Van Oort, Sarah Whetsone, Vania Brightman Cox, and Tanja Andic.

I am grateful for the financial support that enabled the completion of fieldwork and dissertation writing, especially the University of Minnesota's Doctoral Dissertation Fellowship and the Sylvia K. and Samuel L. Kaplan Graduate Fellowship in Social Justice. I would also like to acknowledge the fantastic resource in the Gerber/Hart Library in Chicago as well as the Jean-Nickolaus Tretter Collection in Gay, Lesbian, Bisexual, and Transgender Studies at the University of Minnesota Libraries.

My parents, Kathy and Joel Beam, have shown me such unconditional support over the many years of building the analysis that appears in these pages. My mother in particular has lent me her English-teacher-turned-librarian's keen editorial eye. All mistakes herein are in spite of her valiant efforts. My parents' intellectual and creative curiosity, and their desire to leave the world a better place, were—and are—a model to me. This project would not have been possible without them.

I'm also fortunate to have been welcomed so generously by the Brodbank clan, whose faith in this project has been such a gift.

As I've said, this is a shared project; I share it with no one more than with Kate Eubank. While I write about this from the cheap seats, she works every day in the messy, confusing quagmire of nonprofits. She has read every word, over and over, and given me the gift of her insight, her time, and her patience. There is no one from whom I've learned more, and her strategic mind, integrity, and intention are profound influences on me. She reminds me that it's easy to be critical, and much harder to continue to do what's necessary despite it all. She teaches me every day about what it means to carry on regardless, doing the very best we can. I am honored to work alongside her, and so blessed to share my life with her. She, and our kiddos Toby and Milo, make my life joyful.

Notes

Introduction

1. Nasty Pig, *Shred of Hope: A Fundraiser for Ali Forney Center Presented by Nasty Pig*, video, 2:16, June 11, 2013, https://www.youtube.com/watch?v=mV4bmU8JcO4.

2. Craig Willse ably tackles this pernicious myth, arguing that the family rejection narrative is "not only inaccurate, but politically suspect." Instead of the narrative of familial homophobia, Willse writes, LGBTQ youth homelessness can better be described by "looking at the complex ways that gender and sexual marginalization interact with schooling, state foster care, immigration law, and criminal punishment." Craig Willse, *The Value of Homelessness: Managing Surplus Life in the United States* (Minneapolis: University of Minnesota Press, 2015), 7.

3. See for example "Beyond Same-Sex Marriage: A New Strategic Vision for All Our Families and Relationships," originally released in the July 26, 2006 issue of the *New York Times* with some 240 signatories. (Beyond Same-Sex Marriage Collective, "Beyond Same-Sex Marriage: A New Strategic Vision for All Our Families and Relationships," *Studies in Gender and Sexuality* 9 (2008): 161–71. See also: Ryan Conrad, ed., *Against Equality* (New York: AK Press, 2014); Lisa Duggan, "Beyond Marriage: Democracy, Equality, and Kinship for a New Century" *Scholar and Feminist Online* no. 10.1–10.2 (Fall 2011/Spring 2012); Dean Spade and Craig Willse, "Freedom in a Regulatory State? *Lawrence*, Marriage, and Biopolitics," *Widener Law Review* 11, no. 309 (2005); Kenyon Farrow, "Is Gay Marriage Anti-Black?" *ChickenBones: A Journal for Literary and Artistic African-American Themes* (2006).

4. The organization Funders for LGBTQ Issues, which monitors and assesses philanthropic giving to LGBT organizations and issues, reports that LGBT philanthropies gave very modestly to the marriage campaign. Instead it was overwhelmingly funded by individual donors, with the vast majority of that funding coming from a relatively few number of very wealthy individual donors.

5. See Cathy Cohen, "Punks, Bulldaggers, and Welfare Queens: The Radical Potential of Queer Politics," *GLQ* 3 (1997): 437–65; and Lisa Duggan, *The Twilight of Equality?: Neoliberalism, Cultural Politics, and the Attack on Democracy* (Boston: Beacon Press, 2003). LGBT movement organizers have also long expressed this limitation. See, for example, Urvashi Vaid, *Virtual Equality: The Mainstreaming of Gay and Lesbian Liberation* (New York: Anchor, 1996).

6. Lisa Duggan, *The Twilight of Equality?: Neoliberalism, Cultural Politics, and the Attack on Democracy* (Boston: Beacon Press, 2003).

7. Duggan, 50.

8. Duggan, 65.

9. Illustrating this paradoxical nature has been a central project of scholars and activists advancing a critique of the so-called Nonprofit Industrial Complex, including Dylan Rodriguez, Andrea Smith, Ruth Wilson Gilmore, and David Wagner, along with many others. See in particular the anthology *The Revolution Will Not Be Funded*, edited by the collective Incite! Women of Color Against Violence.

10. Internal Revenue Code, Section 501 subsection C lists twenty-eight different kinds of organizations or exemptions from federal taxes, including, but not limited to, federal credit unions, fraternal organizations, labor organizations, the National Football League (oddly)—but not its pension, mutual life insurance, or retirement funds "of a purely local character" — various kinds of local utility cooperatives, and many kinds of trusts. However, the organizations most commonly referred to as "nonprofits," and those analyzed in this project, are covered in subsection 3—what are, therefore, often called 501(c)(3)s. Subsection 3 covers two distinct kinds of organizations, both of which I will address: public charities and private foundations. The code states:

> (3) Corporations, and any community chest, fund, or foundation, organized and operated exclusively for religious, charitable, scientific, testing for public safety, literary, or educational purposes, or to foster national or international amateur sports competition (but only if no part of its activities involve the provision of athletic facilities or equipment), or for the prevention of cruelty to children or animals, no part of the net earnings of which inures to the benefit of any private shareholder or individual, no substantial part of the activities of which is carrying on propaganda, or otherwise attempting, to influence legislation (except as otherwise provided in subsection (h)), and which does not participate in, or intervene in (including the publishing or distributing of statements), any political campaign on behalf of (or in opposition to) any candidate for public office.

11. Raymond Williams, *Marxism and Literature* (Oxford: Oxford University Press, 1977), 132. There is an important distinction between the work of Raymond Williams, which I follow, and some contemporary scholarship on affect, most notably that of Brian Massumi. In particular Massumi, in his book *Parables of the Virtual*, argues that affect should be differentiated from emotion, which should further be differentiated from feeling. Massumi understands affect as the capacity to act, a capacity that originates in the body and exists on two levels: one is simply an intensity, the potential of disruption, and the other is semiotic, is nar-

rative, is social. In other words, according to Massumi and those scholars who follow him, affect is both "before and other than meaning." In other words—and this is, in particular, where my approach diverges—Massumi understands affect to be "presocial." I join Sara Ahmed in resisting this splitting, and more broadly in resisting the idea that something is, by virtue of originating in the body, prior to the social. Instead, Ahmed argues that we "shouldn't look for emotions 'in' . . . bodies. Emotions shape the very surfaces of bodies, which take shape through the repetition of actions over time, as well as through orientations towards and away from others." Following Ahmed, I use an approach that places affect, emotion, and feeling within a terrain of contested social meaning. See Brian Massumi, *Parables of the Virtual: Movement, Affect, Sensation* (Durham, N.C.: Duke University Press, 2002); Patricia Clough and Jean Halley, *The Affective Turn: Theorizing the Social* (Durham, N.C.: Duke University Press, 2007).

12. Anna Agathangelou, Morgan Bassichis, and Tamara Spira, "Intimate Investments: Homonormativity, Global Lockdown, and the Seductions of Empire" in *Radical History Review* no. 100 (Winter 2008): 122. Agathangelou, Bassichis, and Spira are, in turn, reliant on Sara Ahmed's theorization of affective economies, especially in her book *The Cultural Politics of Emotion* (New York: Routledge, 2004).

13. Deborah Gould, *Moving Politics: Emotion and Act Up's Fight Against AIDS* (Chicago: University of Chicago Press, 2009).

14. Gould, 3.

15. Ann Cvetkovich, *Archive of Feelings* (Durham, N.C.: Duke University Press, 2003), 7.

16. Ahmed, *The Cultural Politics of Emotion*, 11.

17. See Soo Ah Kwon, *Uncivil Youth: Race, Activism, and Affirmative Governmentality* (Durham, N.C.: Duke University Press, 2013); and Nikolas Rose, *Governing the Soul: The Shaping of the Private Self* (London: Free Association Press, 1999).

18. Michel Foucault, *Society Must Be Defended: Lectures at the College de France, 1975–1976* (New York: Picador, 2003), 256.

19. Jasbir Puar, *Terrorist Assemblages: Homonationalism in Queer Times* (Durham, N.C.: Duke University Press, 2007), xii.

20. See, for instance, Lisa Duggan, *The Twilight of Democracy* (Boston: Beacon Press, 2004); and Alexandra Chasin, *Selling Out: The Gay and Lesbian Movement Goes to Market* (New York: Palgrave MacMillon, 2000).

21. See, for example, Michael Hardt and Antonio Negri, *Empire* (Cambridge, Mass.: Harvard University Press, 2001).

22. The Movement Advancement Project concluded in their "2016 National LGBT Movement Report" that there were some 588 LGBT nonprofits in the United States. They came to that number based on the GuideStar database of charitable IRS filings, and using the search terms "LGBT," "gay, lesbian, bisexual, transgender," "gay men," "lesbian," "bisexual," "transsexual," and "transgender," found 588 LGBT nonprofits. This excluded new organizations and those with very small budgets who are

not required to file an IRS form 990. It also excluded those whose last 990 filing was prior to 2012 and those showing zero revenue.

23. I was a case manager at the Broadway Youth Center, a program of Howard Brown Health Center in Chicago, from 2006–2008, during which time I worked in collaboration with staff of the Center on Halsted. Further, many clients of the Broadway Youth Center attended programs at the Center on Halsted, so I had even greater access to information about that organization through the stories that were shared with me by those clients. A few years after my time as an employee of Howard Brown I returned to Chicago to conduct approximately thirty one-on-one interviews over a period of four years, from 2010 through 2014. In Minneapolis I also conducted one-on-one interviews with former youth participants, staff, board members, and donors of District 202. Further, I conducted participant observation ethnography as a volunteer and then board member of the Trans Youth Support Network (TYSN) in Minneapolis from 2009–2014. These interviews were augmented by archival research at the Gerber/Hart Library in Chicago and the Jean Nickolaus Tretter Collection at the University of Minnesota Library.

24. Ahmed, *The Cultural Politics of Emotion*, 14.

25. Johannes Fabian, "Presence and Representation: The Other and Anthropological Writing," *Critical Inquiry* 16, no. 4 (Summer 1990): 770.

26. Marion Goldman offers an example of this kind of "composite" narrative intended to protect the identities of the women whose lives she traced in her ethnography investigating women's experiences with a Pacific Northwest cult. See Goldman, *Passionate Journey: Why Successful Women Joined a Cult* (Ann Arbor: University of Michigan Press, 2001).

27. Avery Gordon, "The Prisoner's Curse," *Towards a Sociology of the Trace*, ed. Herman Gray and Macarena Gomez-Barris (Minneapolis: University of Minnesota Press, 2010), 18.

1. Neoliberalism, Nonprofitization, and Social Change

1. These statistics are gathered and disseminated by The Urban Institute's National Center for Charitable Statistics, and include primarily information from the IRS, with whom most, but not all, nonprofits must register. Those nonprofits with a budget of less than $50,000, as well as religious congregations, are not required to register with the IRS.

2. "Nonprofits Contribute $887.3 billion to U.S. Economy," *The Nonprofit Times*, October 28, 2014.

3. Giving USA, *Giving USA 2017: The Annual Report on Philanthropy for the Year 2016*, June 12, 2017.

4. The term NGO was coined in the 1945 charter of the United Nations and signifies any organization that is independent from the state and not a profit-

generating business. It is, therefore, like the term nonprofit, capacious and vague. As a rule, however, the terms can be used interchangeably, the only difference is that the term nonprofit is commonly used to refer to domestic U.S. organizations and NGO for those operating globally.

5. Michel Foucault, *The Birth of Biopolitics: Lectures at the College de France, 1978–1979* (New York: Palgrave Macmillan, 2008), 218.

6. Foucault, 243.

7. Foucault, 243.

8. Lee Bernstein, *America is the Prison* (Chapel Hill: University of North Carolina Press, 2010).

9. Ronald Reagan, *Proclamation 5590: United Way Centennial 1887–1987*, December 10, 1986.

10. Janet Poppendieck, *Sweet Charity: Emergency Food and the End of Entitlement* (New York: Penguin, 1998), 5.

11. Poppendieck, 5.

12. Poppendieck, 6.

13. Poppendieck, 6.

14. Wendy Brown, "Neo-liberalism and the End of Liberal Democracy," *Theory and Event* 7, no. 1 (2003).

15. Jennifer R. Wolch, *The Shadow State: Government and the Voluntary Sector in Transition* (New York: The Foundation Center, 1990), xvi.

16. An ideal example of this occurred in 2010 when LGBT activists called for a boycott of Target because of that corporation's $150,000 donation in support of Tom Emmer's Minnesota gubernatorial campaign. Emmer, a conservative Republican, supported so-called Right to Work anti-union legislation, as well as corporate tax subsidies attractive to big business. Through social media, former Target customers told of their return of Target merchandise and intention to stage a boycott until the corporation ceased to support antigay candidates, eventually prompting the retailer to issue an apology. Even as Target fights for anti-union legislation and regressive taxation, they fund LGBT organizations and have a significant presence at LGBT Pride events in Minneapolis—so much so that Pride attendees are often seen wearing a rainbow colored version of the iconic Target bull's-eye brand on their cheeks after wandering past the Target booth.

17. Dylan Rodriguez, "The Political Logic of the Nonprofit Industrial Complex," in *The Revolution Will Not Be Funded,* ed. Incite! Women of Color Against Violence (Cambridge, Mass: South End Press, 2007), 21–22.

18. Sangeeta Kamat, "Foreword," *NGO-ization: Complicity, Contradictions, Prospects,* ed. Aziz Choudry and Dip Kapoor (Chicago: University of Chicago Press, 2013).

19. The campaign cites *The Global Journal* as the source of the statistic, though I am unable to confirm the exact number with available statistics.

20. Michael Edwards and Alan Fowler, "Introduction: Changing Challenges for NGO Management," *The Earthscan Reader on NGO Management* (London: Earthscan Publications, 2002).

21. See for example Aradhana Sharma, *Logics of Empowerment: Development, Gender, and Governance in Neoliberal India* (Minneapolis: University of Minnesota Press, 2008).

22. Sangeeta Kamat, *Development Hegemony: NGO's and the State in India* (London: Oxford University Press, 2002).

23. See for example Arturo Escobar, *Encountering Development: The Making and Unmaking of the Third World* (Princeton, N. J.: Princeton University Press, 2011).

24. James Ferguson, *The Anti-Politics Machine: Development, Depoliticization, and Bureaucratic Power in Lesotho* (Minneapolis: University of Minnesota Press, 1994). See also, David Mosse and David Lewis, *The Aid Effect* (London: Pluto Press, 2005); Timothy Mitchell, *The Rule of Experts: Egypt, Techno-Politics, Modernity* (Berkeley: University of California Press, 2002).

25. Tania Murray Li, *The Will to Improve: Governmentality, Development, and the Practice of Politics* (Durham, N.C.: Duke University Press, 2009).

26. David Wagner, *What's Love Got to Do with It? A Critical Look at American Charity* (New York: The New Press, 2000).

27. Wagner, 44.

28. Wagner, 44.

29. Mather quoted in Robert Bremner, *American Philanthropy* (Chicago: University of Chicago Press, 1960), 12.

30. Mather quoted in Wagner, *What's Love Got to Do with It?*, 44.

31. Andrew Carnegie, "The Gospel of Wealth," *Pall Mall Gazette*, June 1889.

32. Peter Dobkin Hall, *Inventing the Nonprofit Sector* (Baltimore, Md.: The Johns Hopkins University Press, 1992), 47.

33. Hall, 51

34. Quoted in Hall, 48.

35. Loïc Wacquant, *Punishing the Poor: The Neoliberal Government of Social Insecurity* (Durham, N.C.: Duke University Press, 2009), 42–45.

36. Jacob Hacker, *The Divided Welfare State: The Battle over Public and Private Social Benefits in the United States* (New York: Cambridge University Press, 2002), 3.

37. Hall, *Inventing the Nonprofit Sector*, 70.

38. Hall, 44

39. Quoted in Robert Allen, "Black Awakening in Capitalist America," *The Revolution Will Not Be Funded*, ed. Incite! Women of Color Against Violence (Cambridge, Mass.: South End Press, 2007), 57.

40. Philip Carter, Quoted in Allen, 57.

41. Rodriguez, "The Political Logic of the Nonprofit Industrial Complex," 29.

42. Stanley Aronowitz quoted in Wagner, *What's Love Got to Do with It?*, 149.

43. See Incite! Women of Color Against Violence, *The Color of Violence* (Cam-

bridge, Mass.: South End Press, 2006); Priya Kandaswami, "Innocent Victims and Brave New Laws," in *Nobody Passes: Rejecting the Rules of Gender and Conformity*, ed. Matilda Bernstein Sycamore (Emeryville, Calif.: Seal Press, 2006).

44. Ruth Wilson Gilmore, "In the Shadow of the Shadow State," *The Revolution Will Not Be Funded*, ed. Incite! Women of Color Against Violence (Cambridge, Mass.: South End Press, 2007), 47.

45. Gilmore, 47.

46. Terrence Kissack, "Freaking Fag Revolutionaries: New York's Gay Liberation Front, 1969–1971," *Radical History Review* 62 (1995): 104–34.

47. Kissack, 104–34

48. Katie Batza, *Before AIDS: Gay Health Politics in the 1970s* (Philadelphia: University of Pennsylvania Press, 2018), 112.

49. Batza, 112.

50. Batza, 112.

51. Batza, 96.

52. Tamar Carroll, *Mobilizing New York: AIDS, Antipoverty, and Feminist Activism* (Durham, N.C.: University of North Carolina Press, 2015), 16.

53. Amy Stone, *Gay Rights at the Ballot Box* (Minneapolis: University of Minnesota Press, 2012).

54. Urvashi Vaid, *Irresistible Revolution: Confronting Race, Class, and the Assumptions of Lesbian, Gay, Bisexual, and Transgender Politics* (New York: Magnus Books, 2012), 192–93.

55. Vaid, 38.

56. Vaid, 38.

57. Vaid, 26.

58. The Movement Advancement Project reports that in 2016, the thirty-six organizations that they deem the most important movement organizations received 43 percent of their revenue from just ten contributors, including individual donors, foundations, and corporate funders. Twelve of the organizations surveyed received more than 50 percent of their revenue from their top ten contributors. This illustrates the outsized impact that a very small number of donors has on these movement organizations. Movement Advancement Project, "2016 National LGBT Movement Report: A Financial Overview of Leading Advocacy Organizations in the LGBT Movement," December 2016.

2. The Work of Compassion

1. Larry Kramer, "An Open Letter to Richard Dunne and the Gay Men's Health Crisis, Inc.," *New York Native*, January 26, 1987.

2. Kramer.

3. Kramer.

4. Throughout the chapter I will refer to the organization using both acronyms

HBMC and HBHC, according to the organizational name during the time period in question.

5. Howard Brown Memorial Clinic, *1990 Annual Report*. Howard Brown Papers, Gerber/Hart Archive and Library, Chicago.

6. Lauren Berlant, *Cruel Optimism* (Durham, N.C.: Duke University Press, 2011), 10.

7. Candace Vogler, "Much of Madness and More of Sin," in *Compassion: The Culture and Politics of an Emotion*, ed. Lauren Berlant (New York: Routledge, 2004).

8. Loïc Wacquant, *Punishing the Poor: The Neoliberal Government of Social Insecurity* (Durham, N.C.: Duke University Press, 2004), 42.

9. Wacquant, 41.

10. Lauren Berlant, "Compassion (and Withholding)," in *Compassion: The Culture and Politics of an Emotion*, ed. Lauren Berlant (New York: Routledge, 2004), 2.

11. Marjorie Garber, "Compassion," in *Compassion: The Culture and Politics of an Emotion*, ed. Lauren Berlant (New York: Routledge, 2004), 20.

12. Berlant, "Compassion (and Withholding)," 4.

13. Katie Batza, *Before AIDS: Gay Health Politics in the 1970s* (Philadelphia: University of Pennsylvania Press, 2018).

14. Board Minutes, April 12, 1980. Howard Brown Papers, Gerber/Hart Library, Chicago.

15. Jerry Tomlinson, Resignation Letter to Board of Directors, August 14, 1987. Howard Brown Papers, Gerber/Hart Library, Chicago.

16. Jerry Tomlinson, Resignation Letter to Board of Directors, emphasis in original.

17. Jerry Tomlinson, Resignation Letter to Board of Directors.

18. Howard Brown Memorial Clinic, *1990 Annual Report*.

19. PWA Client Population Data, July 31, 1987. Howard Brown Papers, Gerber/Hart Library, Chicago.

20. HBMC Operational Issues, Photocopy of handwritten document on lined paper, undated, in box with 1987 materials and in a folder entitled "management consultant." Howard Brown Papers, Gerber/Hart Library, Chicago.

21. Proposal to the Chicago Resource Center, undated, in box with materials from 1984 and 1985. Howard Brown Papers, Gerber/Hart Library, Chicago.

22. Proposal to the Chicago Resource Center, undated, in box with materials from 1984 and 1985.

23. Proposal to the Chicago Resource Center, undated, in box with materials from 1984 and 1985.

24. William B. O'Brian, "Arlington Party to Raise AIDS Research Funds," *Daily Herald,* June 14, 1991. Howard Brown Papers, Gerber/Hart Library, Chicago.

25. O'Brian.

26. Script for video presentation for Gala at Arlington Racetrack, "An Unbridled Affair," 1991.

27. This image is the final slide in the slide packet, its number corresponding to the number listed next to the final paragraph of script text.

28. Letter to Howard Brown Director of Development, 1990. In untitled envelope with approximately 80 similar letters. Howard Brown Papers, Gerber/Hart Library, Chicago.

29. Acknowledgment Letter, 1990. In untitled envelope with approximately 80 similar letters. Howard Brown Papers, Gerber/Hart Library, Chicago.

30. Letter to Bette Jackson, Executive Director of AIDS Foundation of Chicago, April 1986. Howard Brown Papers, Gerber/Hart Library, Chicago.

31. Howard Brown, did, however decide to begin offering testing for those applying for marriage licenses at a marked-up rate as an additional revenue stream. "Job Search Firm Hired to Find New HB Director," *Chicago Outlines,* January 14, 1988. Howard Brown Papers, Gerber/Hart Library, Chicago.

32. Executive Director Report to the Board of Directors, July 1987. Howard Brown Papers, Gerber/Hart Library, Chicago.

33. Executive Director Report to the Board of Directors, July 1987.

34. Bylaws Committee Meeting Minutes, July 1987. Howard Brown Papers, Gerber/Hart Library, Chicago.

35. "re: Financial Assistance to PWAs," Memo from Director of Social Services to Executive Director, July 15, 1987. Howard Brown Papers, Gerber/Hart Library, Chicago.

36. "re: Financial Assistance to PWAs."

37. "re: Financial Assistance to PWAs."

38. Timothy Stewart Winter, "Devastating Stigma and Unexpected Intimacies," conference paper at the Critical Ethnic Studies Association, September 2013.

39. Timothy Stewart Winter, "Raids, Rights, and Rainbow Coalitions: Sexuality and Race in Chicago Politics, 1950–2000" (Dissertation, University of Chicago, 2009).

40. "Minority Outreach Program," undated. Howard Brown Papers, Gerber/Hart Library, Chicago.

41. "Minority Outreach Program."

42. "Minority Outreach Program."

43. Timothy Stewart Winter, *Queer Clout: Chicago and the Rise of Gay Politics* (Philadelphia: University of Pennsylvania Press, 2016), 195.

44. Jasmine, interview with author, July 2011.

45. Rex Huppke, "Howard Brown under Federal Probe," *Chicago Tribune,* April 26, 2010.

46. Tom, interview with author, August 13, 2012.

47. Rex Huppke, "Howard Brown Faces Federal Probe," *Chicago Tribune,* August 2010.

48. "Lifelines—50 stories in 50 days—Lance" https://www.youtube.com/watch?v=Ovd3EAnR5B8.

49. Johnna Redmond, interview with author, August 2012.

50. "Lifelines—50 Stories in 50 Days—Lance (Part 2)" https://www.youtube.com/watch?v=Ovd3EAnR5B8.

51. "Lifelines—50 Stories in 50 Days—Lance (Part 3)" https://www.youtube.com/watch?v=_lH1XYNz1hc.

52. Lauren Berlant, *Cruel Optimism* (Durham, N.C., Duke University Press, 2011).

53. "Lifeline—50 Stories in 50 Days," https://www.youtube.com/watch?v=hOkGrGjUpJE.

54. Tom, interview with author, August 2012.

55. Tom, interview with author, August 2012.

56. Montana, interview with author, April 2013.

57. Shelby, interview with author, July 2013.

58. Tom, interview with author, August 2012.

59. Tom, interview with author, August 2012.

60. Tom, interview with author, August 2012.

61. Tom, interview with author, August 2012.

62. Shelby, interview with author, July 2013.

63. Shelby, interview with author, July 2013.

64. Maleeka, interview with author, March 2012.

65. Maleeka, interview with author, March 2012.

66. Montana, interview with author, April 2013.

67. "Lifeline Appeal—50 Stories in 50 Days—Chanel," emphasis mine.

68. Shelby, interview with author, July 2013.

69. Berlant, *Cruel Optimism*, 192.

70. Berlant, 200.

71. Berlant, 200.

3. Community and Its Others

1. Joseph Duggan Lyons, "[Center on Halsted] Transgender Programming Coordinator Resigns in Protest," *Chicago Phoenix*, November 15, 2012.

2. Violet Stanlet, http://www.Facebook.com/violetstanlet?ref=ts&fref=ts, November 16, 2012.

3. As evidenced by her Facebook record, Violet herself had protested the local HRC chapter's yearly gala fundraiser—the very same chapter that offered the meager $250 donation.

4. Violet Stanlet, http://www.Facebook.com/violetstanlet?ref=ts&fref=ts, November 16, 2012.

5. Terry Stone, speaking at an all-day event entitled "LGBT Community Centers: Creating Community, From the Center" at the National Gay and Lesbian Task Force's Creating Change Conference, February 3, 2011.

6. Centerlink has eighty-eight member community centers across the United States and in China, Japan, Mexico, Peru, and Israel.

7. Here I am drawing a distinction between corporate wealth and foundation giving, although there is some significant overlap. The primary difference has to do with what the money means. While family and community foundation money comes from corporate profits, it is not given directly from the corporation itself. In contrast, corporate giving, which has increased in the period I consider, becomes part of the corporation's marketing and brand building, part of the business model itself.

8. Ann Agathangelou, et al., "Intimate Investments: Homonormativity, Global Lockdown, and the Seductions Empire," *Radical History Review* 100 (Winter 2008).

9. David Wagner, *What's Love Got to Do with It: A Critical Look at American Charity* (New York: The New Press, 2000), 116.

10. Miranda Joseph, *Against the Romance of Community* (Minneapolis: University of Minnesota Press, 2002), xiii.

11. Joseph, viii. Emphasis mine.

12. Joseph, xxxiii.

13. Nikolas Rose, "The Death of the Social? Re-figuring the Territory of Government," *Economy and Society* 25, no. 3 (August 1996), 332.

14. Rose, 332.

15. Soo Ah Kwon, *Uncivil Youth: Race, Activism, and Affirmative Governmentality* (Durham, N.C.: Duke University Press, 2013), 9.

16. Rose, "The Death of the Social?, 336.

17. Kwon, *Uncivil Youth*, 8.

18. Jasbir Puar, *Terrorist Assemblages: Homonationalism in Queer Times* (Durham, N.C.: Duke University Press, 2007).

19. Joseph, *Against the Romance of Community,* xxiii.

20. For instance at the January 3, 1979 meeting: "Gloria read the minutes of the Executive Committee meeting. Joe Shure moved that we approve those as written, motion passed."

21. Joe Loundy Papers, February 21, 1979. Gerber/Hart Library, Chicago.

22. Joe Loundy Papers, February 21, 1979. Gerber/Hart Library, Chicago.

23. Grant Application Narrative to the Chicago Community Trust, 1985. Joe Loundy Papers, Gerber/Hart Library, Chicago.

24. Board of Directors Meeting Minutes, March 1985. Gerber/Hart Library, Chicago.

25. Qualifications for Board Members, 1992. Joe Loundy Papers, Gerber/Hart Library, Chicago.

26. Grant Application, Chicago Community Trust, 1985. Joe Loundy Papers, Gerber/Hart Library, Chicago.

27. Application for 501(c)(3) status, filed 1977. Joe Loundy Papers, Gerber/Hart Library, Chicago.

28. This new transparency initiative was instituted by the executive committee in 1980 in response to an increasingly fractious membership. The organization had recently chosen to seek and accept funding from the Hugh Hefner Foundation, angering what few lesbian members the organization had. The notes of the executive committee meeting following a community meeting to discuss the Hefner Grant and decide whether to accept the funding illustrate the difficulty the board of directors had in even communicating the sequence of events regarding the Hugh Hefner grant to the membership—and moreover, simply even keeping the membership informed about who was on the board. The notes from that meeting state "Maintaining good communication channels within the organization was a major concern of committee members. . . . Other items discussed were: the use of a suggestion box; posting of minutes on the switchboard bulletin board; posting and or distributing names of current board members to all volunteers; calling attention to Board meetings times and encouraging volunteers to attend; improving orientation of volunteers and board members to acquaint them more thoroughly with the organization. The counseling supervision groups appear to be a good means of funneling information to volunteers, and the executive committee agreed that this function can be emphasized even more." Special meeting of the Executive Committee, April 20, 1980. Joe Loundy Papers, Gerber/Hart Library, Chicago.

29. Letter to Human First Event Table Captains, 1995. Joe Loundy Papers, Gerber/Hart Library, Chicago. The following year's prices are even more stunning. In 1996, the high-end ticket cost $500 and included a pre-event cocktail reception and preferred seating as well as one thousand American Airlines frequent flier miles!

30. Annual Budget, 1984. Joe Loundy Papers, Gerber/Hart Library, Chicago. The position description for the first executive director position reflects strong clinical/mental health focus, requiring a masters in social service or related field plus three years of "proven experience with, and sensitivity and commitment to, both the philosophy of social services and the needs of gay and lesbian individuals and their community."

31. Annual Budget, 1994. Joe Loundy Papers, Gerber/Hart Library, Chicago.

32. Finance Committee Meeting, March 11, 1992. Joe Loundy Papers, Gerber/Hart Library, Chicago.

33. Finance Committee Meeting, March 11, 1992.

34. Finance Committee Meeting, March 11, 1992.

35. Board of Directors Meeting Minutes, January 27, 1997. Joe Loundy Papers, Gerber/Hart Library, Chicago.

36. Board of Director Meeting Minutes, March 1997. Joe Loundy Papers, Gerber/Hart Library, Chicago.

37. "A Special Message from Holly Offman," January 27, 1997. Joe Loundy Papers, Gerber/Hart Library, Chicago.

38. Gary Barlow, "The Chicago LGBT Center Deals with New Youth-Related Issues," *Chicago Free Press*, March 5, 2008.

39. Barlow.

40. Barlow.

41. Barlow.

42. Chicago Coalition for the Homeless and Survey Research Laboratory at the University of Chicago, "How Many People are Homeless in Chicago? An FY 2006 Analysis," 2006.

43. Nicholas Ray, *LGBT Youth: An Epidemic of Homelessness* (New York: National Gay and Lesbian Task Force and the National Coalition for the Homeless, 2006).

44. Puar, *Terrorist Assemblages*, xii.

45. Puar, xii.

46. Laila Harim, interview with author, March 2012.

47. Laila Harim, interview with author, March 2012.

48. According to the filmmaker of the YouTube video.

49. "Boystown/Halsted Street Stabbing," http://www.youtube.com/watch?v=_Q6j3VF8eGs. Emphasis in original.

50. Take Back Boystown Facebook page, June 28, 2011, http://www.Facebook.com/TakeBackBoystown.

51. Take Back Boystown Facebook page.

52. Take Back Boystown Facebook page.

53. Take Back Boystown Facebook page.

54. Take Back Boystown Facebook page.

55. Take Back Boystown Facebook page.

56. "Videotaped Street Attack Divides Chicago's Boystown," July 7, 2011, http://www.youtube.com/watch?v=mNtMYjT8kzc.

57. Christina Hanhardt, *Safe Space: Gay Neighborhood History and the Politics of Violence* (Durham, N.C.: Duke University Press, 2013), 73.

58. "Gang Intimidation at Boystown Businesses," *Chicago News Report,* June 20, 2011.

59. "Man Stabbed in Lakeview, 1 Suspect Caught by Bar's Security," *Chicago News Report,* June 18, 2011.

60. Michyl Hoffstead, interview with author, June 2011.

61. Dawn Turner Trice, "Some Black Youth Feel More at Home in Boystown, But Get Chilly Reception," *Chicago Tribune*, November 30, 2009.

62. CAPS stands for Chicago Alternative Policing Strategy, a "community policing" strategy intended to mobilize community members to surveille their neighborhoods and act as allies to the police.

63. "Videotaped Street Attack Divides Chicago's Boystown," July 7, 2011, http://www.youtube.com/watch?v=mNtMYjT8kzc.

64. "Videotaped Street Attack Divides Chicago's Boystown."

65. "Videotaped Street Attack Divides Chicago's Boystown." Belmont is the location of the El (elevated train) stop that serves Boystown and houses numerous gay bars and businesses, and is, additionally, a key area for young people to congregate, hang out, and trade sex.

66. Mack Colter, interview with author, March 2012.

67. Mack Colter, interview with author, March 2012.

68. Mack Colter, interview with author, March 2012.

69. Center on Halsted, "Illinois Department of Justice and Cook County State's Attorney Enable Center on Halsted to Expand Anti-Violence Efforts," press release, January 6, 2011.

70. Cook County State's Attorney's Office, "Federal Grant Helps Expand Cook County State's Attorney's Fight Against Human Trafficking," press release, August 26, 2010.

71. Cook County State's Attorney's Office, "Alvarez Applauds Governor's Signature of Illinois Safe Children's Act," press release, August 20, 2010.

72. "Alvarez Applauds Governor's Signature of Illinois Safe Children's Act."

73. Young Women's Empowerment Project, "Girls Do What They Have to Do to Survive: Illuminating Methods Used by Girls in the Sex Trades to Fight Back and Heal," 2009.

74. Incite! Women of Color Against Violence, "No Simple Solutions: State Violence and the Sex Trades," April 22, 2011.

75. Michyl Hoffstead, interview with author, August 2011.

76. Michyl Hoffstead, interview with author, August 2011.

77. Michyl Hoffstead, interview with author, August 2011.

78. Michyl Hoffstead, interview with author, August 2011.

79. Michyl Hoffstead, interview with author, August 2011.

80. George Henderson, "'Free' Food, the Local Production of Worth, and the Circuit of Decommodification: A Value Theory of Surplus," *Environment and Planning D: Society and Space* 22 (2014).

81. Henderson.

82. Sara Ahmed, *The Cultural Politics of Emotion* (New York: Routledge, 2004), 13.

83. Jin Haritaworn, "Queer Injuries: The Cultural Politics of 'Hate Crimes' in Germany," *Social Justice* 37, no. 1 (2010): 69–91.

84. Michel Foucault. *History of Sexuality: An Introduction, 1 (New York: Random House, 1978),* 138.

85. Puar, *Terrorist Assemblages*, 32.

86. Craig Willse, "'Universal Data Elements,' or the Biopolitical Life of Homeless Populations," *Surveillance and Society* 5, no. 3 (2008): 248.

4. Capital and Nonprofitization

1. Carl Dunn, "It's never too late to come out . . . again." Email message to author, October 11, 2010.

2. Lisa Duggan, *The Twilight of Equality: Neoliberalism, Cultural Politics, and the Attack on Democracy* (New York: Beacon, 2003).

3. District 202 pamphlet, undated, Jean-Nickolaus Tretter Collection, University of Minnesota.

4. "Looking Back" in *District 202 News*, Winter 1998.

5. James Sanna, "District 202 Names New Executive Director," *The Colu.mn*, October 26, 2009.

6. Paul, interview with author, January 2011.

7. National Philanthropic Trust, "Charitable Giving Statistics," http://www.nptrust.org/philanthropic-resources/charitable-giving-statistics/.

8. Association of Fundraising Professionals, "AFP: The First 50 Years," http://www.afpnet.org/.

9. Association of Fundraising Professionals.

10. Teresa, interview with author, July 2012.

11. Internal Revenue Service, "Governance and Related Topics," IRS.gov.

12. Yana, interview with author, November 29, 2010.

13. Jax Alder, interview with author, November 18, 2010.

14. Yana, interview with author, November 29, 2010.

15. Yana, interview with author, November 29, 2010.

16. Lauren Berlant, *Cruel Optimism* (Durham, N.C.: Duke University Press, 2011).

17. Yana, interview with author, November 29, 2010.

18. Yana, interview with author, November 29, 2010.

19. Teresa, interview with author, July 2012.

20. Teresa, interview with author, July 2012.

21. Yana, interview with author, November 29, 2010.

22. Peterson Consulting, Inc., "Strategic Planning Report," August 2001. Linnea Stenson Papers, Jean-Nickolaus Tretter Collection, University of Minnesota Library.

23. Peterson Consulting, Inc., "Strategic Planning Report."

24. Peterson Consulting, Inc., "Strategic Planning Report."

25. Peterson Consulting, Inc., "Strategic Planning Report."

26. Peterson Consulting, Inc., "Strategic Planning Report."

27. Peterson Consulting, Inc., "Strategic Planning Report."

28. Peterson Consulting, Inc., "Strategic Planning Report."

29. Peterson Consulting, Inc., "Strategic Planning Report."

30. Peterson Consulting, Inc., "Strategic Planning Report."

31. Peterson Consulting, Inc., "Strategic Planning Report."

32. Peterson Consulting, Inc., "Strategic Planning Report."

33. Peterson Consulting, Inc., "Strategic Planning Report."

34. Jax Alder, interview with author, November 18, 2010.

35. Youth Community Meeting notes, 2003. Jean-Nickolaus Tretter Collection, University of Minnesota Library.

36. Jax Alder, interview with author, November 18, 2010.

37. "District 202 Youth Community Concerns," October 28, 2004. Linnea Stenson Papers, Jean-Nickolaus Tretter Collection, University of Minnesota Library.

38. "District 202 Youth Community Concerns."

39. "District 202 Youth Community Concerns."

40. "District 202 Youth Community Concerns."

41. "District 202 Youth Community Concerns."

42. "District 202 Youth Community Concerns."

43. "The Issues and Policies That Are Constantly Being Broken and/or Discounted Will Be Remedied by January 1, 2005." Linnea Stenson Papers, Jean-Nickolaus Tretter Collection, University of Minnesota Libraries.

44. "The Issues and Policies That Are Constantly Being Broken and/or Discounted Will Be Remedied by January 1, 2005."

45. Aradhana Sharma, *Logics of Empowerment: Development, Gender and Governance in Neoliberal India* (Minneapolis: University of Minnesota Press, 2008), xx.

46. Sharma.

47. Bev Roberts, interview with author, October 1, 2010.

48. One of the consultants hired to conduct the evaluation of District 202 has generously shared with me the products of their year-long assessment, including a compilation of the Task Force Recommendations, findings from interviews and focus groups conducted, which they describe thusly: "Interviews were conducted with: 18 adults—including LGBT community leaders, current and former donors & funders, former Board members, youth workers, Twin Cities civic/political leaders, and former District 202 staff. Of these adult interviewees, 6 are people of color and 12 are white. 19 youth—all of these youth are, or have been, members of the District 202 community. Of these youth interviewees, 13 are people of color and 6 are white."

49. Carl Dunn, writing on Facebook in response to the question "Where are you all located now?" writes, "After the community assessment, transition planning included District 202 becoming a mobile delivery agency." Facebook, October 20, 2010.

50. James Sanna, "District 202 Names New Executive Director," *The Colu.mn,* October 26, 2009.

51. See Raymond Dart, "The Legitimacy of Social Enterprise," in *Nonprofit Management and Leadership* 14, no. 4 (Summer 2004); and Howard Husock, "Nonprofit and For-Profit: Blurring the Line," in *Chronicle of Philanthropy,* June

29, 2006, as well as the rise of such phenomena as "venture philanthropy," in which wealthy but "socially conscious" individuals "invest" in particular projects in order to achieve a particular social "value," or "social return on investment" as a strategy to literally quantify the cost benefit of various social programs. In other words, this strategy—which was required by the State of Minnesota's Department of Employment and Economic Development of all applicants for Federal Stimulus funds—asks organizations to quantify how much money each dollar the state invests in their program will save the state in costs of incarcerating, sheltering, feeding, and providing health care by "diverting" individuals and "empowering" them toward employment and "self-sufficiency."

52. Alex Nicholls, *Social Entrepreneurship: New Models of Sustainable Social Change* (Oxford: Oxford University Press, 2006), 2.

53. Nicholls, 11.

54. Carl Dunn, the executive director of District 202 often commented publicly on how the goal of LGBT youth organizations, now mostly accomplished, is "mainstreaming." For this reason, he says, there is no longer any need for a physical space, as LGBT youth are fully incorporated into the mainstream and are therefore "safe."

55. District 202, email message to author, January 13, 2010.

56. In response to an article on The Bilerico Project by a local progressive queer author and activist, Carl Dunn wrote: "As a gay-for-pay youth worker, I'm seeing more LGBTA youth mainstream these days when they have a supportive network of family and friends." Carl Dunn in response to the article "When Queer Politics Meant No War and Fighting the Body Police," Bilerico.com, March 15, 2010.

57. District 202 website, www.dist202.org. Website is now defunct, but can be accessed via www.waybackmachine.org.

58. The fundraising appeal was entitled "On the Ground in Anoka Hennepin" (the location of the most recent suicide in Minnesota). It came complete with a new graphic and described the "actions" District 202 was engaged in, including "dedicating an intern" and "reaching out to their national partners." It ends with the entreaty that "by supporting District 202 you will directly impact the lives of many LGBT youth in our community." District 202, email message to author, October 6, 2010.

59. Concerned Community Letter, November 4, 2010.

5. Navigating the Crisis of Neoliberalism

1. Laverne Cox, Keynote Address, National Gay and Lesbian Task Force Creating Change Conference, February 5, 2014.

2. Cox, Keynote Address.

3. Ruth Wilson Gilmore, "In the Shadow of the Shadow State," *The Revolution*

Will Not Be Funded, ed. Incite! Women of Color Against Violence (Cambridge, Mass.: South End Press, 2007). Gilmore writes: "The grassroots groups that have formally joined the third sector are in the shadow of the shadow state. They are not direct service providers but often work with the clients of such organizations as well as with the providers themselves. They generally are not recipients of public funds although occasionally get government contracts to do work in jails or shelters or other institutions. They have detailed political programs and deep social and economic critiques. . . . They try to pay some staff to promote and proliferate the organization's analysis and activity even if most participants in the group are unpaid volunteers. The government is often the object of their advocacy and their antagonisms . . . but the real focus of their energies is ordinary people whom they wish fervently to organize against their own abandonment," 47.

4. Loïc Wacquant, *Punishing the Poor: The Neoliberal Government of Social Insecurity* (Durham, N.C.: Duke University Press, 2009), 42.

5. Jasbir Puar, Lauren Berlant, Judith Butler, Bojana Cvejić, Isabell Lorey, and Ana Vujanović, "Precarity Talk: A Virtual Roundtable," *TDR: The Drama Review* 56, no. 4 (Winter 2012) (T216), 166.

6. Puar, et al., 170.

7. Puar, et al., 170.

8. Puar, et al., 166.

9. Herman Gray and Macarena Gómez-Barris, *Toward a Sociology of the Trace* (Minneapolis: University of Minnesota Press, 2010), 4.

10. Gray and Gómez-Barris, 4.

11. Latasha, interview with author, February 2014.

12. Duke, interview with author, March 2014. Emphasis mine.

13. Vienna, interview with author, March 2014.

14. Randy, interview with author, April 2014.

15. Sarah Banet-Weiser, "Traces in Social Worlds," in *Toward a Sociology of the Trace*, ed. Herman Gray and Macerena Gómez-Barris (Minneapolis: University of Minnesota Press, 2010), 289.

16. Lisa Marie Cacho, *Social Death: Racialized Rightlessness and the Criminalization of the Unprotected* (New York: New York University Press, 2012), 6.

17. Cacho, 6.

18. Cacho, 6.

19. Logan, interview with author, March 2014. Emphasis mine.

20. Logan, interview with author, March 2014. Emphasis mine.

21. Sophia, interview with author, February 2014.

22. Harrison, interview with author, March 2014.

23. Malik, interview with author, April 2014.

24. Sophia, interview with author, February 2014.

25. Xavier, interview with author, April 2014.

26. Duke, interview with author, March 2014.

27. Duke, interview with author, March 2014.

28. Duke, interview with author, March 2014.

29. Vienna, interview with author, March 2014.

30. Avery Gordon, "The Prisoner's Curse," in *Toward a Sociology of the Trace,* ed. Herman Gray and Macerena Gómez-Barris (Minneapolis: University of Minnesota Press, 2010), 41.

31. Orlando Patterson, *Slavery and Social Death: A Comparative Study* (Cambridge, Mass.: Harvard University Press, 1982). Quoted in Avery Gordon.

32. Harrison, interview with author, March 2014.

33. Given the small number of progressive LGBT philanthropies, and the significant likelihood that individuals who once worked with TYSN will at some point rely once again on funding from this organization, I've changed the name of the foundation so as to not jeopardize any future relationships with that funder.

34. Harrison, interview with author, March 2014.

35. Vienna, interview with author, March 2014.

36. Harrison, interview with author, March 2014.

37. Harrison, interview with author, March 2014.

38. Harrison, interview with author, March 2014.

39. In November of 2012 the Ford Foundation announced the $50 million "Advancing LGBT Rights Initiative" which will focus on equal rights, bullying, media, and "developing a diverse, coordinated, collaborative and effective field of leaders and organizations working to secure LGBT rights." One local funder who attended the grantee convening at which they announced this new initiative remarked that they foresee very few, if any, organizations in the Midwest actually receiving any of this money because the requirements in terms of evaluation and reporting are so sophisticated only organizations with fairly large budgets already would have the scope to even apply.

40. Vienna Stanton, Out Front Lobby Day Speech, April 24, 2011.

41. Vienna Stanton, National Coming Out Day Speech, October 2011.

42. Vienna Stanton, National Coming Out Day Speech, October 2011.

43. Email received by TYSN Board, October 10, 2011.

44. Email received by TYSN Board, October 10, 2011.

45. Quorum Facebook page, October 19, 2011.

46. Randy, interview with author, April 2014.

47. Nora, interview with author, April 2014.

48. Nora, interview with author, April 2014.

49. Nora, interview with author, April 2014.

50. Vienna, interview with author, March 2014

51. Vienna, interview with author, March 2014.

52. Vienna, interview with author, March 2014.

53. Vienna, interview with author, March 2014.

54. Anna Agathangelou, Morgan Bassichis, and Tamara Spira, "Intimate Investments: Homonormativity, Global Lockdown, and the Seduction of Empire," *Radical History Review* 100 (Winter 2008): 122.

55. Chris Geidner, "Meet the Trans Scholar Fighting against the Campaign for Out Trans Military Service," *Buzzfeed.com,* September 9, 2013. http://www.buzzfeed .com/chrisgeidner/meet-the-trans-scholar-fighting-against-the-campaign-for-out.

56. Geidner.

57. Geidner.

58. According to the National Conference of State Legislatures, in the 2017 legislative session, sixteen states are considering legislation that would limit multiuser facilities like restrooms and locker rooms based on sex assigned at birth. Further, six states are considering legislation that would preempt municipal and county-level antidiscrimination laws. Finally, fourteen states are considering legislation that would limit transgender student's rights at school. National Conference of State Legislatures, "'Bathroom Bill' Legislative Tracking," July 28, 2017.

59. Harrison, interview with author, March 2014.

60. Vienna Stanton, "Fwd: USDOJ trans law enforcement training—please reply ASAP!", personal email correspondence, December 2013.

61. Stanton.

62. Stanton.

63. Kevin, interview with author, April 2014.

64. Duke, interview with author, March 2014.

65. Duke, interview with author, March 2014.

66. Vienna, interview with author, March 2014.

67. Vienna, interview with author, March 2014.

68. Vienna, interview with author, March 2014.

69. Vienna, interview with author, March 2014.

70. Harrison, interview with author, March 2014.

71. Harrison, interview with author, March 2014.

72. Nora, interview with author, April 2014.

73. Sophie, interview with author, February 2014.

74. Kevin, interview with author, April 2014.

75. Kevin, interview with author, April 2014.

76. Kevin, interview with author, April 2014.

77. Kevin, interview with author, April 2014.

78. Gordon, "The Prisoner's Curse," 18.

79. Gordon, 18.

80. Gordon, 47.

Conclusion

1. Trans Youth Support Team, "TYSN has some important news: Our Last Newsletter," email to author, January 20, 2015.

2. Dylan Rodriguez, "The Political Logic of the Non-Profit Industrial Complex," in *The Revolution Will Not Be Funded: Beyond the Non-Profit Industrial Complex,* ed. Incite! Women of Color Against Violence (Cambridge, Mass.: South End Press, 2007), 39.

3. "Queer Dreams, Non-Profit Blues," *Plenary. New York,* January 27, 2013.

4. Dean Spade, comments at "Queer Dreams, Non-Profit Blues," *Plenary,* January 27, 2013.

5. http://southernersonnewground.org/become-a-member/songs-membership -structure/.

6. http://srlp.org/our-strategy/collective-structure/.

7. http://www.cuav.org/history/.

8. Andrea Smith, comments at "Queer Dreams, Non-Profit Blues" Conference. January 27, 2013.

9. Kevin, interview with author, March 2016.

10. Jack Halberstam, *The Queer Art of Failure* (Durham, NC: Duke University Press, 2011), 2–3.

11. Halberstam, 3.

12. Logan, interview with author, April 2016.

13. Logan, interview with author, April 2016.

14. Kevin, interview with author, March 2016.

15. The organization Funders for LGBTQ Issues reports that funding for trans issues increased by more than $5 million, or 40 percent, between 2014 and 2015. This increase comes at a time, following the Supreme Court decision legalizing same-sex marriage, that funding to LGBT issues otherwise slowed considerably. Despite this disproportionate increase, trans issues remain a very small portion of the overall funding to LGBT organizations, receiving only $18 million of the $160.7 million worth of foundation grants to LGBT organizations and issues. See Funders for LGBTQ Issues, "2015 Tracking Report: LGBTQ Grantmaking by U.S. Foundations."

16. Jose Esteban Muñoz, *Disidentifications: Queers of Color and the Performance of Politics* (Minneapolis: University of Minnesota Press, 1999).

17. Muñoz, 74.

18. Judith Butler, *Precarious Lives: The Powers of Mourning and Violence* (New York: Verso, 2004), 22.

Index

Created by Eileen Quam

"Queer Dreams and Non-Profit Blues" (conference), 192

queer homelessness. *See* homeless youth, LGBT

queer identification. *See* LGBT community

queer politics, 13, 34–37

Queers for Economic Justice, 191

Quorum (Minneapolis LGBT chamber of commerce), 170–73, 176–77

race and deservingness, 62–63

RBC Wealth Management, 175

Reagan administration, 22, 23, 24, 37–38, 43, 57, 59

Redmond, Johnna, 68

rendering technical, use of term, 27

Revolution Will Not Be Funded, The (Incite!), 26

Robert's Rules of Order, 49, 89

Rockefeller, John D., 29

Rodriguez, Dylan, 1, 25, 32, 190

Rose, Nikolas, 10, 81, 86, 87

Roy, Arundhati, 26

Russell Sage Foundation, 29

Safe Harbor Act, 105–6

Salvation Army, 104

same-sex marriage. *See* marriage equality

sanctified sector, use of term, 85

Schmitz, Dean, 149–50

shadow state, use of term, 25, 33–34

Sharma, Aradhana, 139

Shepard, Matthew, 180

Shiller, Helen, 94

Siciliano, Carl, 1

slavery, 28

Smith, Andrea, 194

social death, 159–60, 165, 185

social entrepreneurship, 141–42, 145

social movements: civil rights, 31–32; institutionalization of, 39; nonprofitization of, 8–9, 16, 22, 31–34, 159. *See also* LGBT movement

social safety net, 2, 23–24, 34, 37–38, 42–43, 45–46, 52, 59, 103, 153

Social Security, 61

social service model, 162–66

social theory, 8

social trace, use of term, 156

SONG. *See* Southerners on New Ground

Southerners on New Ground (SONG), 192–93

Spade, Dean, 178–79, 191, 192, 199

Spira, Tamara, 8

SRLP. *See* Sylvia Rivera Law Project

Stokes, Carl, 32

Stone, Amy, 38

Stone, Terry, 82

Stonewall Riots, 35

surveillance, 95–99, 102, 114, 126

Sylvia Rivera Law Project (SRLP), 193

"Take Back Boystown" campaign, 84, 98–104

TANF. *See* Temporary Assistance for Needy Families

Target, 175, 211n16

tax-exempt organizations. *See* 501(c)(3) (nonprofit organizations)

Temporary Assistance for Needy Families (TANF), 45–46, 61

Terrorist Assemblages (Puar), 114

Thatcher administration, 22

Theorizing NGOs, 27

Time (magazine), 198

Tomlinson, Jerry, 50–51

Transgender Day of Remembrance, 81–82, 180

trans people: HRC on, 82; important

MYRL BEAM is assistant professor of gender, sexuality, and women's studies at Virginia Commonwealth University.

Lightning Source UK Ltd.
Milton Keynes UK
UKHW021959240322
400569UK00011B/441